Praise for Out Think

"If you want to deliver exceptional outcomes as a leader, read this book! Shawn Hunter has been all over the world uncovering exciting new insights into innovation and leadership, and he shares them here. I highly recommend this book to anyone who is serious about leading others."
—Paul Hiltz, FACHE, President and Market Leader, Community Mercy Health Partners

"*Out Think* is a book that brings the art of innovation near everyone, underlining the practical and making the quest within the reach of leadership."
—Prof. Liisa Valikangas, author of *The Resilient Organization*

"*Out Think* is a great source of concentrated innovation practices, the kind that leaders need in order to drive their businesses forward in these disruptive and challenging times."
—Chip Conley, Founder, Joie de Vivre Hotels, author of *Emotional Equations*

"Shawn Hunter presents actionable strategies for leaders to spark collaborative, innovative thinking within their organizations and tailor it to their needs—just what we need in times like these."
—Matthew E. May, author of *The Laws of Subtraction* and *The Elegant Solution*

"A timely and important book. *Out Think* is a top-notch distillation of ideas to help you build and apply powerful new leadership skills in your organization."
—Garry Ridge, President and CEO of WD-40 Company, and co-author of *Helping People Win at Work*

"*Out Think* awakens the creative mind and lays out a clear roadmap for innovation. In today's competitive world, innovation has become the currency for success and Shawn Hunter helps you unleash it. A must-read for those looking to take their organizations—or careers—to the next level."
—Josh Linkner, Author, *Disciplined Dreaming*; CEO, Detroit Venture Partners; Founder, former CEO, ePrize

"In this powerful book, Shawn provides us with well researched, tested and proven wisdom from diverse international thought leaders, and wonderfully adds his own personal perspective, providing us with a new lens to see the possibility and potential in us all."

—David Penglase, author of *Intentionomics*

"Shawn Hunter has the innate gift of being able to decipher conversations and link insights meaningfully to unveil profound wisdom. This book is a must-read for all those who want to create their own personal armoury of insights, ideas and stories for bringing innovation and purpose to their leadership."

—Sujaya Banerjee, Chief Talent Officer & Sr. VP for Human Resources, Essar Investments Limited

"I've been an entrepreneur for forty years and I can tell you *Out Think* shows you how to mix the key ingredients of success—how to find your dream, be persistent and honest, and the insight to work smarter than anyone else."

—Harris Rosen, President & COO, Rosen Hotels & Resorts

OUT THINK

OUT THINK

How Innovative Leaders Drive
Exceptional Outcomes

G. Shawn Hunter

JB JOSSEY-BASS™
A Wiley Brand

Published by John Wiley & Sons Canada, Ltd.

While the publisher and author have used their best efforts in preparing this book, they make no representations or warranties with respect to the accuracy or completeness of the contents of this book and specifically disclaim any implied warranties of merchantability or fitness for a particular purpose. No warranty may be created or extended by sales representatives or written sales materials. The advice and strategies contained herein may not be suitable for your situation. You should consult with a professional where appropriate. Neither the publisher nor the author shall be liable for damages arising herefrom.

For general information about our other products and services, please contact our Customer Care Department within Canada at 1–800–567–4797, outside Canada at (416) 236–4433 or fax (416) 236–8743.

Wiley publishes in a variety of print and electronic formats and by print-on-demand. Some material included with standard print versions of this book may not be included in e-books or in print-on-demand. If this book refers to media such as a CD or DVD that is not included in the version you purchased, you may download this material at http://booksupport.wiley.com. For more information about Wiley products, visit www.wiley.com.

Library and Archives Canada Cataloguing in Publication Data:
Hunter, G. Shawn, 1969–, author
        Out think : how innovative leaders drive exceptional outcomes
/ G. Shawn Hunter.

Issued in print and electronic formats.
ISBN 978-1-118-50522-9 (bound).—ISBN 978-1-118-50528-1 (pdf).—
ISBN 978-1-118-50529-8 (epub).—ISBN 978-1-118-50527-4 (mobi)

        1. Leadership. 2. Organizational change. I. Title.

HD57.7.H85 2013   658.4'092   C2013-903554-0
                                                      C2013-902894-3

Production Credits
Managing Editor: Alison Maclean
Executive Editor: Don Loney
Production Editor: Pauline Ricablanca
Cover Design: Adrian So
Cover Image: jpa1999 / iStockphoto
Composition: Thomson Digital
Printer: Friesens Press

Printed in Canada

1 2 3 4 5 FP 17 16 15 14 13

To my parents, Hal and Bev Hunter, two of the greatest leaders and innovators I know.

CONTENTS

FOREWORD

Innovation occurs when a creative solution makes its way to market. It runs the world, from business to society. We have problems that need engaged people willing to finish what they start. It's not about coming up with new ideas. That's a recipe for procrastination and nonexecution. To truly harness innovation, you need to leverage a culture that will stop at nothing to fix bad ideas and stomp out mediocrity. And that requires trust-based leadership.

And that's what this book is all about.

How do we get engaged and emerge as leaders and relentless problem solvers? We arrive at a psychological intersection: purpose and passion. We combine our emotions, mental faculty, and sense of spirit. Often, this happens because there is someone in our lives who challenges us or inspires us to dig deep and find energy. When we do, we detect something powerful that draws us in, and we innovate.

Let Shawn be your guiding force, and allow this book to be the device that helps you open your eyes for worthy problems to address; open your ears for feedback about your creative solutions; and open your heart to the importance of your task, and the suffering you are addressing—be it an inconvenience or true misery.

This book will take you on a journey, offering you helpful pieces of advice that will build up to a personal system of innovation mastery. Once you crack the code of self-engagement, finishing what you start will be a snap.

Along the way, Shawn will give you a well-researched glimpse into the future of business, resulting from what he cleverly calls "a marketquake."

It's likely your company is not fully prepared for the Creative Age, the next big wave since the Industrial Revolution.

And this final stop, the tendency and tenacity to execute, is what separates creativity from innovation. Without a result, your ideas are just happy talk. Speaking of talking, the best way to drive innovative thinking isn't by putting out more words. According to Shawn, it's quite the opposite. It's about asking the right questions, then giving others the breathing room to innovate.

Shawn is certainly no pontificator; he's partnered with some of the brightest minds in the business world over the last decade. He's also successfully conceived, built, and sold a start-up—so that means he knows where the bones are buried for entrepreneurs.

So, dive into this book, take notes, and get ready for a new you.

Tim Sanders
Author, *Love Is the Killer App* and *Today We Are Rich*

INTRODUCTION

THEN

In 1993, I was in Korea teaching English. It was fun and adventurous; I was 24. Meanwhile my dad, Hal Hunter, was 58 and had recently been right-sized, downsized, outsourced—fired from his job. He was cooking up a new adventure himself.

My father had been working in the human-resources research and development world for decades, mostly in the Washington, D.C., area for government contractor firms. He had been developing an interest in what was then called "distance learning." A number of emerging technologies were available to deliver such virtual learning, including expensive laser-disk technology (predecessor of CD-ROMs and DVDs) and audiographics (which evolved into WebEx and other online sharing tools).

My dad had assembled a group of key people from around our nation's capital, all of whom had similar interests on the customer side of the equation. The one thing he could get them all to understand and agree on was that television should be a main component in the approach. Television was the one technology everyone easily understood.

My dad contacted me to tell me he was starting a business focused on televising training and was interested in broadcasting it live by satellite to distant, remote audiences. I had no idea what he was talking about, but it sounded like fun. I had saved about $5,000 from teaching, so I jumped on a flight and joined him.

The basic idea was to take talented instructors into television studios and broadcast them live to remote audiences and charge locations

pay-per-view fees to attend. We even made it interactive, using telephone lines and fax machines. People could call into the studio and ask
questions.

We made great learning content designed for television, but unfortunately very few people saw it because we had no idea how to prop-
erly market or sell it. As far as I was concerned, we were still having a
blast and learning about a new viable business that, as far as we knew,
was unique. We were never aware of anyone else trying such a business
model, but then we'd never thought to look.

My dad was funding the entire enterprise with his own modest
retirement. At the time I had no idea of the bravado and conviction
of that decision. A year or so after we had started the effort, we were
having lunch one day and my dad looked at me and said, "Tell you
what. I'll put another $20,000 in the business account. When that runs
out, we'll shake hands and congratulate ourselves on having a good
run of it."

I remember thinking, "Oh, right. There's an end to the money!" I
hadn't previously considered the possibility of failing by lack of money.
With this realization, I knew we needed to get inventive—and fast.

We stopped producing the expensive broadcast content that we
couldn't sell and found a couple of small companies that were, in fact,
doing much the same thing we were. It turned out a few companies
in the United States had the same idea we did and had developed a
similar service. We approached them and offered to resell their content.
Our margins were smaller, since we kept only commission on sales, but
the big overhead had vanished. We had managed to lower the immense
financial burn rate and still have a product to sell.

Over the next couple of years, we built a strong customer base and
regained a solid financial position. Then we started producing our
own content again. The winds were with us when the dot-com revolution happened and streaming videos online entered the market in
the late 1990s. By that time, we had an inventory of video content, a
schedule of live broadcasts, and a way to reach a much broader audience by streaming media over the Internet. And still we remained one
of the few providers of such content. In fact, at the time, the few companies that offered competition were in the process of dying out due

to mismanagement or financial collapse. However, unbeknownst to us at the time, a new generation of competitors was soon to emerge.

In this book, I often refer to the learning experiences I had through the company my dad and I founded, which started in the mid-1990s and lasted until 2007, when we sold that business. I didn't know it at the time, but this period would be greatly influential in building what I now call the Out Think process.

Now

My wife and I live in Maine with our three kids, all under the age of 13. The other day I was musing about how to teach gratitude to them and posed this question to my six-year-old as we were sitting at the kitchen table: "Annie, would you name three things you are grateful for?"

"What's grateful?"

"Thankful. Name three things you are thankful for."

She thought for a moment and said, "Santa Claus!" Cute. She also said painting with her grandmother and playing with our dog. A good start. Gratitude, just like innovation, can be learned.

The global economy has moved on, from the Information Age to what some have dubbed the "Creative Age." This book is about the importance and power of engaging ourselves in our work, connecting with the people and world around us, and deviating from convention to reliably create innovative value in this new age.

I believe "innovation" is now what "entrepreneurial" was to the 1990s and what "excellence" was to the 1980s. The pursuit of "innovation" has been urgently added to the business buzz vernacular because the velocity of change demands that companies constantly innovate to remain relevant.

Consider: Disney, CNN, MTV, Hyatt, Burger King, FedEx, Microsoft, Apple, Texas Instrument, 20th Century Fox, Gillette, AT&T, IBM, Merck, Hershey's, Eli Lilly, Coors, Bristol-Myers—the list goes on.[1] All of these organizations were started during economic downturns. Our greatest opportunities exist in such times, but we need to let go of some of the attitudes and attributes, methods and mindsets, that have worked in the past, because they're not working so well anymore.

So how do we, as leaders, deal with this continuing upheaval in the marketplace? How do we out think our competitors and think outside the norm to achieve continuing success? The Out Think process described in this book is not a linear blueprint for success. It's not a series of infallible steps that will lead you, the reader, inexorably toward innovation, market leadership, and world domination. It requires that you participate in the journey.

I've synthesized in this book many of those truths in emerging innovative leadership practices that guide reliable value creation from around the world. Out Think is a set of ideas and practices for generating new value in the form of innovative products and services.

I don't believe in definitive models, but I do believe each idea we find in the world presents certain truths and value, represented in the behaviors and beliefs, the methods and mindsets, that drive results— in ourselves and in others. Having interviewed, collaborated with, and filmed hundreds of successful executives, business leaders, and researchers, I have discovered some consistent guiding methods and mindsets for individuals, groups, and organizations around the world that have been proven to be reliably valuable in today's volatile economy.

You will find within these pages that sense of purpose is a pervasive ingredient within each step of the journey. Passion may drive us, but purpose is what connects us to our community and to the world.

CHAPTER 1

MARKETQUAKE: MOVING BEYOND ARRESTED DECAY

I can't recall a period of time that was as volatile, complex, ambiguous, and tumultuous. As one successful executive put it, "If you're not confused, you don't know what's going on."

— *Warren Bennis, founding chairman of*
The Leadership Institute, University of
Southern California

In 1859, a prospector named William S. Bodey discovered gold high in the Sierra mountains of California, and within 20 years the developing town—named after him—had a population of more than ten thousand people. The town, whose name was eventually changed to "Bodie," was a thriving and rapidly growing community, as the people harvested the rich silver and gold deposits from mines dug into the hills. The residents quickly built all the necessary foundations of a full community, including a town hall, merchants, fire and police departments, and schools. Such was the demand for lumber and materials to support the housing explosion that even a railroad was constructed to deliver building materials to Bodie from the nearby town of Mono Mills.

By 1915, Bodie was labeled a "ghost town"; by 1918, the rail line had been dismantled; and by 1942, the town was completely abandoned. However, to this day first the U.S. National Park Service, then the state's park service in conjunction with a private foundation, has maintained the town in an intentional state of arrested decay to show how life was in the town when it was abandoned. That is, the structures, furniture, streetlights, and even the last markings on the school chalkboard have been kept just as they were left, in an attempt to neither improve upon the town nor allow it to fall further into disrepair.[1]

Many organizations behave in much the same manner. We build processes, operations, behaviors, and cultural habits based on the one good idea or market opportunity that surfaced either when the company was founded or during the last product or service triumph the company enjoyed. Then we congratulate ourselves and reminisce about the good old days instead of moving forward.

If we spend our time and resources focusing on building more of the same, instead of something different, we wind up competing only on price, which is a death spiral. No company will ever remain the cheapest in this world of commoditization. Even if it were possible to maintain having the lowest price, this will almost necessarily mean having the smallest profit margins, as the cost of the goods and services sold approaches the market offering price. The cheapest products and services often have a greater likelihood of suffering from lack of product integrity and early obsolescence. And being the cheapest does not build a secure customer base but instead attracts the discount buyer, a buyer with no loyalty and one who often brings a lot of headache.

The urgency for organizational culture change that supports democratized innovation practices has never been higher. Companies that recognize that there is opportunity in chaos and that traditional structures are no longer the answer are likely to lead the way in innovation, leaving those stuck in yesterday's corporate culture behind.

Science fiction author William Gibson once said, "The future is already here, it just isn't very evenly distributed." We've entered a new era. Call it the age of imagination, ideation, conceptualization, creativity, innovation—take your pick. Creativity, mental flexibility, and collaboration have displaced one-dimensional intelligence and isolated determination as core ingredients of a competitive advantage.

Creative people who can bring innovation to the world are our greatest capital now, and with the right leadership and inspiration, creativity can be nurtured in everyone. In any field, expertise is not only an expectation—it is a given. Success for workers and companies centers on being nimble, creative, and having the initiative to bring unique solutions to unexpected problems.

The new creative class includes people working in all sectors of the economy, including engineering, design, science, poetry, music, technology, and whose economic contribution is to create new ideas and take action that yields innovation. They come from all over the globe, collaborating and easily moving from one challenge to the next. The drivers of those in this creative force have a tenacious curiosity and passion for what they do.

Dan Pink, author of *A Whole New Mind: Why Right-Brainers Will Rule the Future*, has popularized the importance of "symphonic" thinking. This concept dates back to 1907, when composers Jean Sibelius and Gustav Mahler considered the nature of symphonies. According to Sibelius, the symphony is about the "profound logic that created an inner connection between all the motives" and that "the symphony should be like the world: it must embrace everything."[2]

Symphonic thinkers see the big picture; they look at the whole system and take their information from a variety of sources. They take a multidimensional approach to solving problems, seeing connections, and finding effective solutions. Such thinkers include Margaret Mead and Gregory Bateson, who developed interdisciplinary perspectives in systems theory; Amartya Sen, an Indian economist, who made great contributions to social-choice theory and welfare economics, particularly focusing on the poor; George Pólya, a Hungarian mathematician, whose work in mathematics education focused on experience-based techniques for problem solving rather than rote memorization; and Martha Nussbaum, an American philosopher noted for, among other things, her championing the idea of reconnecting education to the humanities, rather than viewing it strictly as an economic tool.

Organizations are succeeding by being open to innovation. Amazon went from being an online bookseller to a powerhouse when it started offering a wide variety of web-based services. Google and Apple have added a host of online services to their core competencies. And Toyota has enjoyed a decade-spanning, market-dominating run owing to its policy and practice of empowering its frontline employees to be innovators and change agents. Management has come a long way since Henry Ford once quipped, "Why is it, whenever I ask for a pair of hands, a brain comes attached?"

Companies that can out think their competitors in this chaotic environment usurp the market position of incumbents consistently: Blockbuster got Netflixed,[3] Borders Books got Amazoned, Tower Records got iTuned, and, if iTunes isn't careful, it might get Spotified, as Spotify offers access to more than 15 million songs that can be streamed for $9.99 per month.

We need to understand that knowledge and expertise are easily accessible, common, expected, and cheap or even free. They no longer represent a lasting competitive advantage. We have moved to the age of creative, symphonic thinking, where the ability to harness seemingly disparate pieces of information and ideas and mash them into wholly new iterations that can be used to create innovative solutions is, in fact, the competitive advantage for individuals and for organizations.

Embracing a creativity agenda is not easy when we have quarterly earnings, deadlines, and clear outcomes at stake. Reading this, you may be tempted to think, "Sounds great. I believe in the value of creativity and conceptual thinking, but how does that possibly affect my company's bottom line?"

As Dan Goleman relates in his seminal book *Working with Emotional Intelligence*, researchers John Hunter (Michigan State), Frank Schmidt, and Michael Judiesch (University of Iowa) conducted a study in 1990 in which they evaluated the economic value of the top 1 percent of contributors to company profits.[4] Their findings revealed that top performers in professions that require dealing with high levels of complexity (business-to-business salespeople, lawyers, doctors, designers, and engineers) contributed more than one hundred times the productivity and productive impact than the bottom 1 percent in those same professions.

As the figure below illustrates, as the level of job complexity increases, so does the productive impact value of those at the top of their game. Being able to conceptualize—to be creative—pays off. And being able to draw that discretionary level of initiative, creativity, and passion out of those around us will distinguish the best leaders of the future from those of the past.

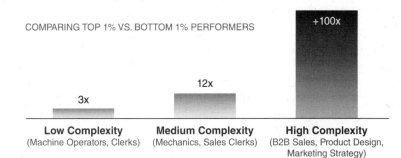

COMPARING TOP 1% VS. BOTTOM 1% PERFORMERS

+100x

12x

3x

Low Complexity
(Machine Operators, Clerks)

Medium Complexity
(Mechanics, Sales Clerks)

High Complexity
(B2B Sales, Product Design,
Marketing Strategy)

Figure 1.1 Economic Value of Conceptual Thinkers

Source: John Hunter (Michigan State), Frank Schmidt, and Michael Judiesch (University of Iowa)

CREATIVITY VS. INNOVATION

This book is about how to lead teams to innovation, so how does that differ from creativity and invention? Paul Sloane, author of *The Innovative Leader*, lays out the distinctions among the various terms:

Creativity is the capability or act of conceiving something original or unusual.

Innovation is the implementation of something new.

Invention is the creation of something that has never been made before and is recognized as the product of some unique insight.

If you have a brainstorm meeting and dream up dozens of new ideas then you have displayed creativity but there is no innovation until something gets implemented. Somebody has to take a risk and deliver something for a creative idea to be turned into an innovation. An invention might be a product or device or method that has never existed before. So every invention is an innovation. But every innovation is not an invention. When your company first published its website, that was a major innovation for the company even though many other websites already existed.[5]

Sloane goes on to say that, while we tend to think of all these terms as applying to a physical product, they can also be applied to services. For our purposes here, "product" means both, unless specified otherwise, and "innovation" includes applying creativity, that is, taking creative ideas to their implementation.

THE INNOVATION GAP SHRINKS

> When the rate of change inside an organization is slower than the rate of change outside an organization, the end is in sight.
>
> —*Jack Welch, former chairman of General Electric*

While we may intuit that creativity is a vital component of innovation, we urgently need a process by which we can accelerate our new-product and value-creation pipelines. Throughout the organizations that my colleagues and I at Skillsoft Corporation have visited in recent years while interviewing executives and collaborating with thought leaders, we've consistently discovered an innovation-delivery gap that is shrinking. This gap is between an organization's ability to create new and distinctive value that the market recognizes and rewards, and the speed at which competitors can emerge and deliver innovative products and services to the market.

Several accelerating forces are influencing this competitive marketplace innovation gap. These include the ubiquity of technologies that enable global collaboration, and the increased accessibility of new ideas and commercial opportunities in emerging markets. Added to these are the broader adoption of open-innovation practices and companies' increasing tendencies to develop capabilities with individuals and groups outside of their own organizations.

Technology Globalizes Innovation

Norm Merritt is the CEO of an internationally recognized business-process outsourcing (BPO) company, iQor. The company helps organizations around the world service their customers and support their operations. In an interview Merritt said:

> Globalization is a lot more about technology and innovation than people often recognize. The reason globalization is happening, in my view, is not because the laws have changed, or countries are suddenly more friendly towards trade. It's happening because the Internet came around in the mid-'90s. And it's making the Philippines as accessible as Phoenix.[6]

In other words, it's now much less about *where* than it is about *how* skills are sourced, services are performed, and innovation is achieved. Merritt goes on to say that globalization used to mean "finding and sourcing the lowest-cost labor." Now, the lowest-cost labor is a moving target; it's more about who can perform the best services and, as a company, be nimble enough to fluidly move operations and innovation to leverage the greatest market opportunity, conduct the most promising research, or deliver the best support services.

Consider that, according to a *Wall Street Journal* article, top information services and consulting organizations in India—including Tata Consultancy Services, Infosys, and the Bangalore-based software developer MindTree—are now all actively hiring employees in the United States.[7] Outsourcing from emerging markets to Detroit, Michigan, or Camden, New Jersey, might sound somewhat absurd, but it's happening quickly as globally agile companies rapidly deploy new initiatives and source projects to the right talent markets. According to Ameet Nivsarkar, vice president of India's National Association of Software and Services Companies (Nasscom), the association's member companies have generated more than 280,000 jobs in the United States over the past five years.

Merritt sums it up best:

> To me, globalization is not about lower wages, or a particular country that you need to deal with. It's about thinking of the entire planet in a seamless way, and constructing your business in such a way that it could move across the globe in a second, that it can leverage talent anywhere, and that it can run processes in a way that is really seamless. To put it another way, for a business, I think the concept of a country or a geography is increasingly less and less relevant. The world of a seamless globe has already arrived for businesses, and the sooner people wake up to it, the better. Paradoxically, in our experience this mindset is a net positive for most U.S. markets.

Going Global Means Going Indigenous

ManpowerGroup is one of the largest providers of human workforce solutions in the world, operating in 80 countries across the globe. It is arguably among the savviest businesses in understanding the highly fluid state of the global talent market. In a conversation, ManpowerGroup chairman and CEO Jeff Joerres—then president of the company—described to me that many companies who claim to be global are not truly global—they just have multiple locations offshore for manufacturing or other operations that are managed by the home office in a highly prescriptive way.[8]

Joerres interprets this as nothing more than changing locations to reduce labor costs or to be close to resources, but this does not harness the real opportunity and value that comes from being a truly global organization, which in his view means providing support, frameworks, and guidelines, not "direct recipes." He claims his strategy of finding and amplifying innovation within his own company is not complicated:

> Our innovation model? Very simple. Innovation is happening every day across the world in our organization. Find it and institutionalize it.

In a conversation in 2011, Bruce Churchill, president of DirectTV's division of emerging business, told me the key to his company's dramatic market growth in Latin America was taking the decision making about how, when, and where DirecTV's services were deployed in Latin America out of the company's U.S. headquarters and instead giving more autonomy to the local operators.[9] Who knows better than the people who live in Bogotá, Rio, and Caracas what television programming to provide that is culturally relevant, how to price it against the local monetary unit, and what kind of marketing would make the programming stick in each locality? As Churchill says, "You have to allow those people to price, market, distribute—do everything that makes sense—within their local market. So we run a fairly decentralized organization."

Therein lies the key to an effective globalization strategy—to be a truly decentralized organization, executives need to trust local operators to conduct the business—to *invent* the business—so that it is locally relevant. Churchill goes on to say:

> People like to consume media in their local language; it's culturally relevant. So therefore, it makes sense to have people running these businesses that

understand the local culture, understand the local media. . . . If you have someone deciding on programming. . . . [i]t's going to make a lot more sense for someone from a local market to make that decision, as opposed to some American guy up in New York or in Miami, or some other place, imposing their opinion.

Similarly, Michael Byrne, CEO of the Australian company Linfox, Asia Pacific's largest privately owned logistics operator, explained that the key to his company's remarkable growth in India, China, and throughout Southeast Asia over the past ten years can be specifically attributed to Linfox tapping into its local talent and giving those employees control over local operations.[10] With more than 2,500 employees in India, Linfox has exactly one Australian regularly working there—and he's not the boss, either. Linfox provides the shared vision and values that are the bedrock of the company by providing a clear and singular vision of commitment to safety, operational excellence, product integrity, and quality, and then gives trust and operating control to the local markets for culturally nuanced execution.

Those closest to the end–user and buyer are often best suited to make discretionary decisions concerning advertising, support, and distribution of products and services. This is especially true in the global market. From enabling such local autonomy, we as leaders can learn how our products and services are deployed, advertised, and supported, which will keep us better informed on how to manage our business overall.

Open Innovation Offers Opportunity

"Open innovation" is a concept made famous by Henry Chesbrough, a professor and executive director at the Center for Open Innovation at the University of California, Berkeley. In his book *Open Innovation: The New Imperative for Creating and Profiting from Technology*, he defined "open innovation" as "a paradigm that assumes that firms can and should use external ideas as well as internal ideas, and internal and external paths to market, as the firms look to advance their technology."[11]

Technology is a chief enabler of open innovation, as demonstrated by the story of Andrew Deonarine. As he tells it on the *Perspectives on*

Innovation Blog, Deonarine has studied public health, medicine, epidemiology, biochemistry, and something called "bioinformatics," which is usually applied to the use of computers for processing biologically derived data, especially relating to molecular biology.[12] He has a keen interest in solving public-health issues in developing economies around the world.

A few years ago, when he was a third-year medical resident at the University of British Columbia and a junior fellow of St. John's College in Ontario, Deonarine visited India. There he became interested in helping find a solution to the struggles that people in emerging populations around the world have with basic math and literacy. Having been inspired by Nicholas Negroponte's One Laptop per Child initiative to improve literacy and learning by providing inexpensive solar-powered laptops in rural areas, Deonarine wondered if there wasn't an even easier and more ubiquitous platform for delivering literacy learning.

Also a programmer, he worked with colleagues to develop a simple application based on phone-casting technology in which anyone can author a brief math or reading script and send it out to potentially millions of people over their cellphones at no cost. He calls it "EduCell."

The EduCell authoring software accepts and understands multiple languages, including some indigenous to the geographies targeted. This democratizes software development by making basic literacy and math learning accessible to hundreds of millions of cellphone users, and their children, around the world. This EduCell solution is both inventive and beautiful because it leverages the one mobile technology that many in rural India or sub-Saharan Africa have—a cellphone. It also demonstrates the rapid pace of technology change, where recent creative solutions can be applied to emerging technologies, which leads to more innovation. As Deonarine explains, EduCell took its first step into becoming a reality through a challenge presented by InnoCentive.

InnoCentive is a global leader in the art of crowdsourcing innovative ideas from the people around the world who are best suited to solve the particular problems needed by organizations today. InnoCentive provides a platform for any organization to post a challenge or problem to be solved, and the world's engineers, innovators, and entrepreneurs submit proposals to solve them. Those with winning solutions are awarded contracts. Deonarine applied, and his EduCell proposal won. He is now in talks with Nokia to develop and deliver EduCell universally on the company's network.

In this example of open innovation, one individual with a big idea had the capacity to affect the lives of millions and, through the crowdsourcing and open-innovation engine that is InnoCentive, problems are being solved everywhere around the world.

GEN Y TURNS TO ENTREPRENEURIALISM

At the close of the last century, the word "entrepreneur" brought up images of individuals making a lot of money through taking a chance on cutting-edge industries, usually high-tech ones. They were cowboys at a roulette wheel. Andrew Deonarine is an example of a new kind of entrepreneur—someone who launches a business on the basis of a good idea instead of a fat bankroll.

For decades the idea of job security has been disappearing, and kids coming out of high school and college now no longer see bright prospects for getting a secure job with good pay. The option of just working hard for a company for 20 to 30 years, rising up the managerial ladder, adding incrementally to your paycheck, and then retiring in security is an anachronism.

Today's youth tend to see themselves as different in many ways, and on their own in an economy that is not likely to improve in the near future or possibly at all. Now even the brightest with good educations who are coming into the workforce are not finding the job they want—or many job choices in general. They also don't envision having pots of money to become high rollers in the tech or any other industry. They believe it's up to them to blaze their own paths into this challenging and scary new frontier.

National Public Radio (NPR) reported that a new form of entrepreneurialism is emerging from today's bleaker economy.[13] Those in Gen Y are creating their own opportunities, often on a small scale. They're identifying a need and forming their own businesses. And these needs are not necessarily for cutting-edge technology or some other next big thing.

Columnist Michael Malone, in a *Wall Street Journal* op-ed piece, says 18- to 24-year-olds are starting their own businesses at a faster rate than 35- to 44-year-olds.[14] Whether it's picking up trash, marketing for a niche business, or organically producing a particular food, these young entrepreneurs are grabbing that opportunity—no matter how meager—to earn their living on their own hook.

INNOVATION DEMANDS CHANGES IN ORGANIZATIONAL CULTURE

In developing EduCell outside of an organizational structure, Andrew Deonarine avoided some common barriers to innovation—organizational politics, dysfunctional team dynamics, bureaucracies, and NIH ("not invented here") cultures. In a May 2011 interview, InnoCentive president and CEO Dwayne Spradlin characterized NIH thinking as possibly the greatest barrier that executives need to overcome in driving innovation in the organization:

> While the C-level suite may be intent on taking bold action, real change means organizational and culture change and change is something firms don't do easily or quickly. The organization and many of those that make it up will fight, like an immune response, to maintain the status quo, ultimately frustrating efforts and diminishing the benefits. Change is an unnatural act for organizations, but it is possible with commitment and resolve. And the reality is that, increasingly, organizations have no choice in the matter. They must adapt or will fail. This is the reality of many businesses today in this hypercompetitive twenty-first century. The organizations will adapt their cultures or they will lose ground rapidly.[15]

Spradlin goes on to say that getting past the NIH culture has been more difficult than previously understood, which means one of the biggest challenges to corporate innovators and those in the C-level suite is, in fact, culture change.

The volatility of the current economy—something I like to call "marketquake"—is demanding that organizations become agile in order to survive. This mandate is giving rise to a new revolution in management, one just as profound as the one that gave birth to the Industrial Age. The companies—large and small, old and new—that are emerging from the global financial ash of five years ago are those that are embracing new management practices.

Last year, more than 1,100 individuals from organizations around the world participated in the Skillsoft 21st Century Leadership survey.[16] In short, the survey reveals that today's workers understand the attributes and behavioral trends—curiosity, creativity, relationship building, global awareness, and integrity—that will drive success and innovation into the future, yet acknowledge that their organizations are instead celebrating and encouraging those behaviors and practices—ambition, determination, and intelligence—that created the iconic leaders of the twentieth-century. While these are indeed valuable and important traits for any successful leader, they are being usurped by more collaborative, creative, and relationship-building behaviors that can more effectively bring together people and ideas from around the world to drive innovation.

Leadership moving forward must emerge, as needed, from all corners of an organization. The Skillsoft study reveals that people both understand the need for, and want to develop, those emerging competitive behaviors, yet often their organizations are behind the curve in building the habitats that create and foster twenty-first-century leadership methods and mindsets.

One of the primary influencing factors in today's marketplace is the compounding rapidity of change we're facing. Product innovation and speed-to-market life cycles are compressing in this new economy, with upstarts being able to enter markets unencumbered by the legacy costs that organizations have had to bear. To compete we need to create new value more rapidly. As the saying goes, "fail faster."

IBM conducted a study in 2010 in which 1,500 CEOs were asked, in face-to-face interviews, to enumerate those skills that were of paramount importance to the leaders in their organizations, to their businesses, and to global competitiveness.[17] The premise of the study is that change is accelerating and complexity is deepening in all markets around the world. Add to this the fact that the world has become increasingly volatile and the future, ambiguous. Yet companies have been able to capitalize on these seismic changes and turn turbulence into innovation and advantage. In a nutshell, CEOs from the study said they cared most about creativity, the ability to borrow brilliance from all sectors, and the willingness to act despite uncertainty.

CONSUMERS CHANGE

Consumers—the ultimate target for product innovation—are also changing. They've never had so much information or so many options. More and more, they want to be involved in the creative process and, with the ability to post reviews to many e-commerce websites that solicit them, they can collectively bring a company down. While having customers involved may challenge traditional processes, it also offers great opportunity. Some of the most success-ful recent innovations are built on the collaborative interactions of the product and consumer, but we need to understand the changing role of the consumer to leverage it.

Today's consumer . . .

- **Has abundance of choice.** Today's technologies have made competitive shopping and peer-reviewed, real-time evaluations readily available. Because of these technological advantages, con-sumers are well-informed in their decision making and can make decisions much later in the sales process. In this abundant market-place, they have the luxury of choice and the market intelligence to make informed decisions without having to make direct con-tact with potential providers until the point of sale. By the time they do make contact, consumers are far more advanced in their decision-making process than they have ever been.
- **Wants to participate.** Whether or not companies are ready for crowdsourcing, consumers are. From Facebook to Twitter to

personalized sneakers and cars, consumers want, and expect, to be able to tweak, trick-out, and otherwise customize and participate in the products we deliver. Many successful innovations are defined by their ability to invite those in the user community to participate in and define what the product means to them. Google, after all, is nothing but a blank page with a waiting text box.

Or take another fun example, In-N-Out Burger, a famous burger restaurant on the West Coast whose menu is curiously simple: cheeseburger, hamburger, French fries, milkshake, soda, milk, and coffee. That's it. However, the restaurant also has a secret (or not-so-secret) menu generated over the years by creative employees and customers. Customers in the know can order a "Flying Dutchman" or an "Animal" or a "Wish Burger." The list goes on, and is getting longer. Part of the appeal of this innovative restaurant is to be in the know, part of the club, both participating and driving the experience. In this way, In-N-Out has indeed built a user-defined signature—a product and brand that is unique.

The participation of consumers also means that they have great power in a company's success through their own ability to add their two bits on any product into the review pool online rather than relying on a few official review sources. A company's message about its products and culture can no longer be effectively expressed only through advertising, press releases sent to the media, and product testing by a few professional review organizations.

- **Yearns for experiences, not products.** Increasingly, consumers are looking for products and services that reflect their own sense of identity and aspiration. You see this shift reflected in how savvy marketing appeals to the consumer's sense of yearning for experience or sensation. From marketing of cars to hair-color treatments to vodka, advertisers seek to capture our yearning for becoming a better, faster, more attractive kind of self as a result of buying the product. And, indeed, the most innovative companies tailor their interactions with consumers to engage and delight.

- **Is attracted to a narrative.** You walk into a sandwich shop, order the yummy-sounding special, and turn to the cooler to grab a drink. The usual representatives are there from major beverage providers. And then a cool photo on the label catches your eye—something called "Fufu Berry" by Jones Soda. The particular photo you see on the bottle is a woman in a hoodie looking triumphant. You look at the sodas again and realize that the photo on each bottle label is different. And every photo is contributed by a Jones Soda fan somewhere around the world.[18] Suddenly the product reaches you at an emotional level that goes beyond the product's utility—it tells a personal story.

  Jones Soda is building the customer story line into the product itself. You can go to the company's website, submit your own photo, and contribute to the community experience. Not only are you participating in the experience, but you have become part of a story, part of a compelling narrative. The labels are also cool, unique, and intriguing—and the soda isn't bad either.

In almost any buying circumstance in which products seem comparable, today's consumer is more likely to be drawn to those with a compelling story behind them.

INNOVATION IS THE ANSWER: OUT THINK COMPETITORS

As I've mentioned, innovative people are our greatest capital now. It's not manufacturing capacity, distribution networks, hardware, or infrastructure that holds the greatest promise of our future, but rather the innovative capacities of the people in our organizations. The good news is that, while people with certain traits may be more creative by nature, innovation can come from anyone and—with the right mindset—the ability to innovate can continue to grow in anyone. First we have to understand how this is possible.

The Story of Peter Georgescu

Over the past few years, I have had the pleasure to work with Peter Georgescu, chairman emeritus of Young & Rubicam, one of the premier marketing and branding organizations in the world. He tells a harrowing story of his childhood in Romania.[19]

Georgescu's father, a Standard Oil executive, was imprisoned by the Nazis when they invaded Romania. Released after the allies won the war, Peter's father found the Russians that followed the Nazis to be no better. Although Peter's father went back to work for Standard Oil, he and Peter's mother were denied reentrance into Romania after a business trip to the United States, and would face harsh treatment if they returned.

Peter and his brother, now separated from their parents, went to live with their grandparents in a small town in Transylvania until, one day, Communists burst into the house to arrest Peter's grandfather. Peter would never see him again.

Peter, his brother, and his grandmother were sent to a small town on the Russian border and given "a series of humiliating, dangerous jobs" by the Communist government. They served long, hard days as virtual slaves. For years the boys received only an occasional letter from their parents that had to be smuggled in. Eventually, even those communications stopped.

Six years later, in a story of political intrigue that was featured in popular media of the time, the boys were rescued and reunited with their parents in the United States. Peter earned his way into Princeton, then Stanford Business School, where he graduated with an MBA in 1963. He was offered a job at Young & Rubicam right out of Stanford, and would end up staying there for his entire career—37 years.

Peter Georgescu rose through the ranks at Young & Rubicam to become president of Y&R Advertising and president of its international division. This was accomplished through his loyalty to the needs of the company's customers and his innovations in marketing communications. Under his leadership, the company transformed from a private to a publicly held company and developed the most extensive database on global branding in the world. From its findings, Young & Rubicam built a proprietary model for diagnosing and managing brands. In 2001,

Georgescu was elected to the Advertising Hall of Fame for contributions to the marketing and advertising industry.

Georgescu is currently the chairman emeritus of Y&R—now a part of the WPP Group, the second-largest marketing and communications company in the world—and serves on several corporate boards of directors. His belief in the power of and commitment to education has also led to his serving on the boards of directors for a couple distinguished universities.

In an interview, Georgescu, like many other executives and leaders interviewed for this book, described creativity and innovation as being of paramount importance for any organization that intends to remain competitive.[20] He also reiterated the importance of not relying on strokes of genius or flashes of insight but rather on building a sustainable and reliable process for generating innovation on a consistent basis:

> If you are the low-cost producer, since the consumer is very sophisticated, yours will be the brand of choice because the consumer will shop you on price. The alternative is you are going to be different, you are going to be an innovator—you are going to invent added-value products and services, and do so on a consistent basis over time.

Georgescu observed that cutting-edge development technology has become increasingly cheaper to acquire and ubiquitously available. Whenever something new is introduced to the marketplace, the forces of the market rush to copy that innovation and, in this way, technology becomes the great equalizer.

Peter went on to describe the role of creativity in the innovation process as being a craft, not an art form. In his view, it's craftsman-like discipline of exercising our creativity that leads to real innovation:

> The right context to look at creativity is the process of differentiating product and services and creating that difference to be relevant and meaningful to consumers, because ultimately a consumer has to be willing to pay a higher price for that difference. And so, that's the nature of the kind of craftsman-like creativity. It's not an art form; it's a craft. You have to make creativity work to solve a specific problem, to make a better product, to add value.

The Out Think Journey

This mandate to innovate is bigger than just us, our teams, and even our organizations. The standard and quality of living of a nation ultimately depends on the ability of each of us, as citizens, to add value to the products and services with which we interact each day.

From my experience working with numerous organizations, leading executives, and thought leaders, I have come to believe it's possible to define, and engage in, an innovative process—one that has clear components and methods. Using intentional, deliberate methodology might feel contrary to finding the eventual "eureka" moment we look for in an innovative breakthrough, but I believe that innovation can only be consistently achieved by thoughtful and active participation in a process.

The ten elements of the Out Think process that are described in the following chapters—trust, inquiry, exploration, aspiration, edge, connection, mash-up, action, signature, and purpose—are not necessarily sequential or discrete from one another. They are parts of a journey that may start from an unexpected place, go off in tangents, and circle back to the beginning. And it is never really over, since the marketplace is constantly in motion and demands continuing innovation.

Exploration, for example, isn't necessarily a step to be completed and abandoned but instead applied throughout the innovation process, with deeper and deeper inquiry. Similarly, a sense of aspiration and reaching toward a more audacious goal or desired outcome should be revisited along the Out Think journey as we gain greater understanding of the innovation we seek. Each part of this journey is dynamic and interactive with the next, in the same way that we are always building upon the skills we have acquired while constantly reinforcing and honing those same skills, which have brought us this far.

In developing the Out Think model, I've factored in changing global paradigms, accelerated technology, and seismic demographic shifts that require new approaches. The chart below highlights aspects of leadership in the twentieth-century that no longer work and the corresponding aspects in the Out Think approach that I have discovered empirically do work.

Out Think Model

Activity	What Worked Before	Out Think Leadership
Driving engagement	Celebrate rewards	Celebrate meaningful progress
Developing strategy	Marshal efforts toward the ideas of a few in power	Listen to the ideas of many Execute on the strongest ideas
Finding new ideas	Ask experts in parallel domains	Ask experts in tangential domains
Enhancing productivity	Increase efficiency of transaction volume and workload	Increase mindfulness and time for focused work
Achieving purpose	Create value for owners	Create value for all stakeholders
Overcoming adversity	Focus on the problem	Identify the problem Focus on new opportunities
Building teams	Aspire to please the boss	Aspire to work well together
Accelerating learning	Immerse in content, and practice periodically	Immerse in content, and practice constantly
Taking risks	Fail less	Fail faster
Hiring	Hire for resume and past accomplishments	Hire for values and growth mindset
Allocating talent	Have managers place people according to their skills	Have people place themselves according to their strengths
Building process	Create and preserve processes	Create new processes and selectively abandon outmoded processes
Collaborating	Deepen close-knit groups	Deepen widely distributed networks
Innovating	Introduce novelty into existing products	Borrow brilliance to develop new value
Assessing performance	Ask "Who is the hero?" Ask "Who dropped the ball?"	Ask "What did we learn?"
Defining success	Achieve a fixed and immutable outcome	Increase adaptation to changing circumstances

Developing best practices	Study and emulate the competition	Build signature solutions
Developing a strong company culture	Copy benefits and policies of past companies	Echo founding vision Encourage unique expression of new personalities
Developing vacation policy	Create clear guidelines	Allow entrusted employees to decide
Chatting with colleagues	Talk about the weekend	Talk about the purpose of the work
Building scale	Adhere to rules	Adhere to values
Investing strategy	Grow fast	Grow far

LET'S RECAP

Remember . . .

- Innovation is creativity in action. Everyone can be creative and contribute to innovative outcomes that create economic value and competitive advantage.
- Innovative leaders nurture, act upon, implement, and take creative ideas into breakthrough change and invention.
- It's not enough to just be ambitious and determined anymore. Leaders must hire, inspire, and develop innovative people while stirring curiosity, creativity, relationship building, global awareness, and integrity.

Your Turn Now . . .

Reach in: Assess yourself in terms of curiosity, creativity, relationship building, global awareness, and integrity. Select one or two of these descriptors that you consider as a strength or passion. Then select one of the descriptors that you are interested in developing more fully. As you learn more about innovation and leadership, reflect on how you are leveraging your strengths and further developing yourself.

Reach out: Conduct a brainstorming session with your team, asking them to complete the sentence "Our team has the potential to be truly innovative because we . . ." Remember that brainstorming means no judging or debating! Simply generate a reasonable list (10–20 items) of qualities or conditions that the team views as their innovative strengths. Then discuss how to leverage these more fully, probing on how technology or human effort can boost team innovation.

Spread out: Ask your team or a cross-functional work group to brainstorm significant innovations achieved by your company or industry. Don't judge or debate anything—just make a list. Then ask the group to jump into the future and create a similar list. What will be different, new, innovative, and inventive years from now? What market or customer factors will impact innovation in your company or industry? Pick one or two ideas that excite people the most and ask them to "test" the idea with contacts and colleagues. Keep the dialogue going!

Remember . . .

- The innovation playing field is so decentralized, global, seamless, and dynamic that leaders can no longer rely on traditional—often limiting—management methods and practices. They must take steps toward and engage others in building a work culture that matches the driving forces of innovation.

- Technology has made it possible to find talent and innovation everywhere. The world of talent and technology is your stage for innovation, and you are the director. Cast the best people, build imaginative sets, provide a rich script, but allow for improvisation and control at the local level.

- Globalization is less about countries and locations as it is about recognizing and capitalizing on rapid, seismic changes. It's about opening up organizational cultures and borrowing brilliance needed for innovation.

- New and emerging generations of workers are blazing their own paths in order to innovate and compete. Companies must engage workers of all ages and experiences in appealing to new consumers who want choice, participation, experiences, and a better life.

Your Turn Now . . .

Reach in: Create a two-column list. On one side, write a list of four or five management practices you believe contribute to your personal success. These might relate to how you plan strategically, manage performance, or solve problems. On the other side of your list, briefly describe how you might change each successful practice to be ready for your own "marketquake"—one that does more than just prop up old ideas. Go beyond "arrested decay"!

Reach out: Go on a research mission. Using the Internet, publications, conversations, and observations, anticipate what your team's product or service will do for customers in the future. What might happen in your customers' world (scope, buyers, technology) that would change the way they view your company's value? Be prepared to share three future scenarios, based on your informal research, which could spark ideas for innovation. Then ask your team members to perform the same assignment, either as a team, in small groups, or as individuals. Have them report on their findings, or put all the ideas into a hat (literally or electronically) and pick some to explore as a team. Look for themes.

Spread out: Consider who or what—outside of your organization— could amplify your innovation efforts with additional ideas, resources, and technology. Use some of the scenarios described above as jumping-off points, and include others. Think beyond centralized control, and don't limit your ideas to those you can afford or access readily.

CHAPTER 2

TRUST: ESTABLISH THE ENGINE OF LEADERSHIP

> At the end of the day it's probably the only thing that matters in any organization. Whether it's your family or your work, trust is the engine of a great life.
>
> —*Howard Behar, former president of Starbucks*

In an interview in May 2011, Paul Hiltz, who is now president of Mercy Health Select, told me about when he became CEO of Mercy Hospital Mt. Airy in Cincinnati, Ohio, in 2007.[1] He was the fifth person to hold that position in less than six years. At that time, the hospital was struggling with serious issues, from financial to employee engagement and retention, and he had been brought in to help it change course. One thing that stood out to him was the skepticism that the employees had: "... There wasn't a whole lot of trust, I don't think, that I would be here, that I would be committed to fixing what needed to be fixed." The hospital employees were tired from the "tons of change" the hospital was already going through, he said, and the financial pressures didn't help. A "sort of sense of hopelessness" pervaded the organization, and a "palpable" fear that closure might be in their future—meaning employees would lose their jobs.

Hiltz was there to help turn the hospital around. He immediately tried to allay fears by assuring the employees that he did not have a "slash and burn" strategy in mind and instead wanted to rebuild around the things that were working. He made it clear at the beginning of his tenure that his approach would be to amplify and encourage what was working, instead of the more common knee-jerk impulse of reducing payroll or programs in an effort to cut costs. Hiltz entered with a new mindset to redirect time, resources, and energies of those people and processes that were not well aligned.

While some CEOs might hunker down in an office and conduct lengthy board meetings that lead to grandiose pronouncements of change, Hiltz instead made himself personally and publicly available throughout the hospital. He asked the doctors and the other employees for a list of the top ten things that needed to be done and then gained their trust by actually starting to work on those things. While he acknowledged that some items would take more time than others, he assured the staff he'd address everything on the list. The important thing, he told them, is that he was committed to working on the list and that there would be a scorecard they could use to give feedback on how well he was doing his job.

This book explores emerging ideas in developing twenty-first-century leadership methods, mindsets, behaviors, and beliefs about driving engagement, building deep collaboration, and deviating from the norm onto new paths toward innovation. However, the expectation going in is that we all have a shared understanding of some of the foundational aspects of leadership, starting with building trust, as Hiltz demonstrated, which means keeping business operations transparent. To be innovative leaders, we must build on this base by constantly reiterating and communicating core ideas, using powerful stories to propel change, modeling the behavior we wish to see, and, above all, creating and sustaining energy in others in the organization. These foundational traits of the innovative leader constitute the terra firma underlying the journey to innovation.

WORK FROM THE BOTTOM UP

Hiltz knew that some of the people in the organization who understood the most about what to change were not executives but rather the rank-and-file staff responsible for the daily operations and management of the facilities and care of the patients. By adopting the practice

of asking the employees throughout the hospital what the most important change initiatives should be, being open with them, and following
up with their recommendations, Hiltz built trust. Employees, he said,
could see he came through on what he said he would do.

Interestingly, some of the changes were not costly but led to an
uplifting of energy and commitment from the staff. For example, Hiltz
replaced old carpeting, added fresh paint to the walls, and repaired broken machinery and medical equipment. When he asked an attending
physician in the intensive care unit what small changes would be valuable to that unit, the doctor said the windows hadn't been washed in
years and gave the rooms a decaying feel to them. So Hiltz arranged for
the windows to be washed. Such small, cosmetic touches weren't time-
consuming or resource intensive but made a tremendous difference to
the people who worked in the hospital every day. To them, it was a
breath of fresh air.

"You come in with preconceived notions that people want you to
make massive change," Hiltz said, but what he found was that some of
the most important changes were "everyday things that really showed
people we were going to breathe some life into the organization."

Because Hiltz spent so much of his time working and interacting
with the people in the hospital, he came to know them and, in many
instances, learned their personal stories and histories. From the cafeteria workers and janitors to the nurses and specialists, he was personally
close to each employee, and because people in the hospital recognized
his sincerity, they were more and more likely to give honest opinions
about what needed to be accomplished. They also gave more of themselves to the growth and reinvigoration of the enterprise. Scores for
both employee engagement and physician satisfaction rose dramatically.

TEACH EVERYONE HOW THE
MONEY FLOWS

To further build trust and engage employees in the process of improving the hospital, Hiltz brought in a medical financial advisor to conduct workshops with the doctors, nurses, and staff. This taught them
how the hospital finances actually worked, from the point at which an

ambulance is dispatched all the way through the system to the point of discharging a patient. They learned how the medical reimbursement and insurance billing systems worked, and what their rates of reimbursement recovery were. They were taught the cost and maintenance of operating expensive and complicated medical devices and diagnostic machines. Through this process, everyone learned where the system worked well, and also where the challenges were.

Many among the staff were astonished to learn that some of the practices and tests they had been prescribing for years, that they believed to be financially sound for the hospital, were actually counterproductive to the financial health of the organization. Hiltz describes that to many it was an eye-opening experience:

> You know, one of the first things we did that I think was a really powerful thing, we brought in a person to help us teach a health care finance class to all of our managers, so we talked to them about how the dollar flows in health care—through insurance, to the doctors, to the hospitals—and what that meant to them and how they could have a big impact on utilization and how we did financially and quality-wise. And people that have been in the business for 20 years came to me afterwards [and] said, "I never knew that that's how we were reimbursed for emergency department visits."

As Hiltz successfully demonstrated in turning around a failing enterprise, an increased level of financial transparency and accountability leads to a more active and aware participation in positive financial practices at all levels of the organization.

USE EMOTIONAL PERSUASION FOR CHANGE

Having worked in hospital environments for many years, Paul Hiltz understands that organizations with deep histories, and often complicated practices, can also be difficult environments in which to create systemic change. Like well-established companies and government institutions, hospitals operate within a long legacy of established practice and code of conduct that can be difficult to change. To get its staff's attention through the power of emotional persuasion, Mercy Hospital used a story that other medical organizations also employ:

In 2001, an 18-month-old girl named Josie King was admitted to Johns Hopkins Hospital with first- and second-degree burns she received from climbing into a scalding bath. She spent ten days in the Pediatric Intensive Care Unit recovering well and soon was scheduled for release to go home and be with her three older siblings. However, over the course of the following few days before her scheduled release, the baby died from severe dehydration and misuse of narcotics as a result of a series of errors and oversights by the attending doctors and nurses.

It's a horrifying story and quite effective at gaining the attention of a room full of medical workers. The energy, focus, and righteous indignation of everyone in the room after hearing such a story were at full throttle. They were appalled, furious, and deeply saddened by the Josie King story. With the staff's full emotional attention focused on the necessity of avoiding this situation, the timing was perfect to introduce specific clinical interventions and practices to correct a particular practice in the hospital.

In an interview, Stanford University Management Professor Bob Sutton called this tactic "hot emotions and cool solutions."[2] The idea is to use a very charged and emotionally engaging story and then follow up with specific tactical solutions and ideas for action. It's a powerful change device because memorable and emotional stories are effective catalysts for action.

If we want those in our organizations to remember the key priorities or to remember the reasons why we're going in a certain direction, we need to develop and share strategic stories that help remind others of the purpose of their work and what they must consider in making decisions. People remember little from looking at data and statistics, yet easily recall compelling stories. If we want people to behave in particular ways when they are away from us—which is much of the time—we should use provocative stories that have a singular message and require a few key actions that are taken to achieve the depicted goal.

SPEAK THE TRUTH

Common sense is not so common.

—Voltaire

I know, this is one of those "Duh!" pieces of advice, but as I have often learned from top executives, common sense does not always translate into common action. In an interview at Starbucks headquarters in Seattle, former Starbucks president Howard Behar told me a personal story of an early life lesson he learned as a young COO of a failing company.[3]

Behar had been brought in to devise a turnaround plan for the suffering company and had come to an early conclusion that it needed to make some staffing cuts to stay afloat. Behar assembled the top executives in a private meeting and asked each to come up with a plan for reducing personnel. After a full two days of closed-door, intense discussion and debate, they constructed a plan to let go of some people and programs. Someone made photocopies of the plan, and unfortunately, the original was left on the copier after everyone went home.

Pretty soon thereafter Howard started to get phone calls from other people in the organization who wanted to know the truth. Howard immediately summoned the private executive group back together to discuss how to handle the information leak, because now people in the company were getting nervous and agitated. Many of these top executives suggested they deny the plan and publicly say that it wasn't true—that it was just an old draft.

As Howard listened to different versions of obfuscating the truth, his assistant in the room turned to him and said, "Howard, only the truth sounds like the truth." And he knew she was right. He assembled the entire company in a town-hall-style meeting and shared everything with them—the good, the bad, and options for next steps. When he disclosed everything, something interesting happened. One by one throughout the room people stepped up with solutions. As Howard recalled in our interview:

> The most amazing thing happened. Blew me away. Here I thought I was going to get shot, figuratively, or maybe literally, and it's not what happened at all. One by one people stood up and started applauding.

People started to ask, "How can we help?" They said, "Even if I'm going to get laid off, I want to help. I want to be part of this process." There I was, in my early thirties, I would have never thought that would happen. It's probably one of the single most valuable lessons of my leadership life.

LEAD WITH INTEGRITY AND HONEST INTENTION

The IBM Global CEO study listed integrity as one of the top three characteristics leaders should have in today's changing business landscape. Integrity is about being true, honest, and authentic with others. It's about being clear about our intentions and basing our actions on them. Our intentions are the platform on which our behaviors, thoughts, habits, and actions stand. Our customers, colleagues, family, and pretty much everyone we interact with generally have keen detectors of our intent.

We need to remind ourselves of the etymology of integrity, which comes from the Latin "integer," meaning a thing that is complete in itself—whole, as in a whole number. Just as we often segment our learning into different disciplines, not benefiting from the synergy that comes with integrating our studies, we also lose out when we partition our lives into work, home, recreation, community service, and other categories. Our greatest strength comes from integrating all the disparate interactions, ideas, and energies into a unified and integrated whole.

A perfect example of someone possessing foundational leadership traits while leading an iconic brand of innovation is Garry Ridge, CEO of WD-40 Company. When I interviewed him in May 2011, he recalled one of his most important foundational leadership lessons.[4] As a boy in Sydney, Australia, Ridge worked in a hardware store privately owned and operated by Warren Knox. One day Warren arrived at the shop and told Garry that his father had died and he needed to leave for a few days to attend the funeral and take care of some family affairs. Warren gave the keys to the shop to Garry and said, "You need to take care of the store. I have to go do family business."

Garry basically ran that store for a number of days until the owner got back, he said. When he turned over the keys, the owner merely thanked him, asking no questions: "He just was confident that sales were made, the cash was banked, the store was taken care of, and we went on with business."

Garry said that, in that moment, he realized the power of trust—not just saying you trust someone but actually giving complete and unconditional trust. This taught him that "people have to be aware of the impact of trust" and that trust means "are you able, are you believable, are you connected, are you dependable?"

In an interview, CEO of World Fuel Services Paul H. Stebbins talked about how powerful early life experiences can be as he described to me an experience that was almost identical to Garry Ridge's.[5] Stebbins had worked for a gas station in Texas for almost three years, starting at the age of 13. The gas station owner was a local man, known to everyone in town. On Paul's 16th birthday, the owner threw him the keys to the shop, asked him to close up as usual at 9:00 p.m., got in his car, and drove home. Paul recalls being deeply humbled and appreciative of this act of complete trust:

> If I do anything, as long as I live, it will be to have that same trust for somebody in my life as well. It certainly changed my view of the world, and I'll never forget it. I was, you know, ten feet off the ground and so proud that somebody would actually trust me with that. But I felt a real sense of responsibility, and that's ultimately the core of it, is the risk to give somebody the freedom to be responsible is a remarkable thing.

TRUST WHAT YOU LOVE TO DO

In his book *The Element: How Finding Your Passion Changes Everything*, Ken Robinson profiles cartoonist Matt Groening (who created the pitch for *The Simpsons* on the spot while in a meeting); rock-and-roll musician Mick Fleetwood (who bailed on high school at 16 to be a jazz drummer in London); noted dancer, choreographer, and director Gillian Lynne (who was deemed an underachiever until she enrolled in a dance school); and many others who eschewed the advice of elders to stick to what is "safe," or who were recognized by mentors for their talents and helped to pursue their passions to great ends.[6]

Coming closer to home, I learned about the value of trusting our passion for the work we do from a story about my great-uncle William F. (Bill) Santelmann, who was director of the "The President's Own" United States Marine Band. The details were related to me by Col. John R. Bourgeois,[7] who was present on the occasion in question and served as the band's director from 1979 to 1996.

According to the colonel, the band plays for heads of state, Rose Garden ceremonies, Arlington Cemetery proceedings, and events throughout the world at the pleasure of the president of the United States.

In the early days, the band consisted mostly of enlisted marines who grew up taking music lessons, but Bill's father, William H. Santelmann, had taken it to a new level when he became director in 1898, ushering in a whole new era for the band. He recruited talented musicians and built up their musicianship and their ability to listen to each other and grow their repertoire. By the end of his tenure, in 1927, the band could play any kind of music—from Dixieland jazz to rock and roll, blues, waltzes, and orchestral arrangements—all with the precision and passion of the greatest bands of the time.

In 1940, Bill followed in his father's footsteps and became the band's director, serving until 1955. At the time he took over, the band was already known to be supremely capable and versatile, but he was recognized for elevating its musicianship even further.

After his stint with the Marine Corps, Bill kept up a rigorous schedule of performing and guest-conducting around the world. In 1984, while attending the American Bandmasters Association's annual conference, "The President's Own" was given the highest honor of being asked to play as the closing band for the conference dinner. And Bill was also honored by being asked to guest-conduct his old band.

For a finale, Bill led the band through Wagner's "Ride of the Valkyries." It was majestic, soaring. The crowd roared their approval, so for an encore he chose "Semper Fidelis," the official march of the Marine Corps, composed by John Philip Sousa in 1888, when he was director of the band. The chamber again thundered applause and, while Bill's own band stood clapping in ovation in his honor, he walked backstage.

With a great sense of joy, Bill sat down where he could see the first few rows of the audience. As they were smiling and clapping, and the band was both bowing to the audience and acknowledging him off-stage, he exclaimed "I love this band!" Those were his last words, as immediately after he said them he died of a heart attack.

Santelmann left this world at the height of his passion and joy, surrounded by friends and colleagues and engaged in something he was passionate about and excelled at. He left the world a better place by sharing his joy. We all leave this world at some point, but this is a beautiful way to go, always engaging and loving what we do.

Great leaders love what they do and feel great purpose in it. That rubs off on those they work with. It's hard not to get caught up in the enthusiasm of the person who is leading us.

LEAVE PEOPLE MORE ENERGIZED

Out Think leaders don't think of themselves as sitting at the top of an organization they oversee, but rather as supporting people and processes from beneath, as a servant to the organization. The Out Think leader has a persistent and unwavering commitment to constantly sustain and grow the energy of others. These types of leaders are known as "energizers."

As shown in Figure 2.1, on the next page, sustaining and growing the energy in others is a paramount characteristic of Out Think leaders.

In most organizations today, if you inquire about a particular person, project, or event, you might hear people talk in terms of the positive energy surrounding it. They might say, "The April conference has a ton of momentum right now!" or "I just got off the phone with Miriam and she totally fired me up. I think I can make this happen." Or perhaps, "Have you talked to Joseph about his new idea? There's a lot of excitement around it right now."

Inversely, people who suck the energy out of everyone around them—who are energy vampires—are often spoken of in terms of dread and apprehension. I'm quite certain you can mentally identify individuals for whom you feel you need to brace yourself for your next interaction.

Rob Cross, an associate professor in the University of Virginia's McIntire School of Commerce, and his colleagues have researched the

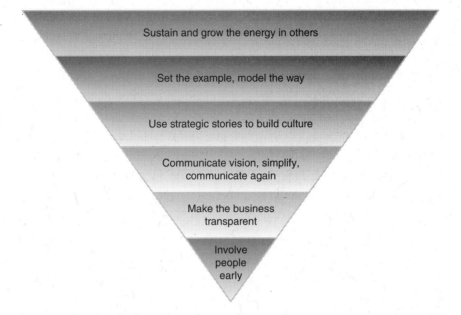

Figure 2.1   Out Think Leaders

impact of what they call "energizers" and "de-energizers" in organizations.[8] He and his colleagues asked individuals in a variety of organizations to rate others on a scale of one (energy-sapping) to five (generous energy-giving). The researchers then interviewed and identified the traits and characteristics of energy creators and their impact on productivity, culture, mood-state in the organization, and innovative capacity.

Not surprisingly, those who create and give energy to others were consistently sought out over de-energizers. According to Cross and his colleagues, top energizers can create and communicate a compelling vision of the future, demonstrate that others are making meaningful contributions, identify and convey a clear sense of progress, and fully engage in each interaction.

Create and Communicate a Compelling Vision of the Future

The key word here is *compelling*. Those energizing individuals capable of instilling a powerful and compelling vision of the future are able to convey a future they envision that is both believable and feasible as a goal. Visions interpreted as overly ambitious or preposterous in scope suck energy and hope from those listening. A true energizer can convey a believable vision of a future state that inspires hope and optimism.

The antithesis of the visioning energizer is the de-energizing naysayer who sees only roadblocks and obstacles. Identifying and presenting ways to surmount real obstacles is critical to becoming a powerful energizer. Those who merely identify problems without looking for solutions become de-energizing leaders and team members.

Convey That Others Are Making Meaningful Contributions

Praise and recognition of individual contribution is a hallmark of strong energizers, but most importantly this requires being specific in praise. Instead of saying "Good presentation!" a gifted energizer might say the following: "You did an excellent job in reframing slides 12 and 14 in your presentation to speak to the specific needs of the customer. You listened well and they appreciated it."

In addition to being highly specific and nuanced in recognizing contribution, skilled energizers also build opportunities for people to make contributions. Not only do they praise with high specificity, but they also offer settings in which people can bring their best skills and make their best contributions to tasks and projects and team environments. In other words, the best energizers understand each player's strengths and create opportunities for players to make their most meaningful contributions.

Identify and Convey a Clear Sense of Progress

I had the opportunity to collaborate with Teresa Amabile, Harvard researcher and professor of business administration and author of *The Progress Principle: Using Small Wins to Ignite Joy, Engagement, and Creativity at Work* in 2011. In person Amabile is affable, yet focused, and also open to suggestions and new ideas. My first meeting with her was when I walked into a conference room where she was working alone.

After I introduced myself, she said politely, "Please just give me a moment to finish this thought," and returned to her writing. She emerged a few minutes later and we entered a discussion about how our production collaboration for the day should play out. It's this kind of determined focus, combined with an open and easygoing disposition, that may be what enables her to uncover more unexpected and nuanced findings while also completing the leviathan research projects she undertakes.

In her work, Amabile affirms Rob Cross's prescription for energizers to convey a clear sense of progress. She and her husband, fellow researcher Steven Kramer, analyzed 12,000 diary entries from 238 employees in 7 companies to come to the qualified conclusion that the most powerful work motivator is indeed a sense of progress in meaningful work. They found from studying this mountain of diary entries that it was not monumental breakthroughs or audacious aspirations that sustained individual motivation. Rather, it was constant progress in work that held meaning for that individual making consistent and measurable steps forward on a daily basis—what Amabile came to identify as "the power of small wins."

Fully Engage in Each Interaction

Anyone who has ever spent a moment with Oprah Winfrey, Bill Clinton, or leadership giant Warren Bennis all share similar stories of feeling these leaders were wholly present, utterly undistracted, and completely immersed in the conversation. In each interaction, energizers, however powerful or important the world believes them to be, will make every person feel as if he or she is the most interesting, important, and valuable person in the room. Energizers present a tone and body language that reflects that they are fully present and attuned to the listener. Put another way, they show great emotional fluency.

LET'S RECAP

Remember . . .

Great leaders lay down a foundation of trust upon which to build an innovative culture. The building blocks are as follows:

- Keep business operations transparent to all staff so they are in the know about the health of the business, financial structures, and the role everyone plays in keeping the money flowing.

- Build trust from the bottom up. Employees who are close to the action have practical, often illuminating, ideas for change and improvement. People are more willing to get involved if you involve them from the start.

- Communicate and reiterate core concepts—principles, values, visions, and strategies. Keep your messages simple, but powerful.

- Use compelling stories and examples to foster and propel change. Share your own stories and elicit stories from others.

- Set the example by implementing desired changes, however small. Make change happen readily, even if it's one step in a bigger change effort.

- Sustain energy and enthusiasm in others. Keep the momentum going through open discussions about progress, achievements, and next steps.

Your Turn Now . . .

Reach in: Assess how solid your trust foundation is right now. For each of the six building blocks, rate yourself in a simple, honest way (e.g., high, medium, or low). Make a personal plan to shore up any trust building blocks that aren't strong enough to support your new innovation culture.

Reach out: Get out and engage with the members of your team. Notice what's working well and acknowledge good work in specific ways, such as the value to the company, team, or customer. Ask questions about what could be done to make "what's working" even better. Ask team members for wish lists and encourage them to share ideas about changing how work gets done or about resources that would help. Make a list of ten to-dos based on what people want, and diligently act on the list to show your intention and accountability.

Whenever you have the opportunity, connect people's words and actions to the company's business metrics, core concepts, and principles. If any of the metrics, concepts, or principles are not crystal clear to your team members, explain them in their language. Take the time to listen to stories. These are like gold—precious, revealing indicators of trust. When you share company news—whether it be positive or negative—do it in person as much as possible. The language of emotion is best spoken person to person.

Spread out: Identify ways that you can spread the news about your team's efforts, achievements, and actions in ways that are valuable to others in the company. Whenever possible, let the people in the team tell their stories to others, while you play a supportive and encouraging role. For example, rather than write about your team's accomplishments, conduct interviews with its members and present their comments and stories.

Remember . . .

- How leaders build trust—their words, behaviors, integrity, and intention—influences the impact they make on others. When leaders are sincere, honest, and willing to show their human side, people reciprocate.

- Success begets success, and the greatest achievements emanate from a burning desire to do the task. If leaders love their work and show how much they love it, they can better engage others in taking action required for change and innovation.

- Leaders should be positive and energizing—but avoid over-ambitious or preposterous schemes that leave others sapped of energy, optimism, and hope. Something as simple as sprucing up the work spaces or fixing broken equipment are tangible signs of positive energy.

- When people take on unfamiliar tasks, step up to new assignments, or make meaningful contributions and achievements, it is important to recognize their efforts in specific, personal ways. Give them opportunities to achieve, try new things, and excel.

- The most powerful work motivator is a sense of progress in meaningful work. When leaders reward small wins and help others experience their role in the progression toward the bigger picture, they stir energy and build trust.

Your Turn Now . . .

Reach in: Recall an event that reinforced how much you love your work. Describe everything—what was happening, who was involved, the feelings you had. What was it about the event that felt so energizing, powerful, or symbolic? Similarly, have you experienced an event that caused you to become unmotivated and made you question your love for your work? Describe that event. Compare these events. How did you experience trust, emotion, intention, or integrity in these situations?

Reach out: Think of a task, project, or initiative that is close to you—one you alone have historically taken responsibility for and claimed as your own. Then think of someone on your team whom you trust to execute this effort—someone you know will similarly take ownership and put his or her own personal stamp on the delivery. The most important part of this exercise is to assign the task in a trusting way, without micromanaging or even expecting that the person will perform or deliver the result exactly as you would. Reward small wins and acknowledge progress. Allow the person to put his or her own signature on the finished results.

Spread out: Ask your team to think about how they can make more of an impact on the company's business metrics, financial health, or competitive position. Assign them the responsibility of selecting some endeavor that not only excites them but benefits the company. Then make a team goal. Use this as an opportunity to help the team celebrate small wins and nourish their steady progress rather than micromanage.

CHAPTER 3

INQUIRY: PROVOKE WITH QUESTIONS, NOT ANSWERS

The most serious mistakes are not being made as a result of wrong answers. The truly dangerous thing is asking the wrong question.

—*Peter Drucker*

A week or so before New Year's Day 2011, my mother, Bev Hunter, was diagnosed with advanced mantle cell lymphoma—a particularly pernicious form of lymphoma. She almost immediately began an aggressive chemotherapy protocol that destroys not only cancer cells, but also healthy ones.

The collateral damage to the body can be devastating, and I was astonished to discover the number of countermeasures that oncologists, nurses, and clinicians use to help bolster the body's ability to withstand the amount of internal damage chemotherapy can inflict. There are various kinds of antibiotics (to aid the suppressed immune system), intravenous hydration cocktails (to help flush the high volume of toxins created by the chemotherapy's destruction of cells), drugs (to support kidney function), and a litany of other supporting countermeasures I can't begin to understand.

My mother has always been a smart, curious person, willing to take on the challenges of life. Instead of being overwhelmed by the complexity and life-threatening nature of her situation, she instead turned into her own advocate and harnessed the talents of those around her to develop a strategy for determining the best way to handle her situation and embark on the greatest innovation journey of her life—saving it. She created a team of supporting players and enrolled friends, family, and the community to help with different kinds of supporting tasks and dove head first into her inquiry, opening up her mind to any course that may be useful in fighting her lymphoma.

Throughout six months of debilitating chemotherapy and another four or five months of slow recovery, Beverly was constantly engaged in inquiry while confronting this new challenge and would often ask herself, "What am I capable of becoming in a year?" To address this question, she had to become open to ideas, opportunities, and experiences that she had not paid attention to in the past.

She attended a charity auction to support a local philanthropic effort. At the auction, one of the marquee items up for bid was a week vacation in Burgundy, France—a sublimely beautiful bucolic region of France southeast of Paris known for vineyards, quaint and beautiful villages, and twisting country roads. She had never been to this region, knew very little of its deep history and remarkable beauty, and yet when the item came up for bid, she raised her hand. Outbid, she raised her hand again—and again and again until she had won this prize.

This distant dream of an adventure in France with extended family represented hope of a future adventure and yet started with a question in her mind—her own new inquiry: "Can I go there?" She had no personal history or memory to draw her to Burgundy, and not much at the auction beyond a few photos to entice her, but she had set herself on this course with her inquiry into her medical situation. She was already open to seeing new things, having new experiences, and inquiring deeply into her life and what the world had to offer her. She had risked making changes, and was embracing them.

"When presented with new and difficult challenges, you have to be open to asking audacious questions that you might have previously been closed to—to take you in new, and innovative, directions," she explained.

In a *Peanuts* cartoon, Charlie Brown once said, "No problem is so large or complex that it can't be run away from." While this may fit his sad-sack character, if we are to succeed in innovation in real life, we need to face challenges head on, no matter how daunting. Challenge and adversity is prevalent and accelerating in our work, and we need to face it with an open mind, a deep sense of curiosity, and a willingness to ask penetrating questions. The journey toward innovation requires curious inquiry. And curious inquiry starts with a growth mindset—a belief that we, and those around us, can constantly grow in skill and talent.

START WITH A GROWTH MINDSET

In a series of studies, Carol Dweck, author of *Mindset*, found that people fall into two general categories—those who believe their intelligence and capabilities are fixed, and those who believe their intelligence and capabilities are malleable and can change over time with effort and constant inquiry. People who believe in learning and growth continually improve their capabilities because they try harder and constantly put themselves in positions where they might fail. They continually improve because of, or despite, the challenges around them. Such a growth mindset can be learned through the inquiry process.

In the inquiry part of the Out Think journey, we ask, probe, investigate, and remain ever open and curious about the paths on which our inquiry may take us. We need to follow the positive idea threads that matter to us, in the context of our work, our team, our organizations, and ultimately what is important in our lives and what leads us to meaningful work. Inquiry applies to the people, the places, and the processes in which we participate—who, where, and how we ask questions. In the context of developing innovation, the power of inquiry can be enhanced in each of these domains. The goal here is to ask those creative questions that will drive tangible innovation that is meaningful and valuable. But first we need to get into the right frame of mind.

GET CURIOUS

Yves Doz, a professor at INSEAD, one of the world's leading graduate business schools, is an immensely prolific and expansive thinker. Having collaborated over the years with numerous leading scholars, he has studied and written about remarkable leaders and innovators the world over. In an interview in 2009, Doz provided valuable advice for those looking to develop strategic agility, which he defines as a heightened and accelerated ability to develop innovative solutions that lead to strategic advantage in the marketplace. First, expose yourself to new external environments outside of your current domain expertise and work groups. Next, become more connected to people and ideas that may positively influence your thinking.[1] As he described in this tennis analogy:

> You need to be willing to engage in true dialogues—in other words, to be in a learning mode rather than in a convincing mode. Sometimes managers go into meetings a little bit like a tennis player goes into a tennis game . . . to win the point with the fewest exchanges and in the shortest possible time. Rather than [thinking] "I want to enlist my colleagues into helping me think about an issue," instead [I] understand some of their starting points and some of their assumptions and have them understand some of mine. And out of our collective understanding, something better will come out.

Finally, *get curious*. Curiosity—a profound, unyielding desire to find out how things work, how problems can be solved—is the main driver of innovation. We're all born with a deep desire to know more about the world around us and our place in it. This curious nature of our species has enabled us—for better or worse—to rise to the top of the food chain, harness nature for our purposes, and continue to invent an endless stream of products and services to suit our needs and desires. Curiosity brings us to delight in the unknown, as it did with my mother when she bid on a vacation in France. And curiosity about the ideas of others can drive innovation in leaders.

In moments of curiosity, we find ourselves extracting the most out of experiences. We ask probing questions, read deeply with intent, manipulate and examine objects, and persist in activities and tasks that we find both challenging and stimulating. If we apply ourselves to learning to be curious, the results can be profound. It can be the sustaining key to happiness, joy, and lifelong fulfillment. Curious people tend to become more curious over time (curiosity breeds curiosity), ultimately find greater enjoyment, and even live longer.

As leaders, we need to learn to be curious ourselves before we can inspire curiosity in others. We can teach ourselves to open up our minds and allow more ideas into our active thinking process by getting outside of our usual domain and experiencing new ideas and new approaches to thinking.

EXERCISE DIVERGENT THINKING

In the beginner's mind there are many possibilities, but in the expert's there are few.

—*Zen Master Shunryu Suzuki*

The great theoretical physicist Richard Feynman once said, "You can know the name of a bird in all the languages of the world, but when you're finished, you'll know absolutely nothing whatever about the bird." His point is that, once we label and partition a thing or an idea, it can curtail our sense of discovery and curiosity to learn more. We have to nurture curiosity continually to enable creativity to emerge. We do this by remaining open to all ideas and new ways of seeing the world.

For example, I once showed a sign of a man throwing litter into a trash can to my five-year-old daughter, Annie, and asked her what she thought it meant. She said, "It's someone putting ice cubes in a hot tub." Well, why couldn't it be? This sense of remaining open to uncovering new truths is a critical component of innovation, and that capacity to interpret the mundane or expected as unexpected is innate in all of us. Before we converge our thinking on a solution, we must first *diverge* in our thinking to find new possibilities and opportunities.

Like creativity expert Paul Sloane, I believe we tend to have "convergent thinking," the default left-brain reaction to stimuli, ideas, suggestions, and circumstances as they occur around us.[2] Our repertoire of experiences, emotions, and understandings of information that confronts us tends to *converge* in our minds as we try to make sense of it. Yet innovative ideas and solutions are often peripheral in our mind and require our thinking to *diverge* out from a central idea or experience. That is to say, once we have acknowledged the circumstance or event in our minds and then made a mental label of what it is, we can use that as a point of divergence to uncover new possibilities or solutions.

Here's an example: While a student in design school in Bolzano, a magnificent village in the mountainous Tyrolean region of northern Italy, Robert Fliri spent much of his leisure time hiking and climbing in the mountains. While he didn't aspire to be a competitive rock climber, he did aspire to have a closer—more natural—relationship with the mountains around him, and particularly the path under his foot. As he describes, he would often try to hike or run barefoot, but his feet were too tender to endure this for very long, and soon he began dreaming of a glove designed for his foot.[3] When he introduced the idea of a "foot glove" to his colleagues and friends, most design suggestions they gave him were modeled after shoes, because, after all, they were to be worn on feet. Innovation in the shoe industry, Fliri says, often means introducing different types of material intended to increase flexibility or cushioning, but what he envisioned was *less* material.

Fliri kept rejecting designs focused on shock-absorbing soles and remained true to his original vision of a foot glove. The result is the Vibram FiveFinger "shoe" later profiled to great acclaim in Christopher McDougall's book *Born to Run*. By diverging to a new mental anchor of envisioning a foot glove instead of a shoe, Fliri eventually arrived at a real innovation in footwear.

To accelerate and sustain our own ability to innovate, we must first change our approach to thinking—step out of cognitive ruts we may have developed or that were imposed on us, and embrace divergent thinking without fear. Below are a few ways we can accomplish this.

Let In Beauty and the Beast

William James, the father of modern psychology, believed that, while we consciously work with only a small subset of ideas, skills, behaviors, and attitudes in our active, conscious mind, we have a wealth of thoughts and ideas at our disposal in our unconscious mind; we just don't allow them into our conscious thought patterns. James suggested in his work that, to harness the unconscious power of creative thought, we need to allow all ideas to surface without bias, without a knee-jerk reaction that the thought is impossible, abhorrent, or fantastical. If we can capture such ideas as they emerge and allow ourselves to consider them, we will have a much greater arsenal of ideas to work with—in other words, more tools for our creative problem solving.

We shouldn't confine our search for divergent thinking to our species. Airplanes would never have gotten off the ground if curious people hadn't looked long and hard, over many centuries, at how birds did it. We need only look down to see another species that has inspired innovation—ants.

Although tiny, ants make up a large and diverse taxonomic family with trillions of individuals. In *Journey to the Ants*, Bert Hölldobler and E.O. Wilson cite entomologist C.B. Williams's estimate of the number of ants alive on the planet at any given time to be ten thousand trillion and extrapolate that "when combined, all ants in the world taken together weigh about as much as human beings."[4]

For millions of years ants have been innovating to solve challenges in their daily lives, and researchers found that they are able to solve math puzzles.[5] Their long list of accomplishments also includes constructing living suspension bridges consisting of individual ants and elaborate underground housing complexes, farming aphids for the "honeydew" they produce and that the ants eat, cutting and storing leaves to grow mold for food (which also offers protection from bacteria), and developing ways to determine and share the quickest route to food sources.

Curious engineers, architects, medical researchers, and others have literally stooped to study these tiny creatures to find ways to, among other things, make architecture more friendly to humans and the environment, find the most direct route for delivering packages on the streets and data packets on a computer network, and develop antibiotics that can stay ahead of mutations in disease-producing bacteria.

And ants make up just one family in the estimated 8.7 million species on earth that can inspire innovation.[6]

Pursue "Accidental" Innovation

What do the following products have in common? Anesthesia, cellophane, cholesterol-lowering drugs, cornflakes, dynamite, the ice-cream soda, the Slinky, Ivory soap, NutraSweet, nylon, penicillin, photography, rayon, PVC, smallpox vaccine, stainless steel, Teflon. The answer is they were all invented by accident. But such happy accidents are more likely to become valued innovation when we're ready to seize on the opportunity.

Percy Spencer, a curious, skilled engineer in the early days of Raytheon, was responsible for scaling up the production of magnetrons for military use in radar equipment. One day in 1946, while walking past one of the magnetrons, he noticed the candy bar in his pocket was melting. Curious, he started experimenting with popcorn and eggs, and immediately discovered the heat-generating qualities of magnetrons. He pursued this idea, and eventually developed the first commercially available microwave oven, the 750-pound Radarange, in 1947. This innovation didn't happen entirely by accident. Spencer had to have the right frame of mind to observe and capitalize on his observation.

In an interview with Sarah Jane Gilbert for the Harvard Business School's website, Professor Robert Austin related his discussions with a number of artists who constantly experiment with their methods to create new work.[7] One artist described finishing a clay piece and then, before it cured, hitting it with a bat to see what new shape occurred. Through such experimentation, innovation emerged. Like these artists, we should build into our organizations a process that varies conditions and spurs curiosity, enabling us to more easily recognize and embrace the value in the change that emerges.

Sometimes we're pushed into diverging from our routine through making mistakes. The relationship between error and progress is undeniable. Often innovation that is the result of an accident, even a mistake, can be the most powerful and profound. We should want to have such accidents, and induce and examine them, to accelerate innovation. To allow and recognize these happy accidents, we have to set up the right conditions and then be mindful of the changes that should be observed.

One caveat: although change can ignite innovation, there is a ceiling at which we are able to recognize and harvest value out of the variation we are creating. We shouldn't let the volume of noise exceed the measurable signal level. In other words, the number of inquiries in progress should be sufficient to create some chaos and keep us thinking, but not so many that we can't extract the value from them. This is also known as being "chaotic by design."

Choose Questions Carefully

We create our world starting with our conversations with others, by the questions we ask and the ideas we pursue in those conversations. My colleague Pam called me the other day, and we were talking about creating and sustaining some real systemic change in our organization— really shaking things up. She closed the call by asking how we can make this happen. We both agreed it had already begun, for change starts the moment we ask the question. Asking creates and deep inquiry sustains the momentum of change and eventual innovation.

Peter Drucker observed later in his life that we spend an immense portion of our time working to solve dilemmas, to unpack problems, and to build solutions, yet we spend vanishingly little of our time exploring the questions that led us there. If we direct more of our energy and time finding the right questions to ask, we might gain closer understanding of how we can apply our personal and collective inquiries toward what will forward the conversation and push the edges of what is possible.

In a world that is increasingly volatile, ambiguous, and complex, the ideas and opinions that vie for our attention have compounded far beyond our abilities to digest them all intellectually. Thus, the questions we choose to ask become increasingly important in directing the shape of our ideas, our identities, and our collaborative communities.

Constantly questioning everything around us can unlock the key to innovation. Often the questions we ask are born of a time and place in which the initial question had consequence and meaning, in terms of our business and market-value gains, but times have changed and we need to examine the question more carefully. Sometimes our inquiries will lead us in totally new directions, to new threads of thought. It's nearly impossible to see future realities, but it is easy to imagine possibilities. We need to allow ourselves to follow the threads that matter to us in the context of our work, our play, and our lives.

Dr. David Cooperrider, a management professor at Case Western Reserve University, popularized the method of "appreciative inquiry." He and coauthor Diana Whitney write about this method in their book, *Appreciative Inquiry: A Positive Revolution in Change*: "In its broadest focus, it involves systematic discovery of what gives 'life' to a living system when it is most alive, most effective, and most constructively capable in economic, ecological, and human terms."[8]

The appreciative inquiry method consists of discussions and brainstorming sessions that are designed to tap into the existing strengths of an organization. It helps us value the ideas and beliefs in what we inquire about. As Cooperrider sees it, the questions we ask reflect our spirit, our tendencies, and our inclinations.[9]

Using the appreciative inquiry method, we can recognize that our questions are indeed creations. That is, each question we pose begets change, and what we anticipate in the world and in each interaction tomorrow reflects our behavior and disposition today.

At the heart of the appreciative inquiry method is the belief that the only antidote to all problems—including the very serious one of resisting change—is a positive approach. Diagnostic exercises, such as "autopsies without blame," are definitely useful at isolating and excising those practices and processes that failed, but such exercises arguably only add to the ever-increasing list of things we should *not* do.

Remediation efforts, such as finding the weakest link, can also certainly work toward our elevating those skills and behaviors that fall below the curve. But again, if we focus our inquiry on correcting defects, impurities, and subpar performances, how will we create the kinds of innovative breakthroughs we need to remain competitive, and do so on a consistently reliable basis? In this rapidly evolving economic landscape, where inspired innovation is what separates one company from another, a more forward, positive, and appreciative approach is needed.

CHOOSE OPTIMISM

In his book *Curious?* Todd Kashdan relates a great story he said he heard on NPR of a guy whose job was to spot irregular potato chips on a moving conveyor belt and remove them to ensure product consistency.[10] Although this job might seem unbearably boring to many, the guy said he loves his job. *Loves it.* Seriously.

Why? He plays a game in which he tries to spot famous faces in the potato chips. (Hey, there's Ernest Borgnine!) Now this may not be everyone's idea of fun, but it was fun for him. By being optimistic and looking for new ideas among the mundane—happily exercising divergent thinking—he ended up loving his job and was successful at it.

In September 1999, Dr. Martin Seligman, then president of the American Psychological Association, gave a speech in which he told of an epiphany he'd had about the field of psychology a couple of years before.[11] Over the previous 30 years, the majority of studies and research inquiries, and resulting psychotherapies and pharmacological agents, he said, had been focused on identifying and treating depression, anger, schizophrenia, impotence, different psychoses, and a variety of other afflictions. While celebrating the remarkable progress having been made in treating mental illnesses, he was appalled at the historical focus on correcting disorders—identifying and remediating what is wrong with people instead of building a discipline that focused on building up people's strengths, hope, future-mindedness, and optimism, and using these as a buffer against depression.

As he said in his presentation, "The problem is that because we have been a profession and a science focused on what was wrong, and what was weak, we know almost nothing about the strengths, about those virtues."

Seligman described some of the research he and his colleagues conducted in which they discovered that, by simply teaching people the mindset of learned optimism, they can make dramatic positive impacts on people's mental health. As he described, they basically teach children and adults the skills of thinking about bad events as being local and specific rather than pervasive and permanent.

"By becoming accurate in their attributions for bad events," he says, "we find that we cut the rate of depression by about 50 percent in both children and adults."

Often we get entranced by the idea that working really hard and then performing well at work will lead to happiness—that our success will make us happy. Yet, if we constantly define our happiness against a future state, it's hard to ever arrive there. What if we *start* with happiness instead?

In a June 2012 interview I conducted with Shawn Achor,[12] author of *The Happiness Advantage*, he pointed to a body of research and evidence emerging over the past couple of decades that confirms that our minds work better in a positive state. He argues that we have developed a preoccupation with becoming successful, which we believe will lead to our happiness. Achor argues that the inverse is a better bet—that the more we focus on our own happiness and personal fulfillment, the more likely success will follow.

We can all be change artists within our organizations if we choose to be optimistic. The importance of optimism in the workplace cannot be undervalued, especially in a recession-hit workforce. The fear of failing can keep people from trying new or challenging things outside their area of expertise. However, when we encourage employees to believe that nothing is impossible, that a solution can always be found, the sheer optimism of this belief will create a positive environment and workforce.

There are lots of ways we can become more optimistic, but moving forward means leaving behind some old assumptions about how our brains work.

Rewire Your Brain

At the close of the nineteenth century, psychologist William James first introduced the idea that our thoughts can change the structure and function of our brains. This shook the very foundations of scientific belief regarding the brain. Scientists of the time saw the brain as rigidly mapped out and believed certain functions are controlled by certain parts of the brain. These scientists thought that if a particular part is dead or damaged, then the function that is controlled by that part is lost or altered.

As Norman Doidge shows in his book *The Brain That Changes Itself: Stories of Personal Triumph from the Frontiers of Brain Science*, at any age, the brain is endlessly adaptable and dynamic, having the capacity to actually rewire itself and form new neural pathways.[13] Even those with severe neurological illnesses have shown great improvement through applying the principles of this neuroplasticity. Repeating positive thoughts and activities can rewire the brain and reinforce and strengthen those areas in the brain that stimulate positive feelings.

Inquiry thrives best when we believe that the questions we are pursuing will make us and those around us happier. Visualizing previous and anticipated positive moments, places, and people can elevate our sense of optimism because our brain has a difficult time discerning between what is real and what is mentally visualized. In cognition studies, researchers have demonstrated that, for this reason, mental practice can be as effective as actual practice for athletes or musicians. The same is true when people interact with each other—by visualizing a positive outcome, we affirm and encourage that result in our mind and thus contribute to an actual positive result.

Get Off the Conveyor Belt

A common story propagated in our culture is that hard work will lead to proficiency, which will in turn lead to success, which will ultimately make us happy. Much recent research suggests the inverse—that behaviors, communities, and practices that develop our happiness contribute to talent and performance, which in turn fuels success in all aspects of our lives. Happiness actually *precedes* success, not the other way around.

But how do we make ourselves happy? Researchers have shown that we are poor predictors of what will make us happy. The world is full of miserable lottery winners, and yet we still think that, if only we have the house, the car, the spouse, the job, the vacation—the whatever— we'll be s-o-o happy. And yet consistently many of these dreams fail to deliver joy upon arrival, or at least to deliver sustainable joy.

Turns out we aren't very good at remembering how we felt in the past. We fairly consistently remember the past as a joyful time, when in fact the majority of the actual time spent was more mundane. We have the *experiencing* self in real time that has opinions and emotions, and we have a *remembering* self that recollects events and provides us with advice about the quality of that experience and how to make future choices.

Daniel Kahneman and his colleagues conducted a study in which the researchers asked participants to categorize their days into 15-minute increments and value them on the basis of how they felt at those moments.[14] It was found that we really only spend less than 30 percent of our day engaged in activities we characterize as either enjoyable or meaningful— ouch!! And our most enjoyable or meaningful moments are almost always in the company of others and in pursuit of a purpose greater than ourselves. In the study, the activity of volunteering was evaluated as being among the highest in terms of happiness quotient. Sadly, almost a third of our day is spent wandering through what Todd Kashdan refers to as the "conveyer belt" of life, which, to most of those interviewed, meant work or school.[15]

Increase Your Luck through Optimism

We tend to think of innovators as lucky, coming up with the right idea at the right time. But as I mentioned above, often it comes down to having the right mindset—being open to new ideas and taking an optimistic approach to events in our lives.

When I was about 16 years old, my family owned a car I used to drive around the countryside. One night I ran out of gas on a country road. I had just come over a small rise in the road, and instead of pulling over and considering my next move, I put the car in neutral and used the hill decline and my own momentum to coast along. Luckily, I managed to coast almost a quarter mile to a gas station and roll directly up to the pumps without ever stopping. Pretty lucky, right?

We don't have much control over whether we win the lottery, but it turns out we do have control over what we perceive as "luck." To a great extent, we can also control our own happiness by how we interpret and respond to events and situations. When events occur that affect us, we can choose whether we believe they just happened to us, or we caused them to happen—whether we were passive participants or instigators. Bronze-medal winners are consistently found to be happier with the result than silver-medal winners—they are celebrating that they are on the podium, while silver-medal winners are disappointed they didn't win the gold.

In his book *Thinking, Fast and Slow*, Daniel Kahneman describes a survey in which a bank experimented with two different questions in its advertising efforts:[16]

- How much would you pay for $100,000 life insurance that will pay in the event of death for any reason?
- How much would you pay for $100,000 life insurance that pays in the event of death by terrorist attack?

Survey respondents said they would pay much higher rates for the second type of life insurance. This is deeply irrational, since death is death, but thinking generally about it is likely to have much less of an emotional impact as envisioning the specifics of a terrorist attack. This speaks directly to how negative emotions and ideas can cause us to overvalue or overemphasize the likelihood of a specific scenario, because of our emotional response to the idea.

In his book *The Luck Factor*, Richard Wiseman describes luck in terms of choice.[17] In his research working with more than 400 individuals, he found several key attributes of those who describe themselves as "lucky":

- **They harness the power of curiosity well.** They are creative and curious. Wiseman has a fun game in which participants write down six activities or experiences they have not tried but would be willing to try, then roll a die and do the activity that corresponds to the outcome.

- **They make good decisions without consciously knowing why or how they did.** Those who describe themselves as lucky make better gut decisions. Intuition-driven decision making seems impossible to control, yet Wiseman discovered those lucky decision makers actually spent more time reflecting and meditating on the decision once considered, and spent more time envisioning hypothetical circumstances in which they may have to make decisions. So when the situation arose, those who were "lucky" were actually better prepared to make a decision in the moment.

- **They have dreams and ambitions that have a knack of coming true.** Lucky people expect the best outcomes, despite any negative past experiences, whereas unlucky people allow past negative events to dictate future expectations. The lucky people also described their expectations of upcoming interactions with other people as generally positive.

- **They turn their bad fortune into good luck or opportunity.** Wiseman describes two primary ways people turn bad luck into good luck. Basically they interpret the bad as "could have been much worse." And when they reflect on past events, they spend a greater amount of time visualizing and selectively remembering the positive. In other words, the bad wasn't all that bad, and the good was pretty great.

Basically, people who consider themselves lucky put themselves in the position of having chance encounters that lead to interesting new possibilities and opportunities, see the upside of the experience, and harness the power of curiosity to be creative. We can all be lucky in this way.

Share Optimism through Expressing Gratitude

One of the keys to fostering optimism is reflecting on things for which we are grateful and then sharing that gratitude with those around us. According to Jaak Panksepp and Lucy Biven, authors of *The Archaeology of Mind: Neuroevolutionary Origins of Human Emotions*, by recollecting and expressing gratitude, we activate endorphins that have the power to fight fatigue and pain and increase happiness.[18] By sharing that positive experience socially, we also invoke a positive endorphin response, through neurons in our brains that mirror the emotional state of others. Through this sharing, we not only make someone else happy, but we also feel a sense of purpose and meaning. This reinforces our sense of community by affirming that our actions matter.

CLOSE THE ORGANIZATIONAL INQUIRY GAP

Matthew May is the author of *The Elegant Solution: Toyota's Formula for Mastering Innovation*, a consultant, and a leader in innovation. In an interview in October 2009, he shared a telling anecdote with me about the importance of creating an organizational culture that is open to inquiry, and what happens when the leaders are out of sync with the culture.[19] When May was a consultant to a car company—before joining Toyota—he tried to tell the leaders that their culture stifled ideas by managing the organization through a command-and-control hierarchy. The company leaders didn't believe him, rejected his suggestion, and insisted they had an open environment where all ideas were welcome.

When May was asked to conduct a workshop session for the company, he created an exercise in which diverse employees from all strata of the organization had to work in teams to solve a puzzle. The puzzle was to determine the right balance of fuel, food, people, and resources for a successful trip to the moon. In the exercise, only one configuration of resources solves the problem.

Before the exercise started, May took aside the most junior member of each team and gave that person the answer. He told those selected that they were free to do anything they chose to make their voices heard and make their teams win the game except to disclose that they were given the answer.

Not one team solved the puzzle. At the conclusion of the session, May asked the member of each team who held the answer key to stand up. The leaders attending the meeting were both appalled and enlightened to discover that, contrary to what they believed, voices from all levels of the organization really weren't listened to thoughtfully and appreciated. After all, for each group the answer was sitting right at the table, yet no team delivered the correct solution.

This is what I call the "inquiry gap"—the divide between what the leaders believe is an open culture of inquiry and debate, and the reality. In this case, the exercise May conducted clearly showed that people at different strata of the organization didn't feel listened to, didn't feel as if their opinions were valued—the inquiry gap was wider than the leaders thought.

The innovative organization is one in which the culture encourages— even demands—active and constructive participation in dialogue from all its members. The innovative leader models this by first asking provocative questions, then allowing and encouraging deep inquiry by contributors throughout the organization and mining that for innovation.

Ask "If It Were Possible . . .?"

In an interview in September 2010, I asked Lincoln Crawley, managing director of ManpowerGroup, if he could point to a watershed learning event in his career.[20] He recollected a moment more than 15 years ago when he was trying to win a service contract. He was acting as the lead on a proposal in which his company was competing against a company with an enormous infrastructure advantage.

The client required having a redundancy system in place as a security measure—something Crawley's competitor had but his employer didn't. Crawley seemed sure to lose the contract, as the task to replicate the competitor's infrastructure in the time required seemed nearly impossible.

In discussions during the proposal process, the people around Crawley described the technical and financial obstacles the company faced as insurmountable. In a conversation with an external mentor, he said, "I understand the issues and concerns you are raising, but tell me, if it were possible, what would the solution look like?"

That simple phrase "if it were possible" gave the team permission to speculate, and opened up a whole new conversation. It was an invitation to dream. Crawley and his team conceived of a plan and proposed it to the prospective client. They won the contract.

"I've taken those few words with me all through my career," Crawley says, especially when he can't see his way around a particularly difficult situation, when the competitor seems unbeatable. At that point he asks, "If it were possible, what would it look like?"

"It puts you in a completely different environment where you're not now talking about why haven't you done [something]," Crawley says. "You're actually talking about how can we make this happen? It changes the conversation."

Here's the interesting part: Crawley said he didn't fully recognize the power of the suggestion "if it were possible" until years later when, as a leader, he started using the expression with his own team. Only then did he recognize that these four words opened up the capabilities and imagination in his team. When we see that our teams are stymied, we should try asking them to use their imagination.

Mine Curiosity

Recently, I was treated to hearing my son play the piano. It was not the pounding, childish, make-noise kind, nor the rote, practice kind assigned by music teachers. (I take nothing away from either version of playing the piano, since both approaches are quite valid in figuring out this instrument.) My son was exploring the piano in a moment of utter focus, totally engaged in finding his own melodies.

My son's exploration of the piano was nothing Mozart-like of a young prodigy; he was simply investigating the possibilities that the piano offered in a very present and engaged way—finding rhythm and notes on his own. He's never had piano lessons beyond watching and listening to my playing tunes I learned long ago. He was simply curious about what sounds he could get the piano to make and totally engaged in his exploration of the instrument.

Study after study reveals that true and lasting competitive advantage comes from having people who are talented *and* engaged—who mine their curiosity. Engagement is the intersection of curiosity, expertise, passion, and an understanding of how our contributions fit into the bigger picture. Having one or two ingredients isn't enough. A passionate contributor with little expertise won't make a measurable impact. Likewise, a skilled worker without passion for the organization's purpose and mission will likely lack allegiance and easily jump to a competitor.

NARROW CHOICES

I've devoted quite a few pages to the importance of exploring possibilities and exercising our curiosity. However, sometimes facing a wealth of choice can undermine the innovation process. Sheena Iyengar, author of *The Art of Choosing*, demonstrates through a series of studies she covers in her book that too much choice can often lead to both slower decision making and ultimately poorer choices.[21]

Iyengar, in a conversation with one of my colleagues at Skillsoft, Taavo Godtfredsen, in April 2012 about the studies in her book, described what she learned from a study in which a manager provides six choices instead of only two:

> Well, what happens in this case is, rather than feeling empowered, the employees perceive their manager as warm and nice, but utterly incompetent, because they're left feeling as if they're holding the bag. They don't know how to go forward.[22]

However, when the manager offered only two choices, the engineers performed better at the task and perceived their manager as more competent and effective. The obvious point being that, if we can eradicate distracting, time-consuming, and exhausting abundance of choice, we can often reach a faster and better decision.

Anyone who shops at a store that is rich with options, such as a Whole Foods grocery store, without a clear list of things to buy can easily be overwhelmed by the experience, and might even leave, defeated by too many options. However, even when encountering the rich abundance of choice within such a store, if we arrive with a prepared list of items to purchase, we can make faster and better choices that make the shopping experience more enjoyable.

We are tightening our scope of inquiry now as we prepare to move into the exploratory phase of the Out Think process, where we focus more deeply on our journey toward innovation.

LET'S RECAP

Remember . . .

- Innovation results—often accidentally—from facing tough challenges with an open and curious mind.
- Appreciative inquiry is a powerful way of questioning that demonstrates value for what we inquire about and taps into existing strengths of people and organizations. This type of positive, optimistic inquiry is far better and more apt to lead to innovative outcomes than blaming or faultfinding. Our minds work better in a positive state, and focusing on happiness and fulfillment increases the likelihood of success.

- Asking careful, thoughtful questions and inquiring deeply automatically creates momentum for change and innovation.

- People with a growth mindset believe that intelligence and aptitude are malleable, and even in the face of obstacles or potential failure, they can still learn and improve. This mindset starts with a strong sense of inquiry, curiosity, and openness to new ideas.

- Inquiry involves examining, observing, and discovering things that are interesting, intriguing, and stimulating. This may require stepping away from the norm or the routine, getting out of your cognitive rut and into a more divergent way of thinking that includes an openness to making mistakes.

Your Turn Now . . .

Reach in: Recall some of the tough challenges, failures, or mistakes you've experienced in your life or career, and how they led to deeper understanding or change. What are you facing now that is—or could be—a tough challenge that requires a curious, open, and inquisitive mind? Draft three questions to ask others that will deepen your understanding and clarity related to this challenge. Ask the questions and think deeply about the answers and your reaction to them. If you are not facing any particular challenge, ask questions of someone who is—a colleague, your manager, or a member of your team.

Reach out: With your team or work group, elicit concerns, challenges, or obstacles that currently exist in relation to a specific effort or project. Model appreciative inquiry, divergent thinking, and a growth mindset as you remain aware of what you are learning and experiencing from the team's responses. Ask your team these two questions, and give them time to think about and discuss them: "What are we learning through this project experience?" and "What could we do differently to reframe some of our challenges or pressures into positive, energizing opportunities?" Encourage them to think beyond perceived limitations.

Spread out: Select an issue or challenge that is particularly problematic for one or more members of your team. Make an assignment for them to inquire as deeply as possible into this issue, asking others whom they trust about how they have faced similar challenges, what ideas they have for overcoming obstacles, and how they perceive the challenge, from their "outside" perspective. Schedule a follow-up date to review what was asked and, more importantly, what was learned.

Remember . . .

- Bombardment with today's information overload can confuse our perceptions, so persistent inquiry and appreciation becomes even more important. Creating a quiet mental space for inquiry and taking time to focus and settle your mind will stimulate creativity and synthesize ideas toward innovative solutions.

- The brain can be rewired, making new neural pathways that will reinforce positive thought. This enhances physical performance to much the same extent as actual exercise and practice.

- Reflecting on and sharing gratitude activates endorphins that fight fatigue and pain and stimulate well-being. Studies show we spend only around 30 percent of our time engaged in "enjoyable or meaningful" activity and, almost always, this occurs in others' company, or in pursuing a purpose greater than ourselves.

- We can control our happiness by how we interpret events and situations. "Luck" increases for those who harness curiosity well and unconsciously make good decisions, reflect on consequences, and are ready when choices arise. They have dreams and ambitions that often materialize because they expect a positive outcome. They ask: "If it were possible . . .?"

Your Turn Now . . .

Reach in: Schedule "quiet time" into your daily calendar—even if only 15 minutes when you take a walk, sit quietly, or write in a journal—focusing only on positive thoughts, ideas, and possibilities. Avoid distractions such as phones or computers—just be present, and calm your mind. You might also use this time to share with another person and ask him or her to engage in an optimistic conversation or an activity that is enjoyable or meaningful. Alter your routine!

Reach out: Teach your team members some of the fascinating findings about happiness, optimism, and appreciation—about the brain's potential for rewiring, the role of happiness in a person's success, the small amount of time we typically spend performing the enjoyable, purposeful activities that can make us more productive, creative, and happy. Suggest that whenever the team meets, there is time set aside for quiet time or appreciative, optimistic conversation. Rotate the assignment among team members to lead 5–10 minutes of every team meeting in this type of activity.

Spread out: If your organization supports a charity or aspires to a meaningful cause (e.g., health, ecology, invention, or safety), decide on an action that you and your team can take to contribute to that charity or cause. It might be as simple as volunteering as a team for a few hours, inviting charity representatives to your team meeting to share his or her stories, or including one goal per year that involves some type of community service or volunteerism.

CHAPTER 4

EXPLORATION: GO TO
THE WOODSHED

Every organization must prepare for the abandonment of everything
it does.

—Peter Drucker

As the legend goes, in 1937, drummer Jo Jones threw a cymbal at
Charlie Parker's feet, indicating it was time for Parker to leave the stage.
Humiliated, Parker worked even harder at the instrument and that summer he famously secluded himself at a resort in the Ozark Mountains
to work on his playing. Known in jazz circles as "going to the wood-
shed" or "woodshedding," the term means secluding oneself to develop
virtuosity through practice and hard work.[1]

Six years ago, before engineering the sale of Targeted Learning
to Skillsoft, I had been accustomed to working in all aspects of the
business. These activities ran from designing the user experience,
to technical delivery, marketing, pre- and post-sales efforts, and of
course the customer-service aspect of building relationships with the
people and organizations that would actually use our products. In
short, I was accustomed to being an entrepreneur in every sense of
the word.

Among our small band of 11 employees and our various contrac-
tors, there were other immensely talented and remarkable people who
had much greater expertise, and each had his or her own focus in the
company. Amidst all their effort, I always stayed close to every aspect of

the business. I enjoyed it and thrived, actively participating in the entire entrepreneurial process. In fact, I had to be able to take responsibility wherever it was needed *because* we were small.

Taking an entrepreneurial approach to Targeted Learning had worked, but had not completely prepared me for navigating a more densely populated corporate environment that had richer core expertise. Although the environment in which I was working had changed, I was still trying to make contributions in as many places within the company as I could, and in doing so, I wasn't leveraging my strengths. In short, I hadn't yet found my voice in this new environment.

It took me a while to truly realize that I was no longer a CEO—that now I had one, Chuck Moran, who sat a couple levels above me. What Skillsoft needed from me was not a broad range of entrepreneurial and managerial skills but rather for our team to focus on creating the content itself—identify, film, and produce great new content that would eventually surface in the product line we were responsible for developing. The company had seasoned experts to handle the marketing, sales, engineering, design, and other process areas that I had previously managed at Targeted Learning.

Initially, I felt a touch undervalued, but I soon realized that, while I had some expertise in these other areas, my knowledge didn't compare to the dedicated Skillsoft professionals who specialized in them. Being aware of these new stakeholders in the work I was now doing for Skillsoft, and being committed to delivering a successful new product for Targeted Learning's new owners, I initially began to try to intuit what this new company expected of me.

In terms of new-product creation, I began asking myself, "What content will deliver a big win for this company?" This is a very different question than "What have we discovered our customers want?" or, better, "What do *I believe* will be wonderful new ideas and content to produce?"

The effect of focusing on the big win was that I began to gravitate toward safe choices. I would champion speakers, ideas, and content that was mainstream and popular. Instead of trying to find the next new voice in cutting-edge thinking or looking for ideas and content that resonated with me—that I found honest and valuable—I looked at the *New York Times* bestseller list and picked seasoned, venerable, known contributors whose ideas and voices had been well established. It was akin to picking the Rolling Stones instead of trying to find cutting-edge artists at that time, such as the Black Keys—an innovative, popular garage-band duo.

It took months of casting about, and making choices that weren't entirely mine, to decide that our small tribe of entrepreneurs from Targeted Learning had indeed delivered the success we promised to Skillsoft. We had created the valuable and scalable product and service that was novel in the marketplace and valued by the customers. Now adopted as a Skillsoft product, the service has consistently enjoyed annual double-digit growth. And yet, because I had been pursuing a product-development strategy that didn't feel entirely my own, I felt somewhat empty in the content choices I was making. We were creating what we believed our company and customers expected of us, instead of creating the content and ideas we most cared about and believed in.

Not being satisfied with the approach I was taking, I spent a weekend thinking this over. I decided to start choosing what I personally cared about—what I passionately believed could work in an emerging market. I embarked on a journey of exploration to see how I'd fit into this new stage in my life, shifting my path to continue to maximize my own ability to innovate in this new situation.

Accomplish More through Grit

What we hope ever to do with ease, we must learn first to do with diligence.
                                        —Dr. Samuel Johnson (1709–1784)

Imagine a race in which you don't know what you will have to do, where or how long the course is, or even when it will end. Imagine that, once you sign up for this race, you are told immediately and repeatedly to quit before you even start. You are warned you might die, and even if you don't, you don't have what it takes to finish, so you shouldn't even bother showing up.

During the course of the race—which has no finish line—you are asked to dig up a tree stump with your bare hands and then drag it ten miles to the top of a mountain, where you will be greeted by someone who asks you to memorize passages of the Bible. You then drag the tree stump back down the mountain to another location that is miles away, where you recite the lines. If you get it wrong, you hike back to memorize it until you get it right. You may sleep only when allowed. And during your sleep-deprived stupor, you may be asked to count out exactly 5,000 pennies, only to have them thrown in an icy pond. Your next task is to retrieve them.

During the event, you are constantly berated by race organizers who tell you to quit. And you have no idea when this will all end or where the finish line is, until they tell you it's over.

It's called The Spartan Death Race (www.youmaydie.com). The 2012 version lasted three days. Fewer than 15 percent of the contestants finished. Intelligence may be the least of the discerning factors in finishing. Grit may be the biggest.

Innovation may start with a spark of inspiration and be fed by aspiration, but every new idea needs to be probed, prodded, and explored in detail. This component of the innovation journey requires work, grit, determination, and unflagging perseverance to maximize innovation within ourselves, inspire others to do the same, and ultimately contribute to the innovative end result to which we aspire. It's in this part of the innovation journey that we are most likely to get distracted or lose momentum.

Why do some people accomplish more than others of equal intelligence? This was the question Angela Duckworth and her colleagues posed in 2004 when embarking on a study to measure people's level of "grit."[2] Surveying the available research regarding traits beyond intelligence that contribute to success, Duckworth and her colleagues found it lacking in the specific area regarding the influence of possessing this quality, which they defined as follows:

> We define grit as perseverance and passion for long-term goals. Grit entails working strenuously toward challenges, maintaining effort and interest over years despite failure, adversity, and plateaus in progress. The gritty individual approaches achievement as a marathon; his or her advantage is stamina.

Basically, Duckworth identified grit as the combination of two distinct characteristics: consistency of task and perseverance through adversity.

The researchers initiated their own study to develop something they call the "Grit Scale." After generating a series of questions intended to measure "grittiness," (for example, "I have overcome setbacks to conquer an important challenge" or "I finish whatever I begin"), the researchers set up a questionnaire on their website, www.authentichappiness.com. Their results reveal that higher levels of grit correlate with higher levels of education. The results also show that grit tends to increase with age. Those individuals with high levels of grit also tend to have fewer career changes. More surprisingly, those identified as possessing high levels of grit often had high grades in school, yet scored more poorly on standardized achievement tests, suggesting that, despite lower scholastic aptitude, their perseverance and tenacity yielded stronger overall academic results.

The study gets even more interesting when the researchers decided to apply their Grit Scale to the 2004 incoming class of the United States Military Academy at West Point. Just getting into West Point is famously difficult. Entrance requires a nomination from a member of Congress or the Department of the Army. Once accepted, each entering cadet is evaluated on the Whole Candidate Score, which takes into consideration school grade-point average, SAT results, physical fitness, class rank, and evidence of demonstrated leadership ability.

This comprehensive evaluation process for those applying to the academy is necessary to help the academy predict not only the graduation rate, but also the likelihood that entering freshmen will finish an arduous summer entrance session known as "Beast Barracks," or more simply "Beast." Nearly 100 percent of the freshman cadets also took the Grit Scale test in 2004, and its results proved to be a better predictor of whether or not a cadet would survive Beast Barracks than the military's own sophisticated and complexly designed evaluation tests.

It is grit—perseverance and passion for long-term goals, plus a willingness to remain tenacious in the face of adversity—that leads to deep expertise and mastery necessary to propel innovation.

PUT A STAKE IN THE GROUND

A key component of companies that differentiate themselves well from their competitors is the ability and willingness to put a stake in the ground on key market expertise. As I learned in moving from a small to a much larger organizational environment, developing deep niche expertise is critical to making valuable contributions. The same is true at scale when we compete in the larger marketplace.

John Grant is CEO of Data#3, in Australia, a company that has grown from a tiny technology-solutions firm in the early 1980s to one of the leading providers of information and communication technology throughout Australia and Asia, with more than $600 million in annual revenue. The company has differentiated itself by focusing on its core strengths and expanding and deepening its product position in the market.

In September 2010, I had the opportunity to sit down with Grant.[3] He said that, while Data#3 prides itself on its flexibility and its ease in working from a customer's standpoint, behind that easy human interaction is complex technology and proprietary methodologies that drive the company's unique solutions. He described the balancing of human support with strong technology solutions:

> We are a reasonable business to work with, that is, culturally. We have a strong set of values, and the values are what we will guarantee we will bring to bear during the implementation. . . . Yet, in order to handle the complexities associated with [our customers' needs], we've driven a big stake in the ground around expertise.

Creating such deep expertise requires developing the right kind of cultural environment and expectations, including clearly defined and valued products and services in the market. To develop such deep expertise, employees need the time and space to fully explore their ideas.

ALLOW TIME FOR FOCUSING

Recent research has undermined another conventional thought—that imminent deadlines and crisis thinking can lead to solutions that are more innovative. In a 2002 interview, Leslie Perlow, professor of leadership in the organizational behavior area at the Harvard Business School, described that a vicious time–work cycle of crisis mentality, rewards for individual heroics, and constant interruption is considerably less conducive to fostering real creativity and innovation than good old-fashioned focus and uninterrupted attention.[4]

In the same interview, Teresa Amabile, who is also Perlow's colleague, described her and Steven Kramer's own investigation into how time pressure in a corporate setting affects creativity. They asked participants to reveal their activities in daily questionnaires throughout the entire project, so they could monitor what participants were doing as they were doing it.

Perlow introduced into her study a mandatory quiet time interspersed with collaborative interaction. Overwhelmingly, the participants reported a higher level of productivity and creativity when the strict quiet time was imposed. Such peaceful intervals offer a time for regrouping and incubating thoughts and ideas, while refreshing and rejuvenating the mind.

After feeding our minds positive, constructive ideas, we need a pause in our efforts. In actively creating pauses in our puzzle-solving process, we allow new ideas to come in and ideas that are working below the surface to incubate. This incubation period is crucial to synthesis, to mentally pulling together the ideas that will create an innovative solution.

Taking a break isn't always easy. According to Buddhism, the mind is unsettled, restless, capricious, whimsical, inconstant, confused, indecisive, and uncontrollable—a "monkey mind" that chatters endlessly and jumps from one thought to another. Each of us has an internal running dialogue in his or her head. It feeds our thinking and ultimately our output, behaviors, and decisions. We analyze personal and professional relationships until they are threadbare; we worry endlessly about the future; we dissect every word that we speak or that is spoken to us. What we tell ourselves can become habitual. And what we think consistently and then say out loud affects our conversations and others around us. The mental cycle becomes reinforcing and may feel beyond our control.

We can create a creative space to jump-start the creative process by getting up from our desks, engaging in physical activity, attending an art exhibit, having lunch with someone who works in a different field, or taking a nap. Thomas Jefferson, Teddy Roosevelt, Isaac Newton, and Albert Einstein included long walks as part of their daily routine.

Meditation and focusing can help us get off the conveyor belt and ease the monkey mind. By relaxing our bodies, calming our minds, and focusing on single mental or physical activities, we gain greater proficiency, talent, and success in all activities—which leads to greater happiness.

Through meditation, we can become aware of each thought gradually and either accept it or let it float away, instead of pulling us in an unwanted direction. Gradually, we can focus on the thought we have chosen, allowing it to flower into innovation.

As mentioned in chapter 2, in her book *The Progress Principle: Using Small Wins to Ignite Joy, Engagement, and Creativity at Work*, Teresa Amabile and Steven Kramer conducted an enormous study, analyzing thousands of diary entries.[5] They found that the most productive kind of deadline expectations were those in which a clear deliverable was needed and expected but not urgent. The task had a sufficient time horizon to enable the individual responsible for the task to give thoughtful consideration to the project. When this was the case, the resulting deliverables were consistently more creative and of higher quality. Unfortunately, upon reviewing the diary entries, Amabile discovered that most contributors worked under a state of constant demands that allowed little time for either thoughtful effort or for contributors to stretch their abilities.

Shortly after her book came out, I had the opportunity to collaborate with Amabile and spend a day working with her and understanding her ideas. She described her findings that day:

> Unfortunately, the most frequent form of time pressure that we saw in organizations in this research is what we call being on a treadmill. And that is where people are running constantly all day, feeling that they have to juggle a bunch of balls in the air, many of which are being tossed at them unexpectedly. And yet they're not actually getting anywhere. That, on a treadmill time pressure, is really deadly for creative productivity. People might be getting a lot done, but it's not the most important work, the most creative work that they should be doing. And that kind of time pressure is not nearly as conducive as the low-to-moderate time pressure that we see when people are on an expedition for those better solutions.[6]

MINE THE ORGANIZATION FOR EXPERTISE

If only HP knew what HP knows, we'd be three times more productive.
—*Lew Platt, former CEO of Hewlett-Packard*

When Sir Howard Stringer first joined Sony in 1997, he coined the phrase "Sony United" to express the idea that, in this large and highly technically skilled organization, Sony employees needed to collaborate with each other internally much more than they did. He knew that there were extraordinarily talented engineers working in isolated pockets throughout the Sony organization. He knew building applications were at the heart of the future of the company, and yet there was extensive duplication of effort and a lack of collaboration. As he put it, "We couldn't get the company to understand that software was about cooperation."

Stringer held a cocktail party to which he invited 120 engineers from throughout the organization and said to them:

> From now on this company is going to talk to each other. People are going to talk to each other and are going to communicate. The next two hours you will exchange business cards and you will meet each other, because you will find that each of you is doing similar things in different parts of the company and you are duplicating your own experiences. This is the grassroots revolution, so don't wait for management, because I can't fire enough managers to get to you.[7]

With this message, he was saying to the engineers and software developers that he was expecting them to reach out to each other directly to collaborate and accelerate productivity and innovation by jumping across traditionally partitioned operational teams and internal boundaries.

Once we identify remarkably talented people within our organizations and create environments for them to effectively collaborate, we need always to be building and accelerating the talent that is developing and emerging so as to nurture the next generation of deep expertise and talent. A valuable way to accomplish this is by capturing something I call "voices of distinction."

REINFORCE COMPANY CULTURE BY CAPTURING INTERNAL VOICES OF DISTINCTION

People and relationships are at the core of a company's identity, embedded in its fabric and essential to its success. Great stories are at the heart of the world's best businesses and an integral part of any successful communication strategy. They create the connections that propel people to act.

By identifying individuals within our organizations who have led innovation over many years as well as newer employees that share this same vision of innovation, capturing their stories, and sharing them with new employees, we perpetuate the values of an organization. To develop these stories, we can ask a series of questions of those we have chosen as examples, such as the following:

- What does the corporate mission mean to you?
- How do you embody that mission in the way you work and how you live your life?
- What positive outcomes do you feel you have achieved, and how did you achieve them?
- What advice would you give to new employees or those being promoted?

By capturing and amplifying the powerful voices of distinction throughout the organization of those who are projecting the mission and culture of an organization, we can tap into three key ingredients for building success for the business:

- **Use of strategic stories.** One of the most important mediums we have as leaders is that of communicating through telling strategic stories. Stories that illustrate a concept tend to be more memorable than just describing the concept. Strategic stories are targeted stories intended to elicit a specific outcome.

- **Tapping strong internal credibility.** By leveraging those known experts and internal voices of distinction, we can tap into one of the most valuable aspects for translating mindsets and skillsets by presenting a familiar and credible person to deliver the message. While we must always introduce external ideas and leading experts from a variety of academic and professional domains, these ideas are well reinforced when shared through real stories told by familiar people in the company.

- **Sustaining company identity.** When faced with adversity, market pressures, or negative press, sometimes organizations need to change their culture and brand. To build a truly iconic, signature brand, successful companies understand the importance of not only leveraging emerging technologies, market opportunities, and relationship building, but also that a key guiding force comes from the existing people and the stories readily available in the company. By capturing and sharing those voices of distinction, a company can sustain and reinforce the culture in a highly scalable manner through the power of engaging video interviews.

Learning about tested ideas from voices of distinction in our organizations is the first step toward applying those ideas. Ultimately, developing the expertise necessary to yield valuable innovation requires taking that knowledge and digging in and doing the work. Innovation can happen by accident, and insights can fall from the sky, but not often and not reliably. Developing deep expertise requires consistent and dedicated work.

DEAL WITH INNOVATION BLOCKERS

All too often the act of the innovator, that stroke of genius, is in spite of the company system, not because of the company system.

—*Craig Wynett, chief innovation officer, Procter & Gamble*

As we continue to probe and immerse ourselves in potential paths of action, we'll be constantly sharing potentially provocative ideas that those around us may find jarring—so much so that they may become detractors, naysayers, path-blockers, pessimists, and other enemies of change. To surmount the attitudes and ingrained behaviors of these innovation blockers throughout the organization, we must first start with some level of understanding and sympathy—emotional fluency—of their disposition.

I interviewed Chip Conley, founder of Joie de Vivre Hotels, in April 2011.[8] He is one of the more thoughtful and gracious people I've ever met. Also the author of *Emotional Equations,* he defined emotional fluency in the interview as "the ability to understand, be literate and fluent about emotions with others." As he describes it, if we want to enroll others in our vision (we do), magnify our vision (yes), and have others magnetized to the vision we are exploring (indeed), we need to develop greater fluency with our own emotions and our interactions with others.

We all have running internal dialogues in our minds—that mental input that feeds our thinking, and ultimately our own output, behaviors, and decisions. It might be opinionated: "I can't believe how slow these people are to respond!" Or comment on life: "Wow, what a beautiful piece of music." Or perhaps be our own personal tormentor: "There's no way I'm going to get this done."

We need to keep this voice from taking us down a path of defeatism and infecting not only our own optimism but also creeping into our conversations with others and creating an atmosphere of defeat. According to Conley, we need to understand our own internal dialogue and emotional range before we can understand what goes on in the minds of others. While the constant stream of internal dialogue may feel beyond our control, we can choose to take a positive, constructive tone with ourselves, instead of a negative, derogatory one. By simply choosing our initial reaction, we begin to alter the shape of what happens next—the unconscious mental gestation period. When wrestling with any puzzle, professional or personal, there is typically a period of mental churning before the "A-ha!" moment. That's the "sleep on it" period of time.

Next we can apply what we've learned about our own approach to potentially threatening thoughts to understand the orientation of innovation blockers. We just have to listen to the cues they provide. Below are descriptions of a few of the personas that are likely blocking your path on the road to innovation.

The Bureaucrat

The Bureaucrat builds consistency and sets limits to ensure rule adherence. This persona's favorite responses to new ideas are "Has this been approved?" "Fill out this form," or "That's not in this budget cycle." Bureaucrats are well-intentioned and important to scalable success. Any organization that aspires to scalability and developing size beyond the fun, start-up phase requires a certain level of protocol and operational systems thinking, which necessarily means implementing processes and procedures. Everyone in such an organization can't simply "wing it" on his or her own personal path to developing innovation. However, Bureaucrats go too far, and when they do, we need strategies for working with them:

- **Prepare before going to them.** Write down what you believe you need, being as specific as possible, and have a paper trail to back up your efforts.
- **Participate in the process.** Don't be content to wait for a Bureaucrat to respond. Ask what steps are needed and then ask to participate in the process. As a primary stakeholder, you may be able to chase down information faster.
- **Check in.** The Bureaucrat might give you a vague answer, such as, "It takes between five and ten days." Say you will check back in five days, then do it. Your punctuality will send a message that you expect the same from them. To them, your persistence will elevate the importance of your project.

The Wimp Sponsor

A sponsor is typically someone at a managerial or executive level who will champion new efforts and projects by supporting them publicly within the company and being a project advocate to senior management.

Wimp Sponsors are project managers who lack the attention, interest, or clout to legitimately carry the effort forward. Their favorite responses to new ideas are "Can you rework the business plan on this?" and "Let's study this some more." Forever terrified of social risk and losing political capital, your Wimp Sponsor is either unable or unwilling to champion your efforts. Consumed with cowardice, these impotent and ineffective sponsors need to be identified and addressed from both above and below.

If you work for a Wimp, take the initiative. Take the first few steps in your project and report on your progress. Wimps aren't likely to ask you to stop or retrace your steps. They don't have the courage to ask you to move forward because they don't want to be responsible for your actions.

If you manage a Wimp, create specific targets and deadlines together, but let them lead the way. Wimps often know their weaknesses, and it's best to allow them to state out loud what they believe needs to be done. Ask them "What are you trying to accomplish that requires more than just you?" "Who would be the best people to help?" and "What stands in your way?" By answering those three questions out loud, you will help the Wimps build their own accountability and publicly take the first step in developing a successful project initiative.

The Power Monger

Power Mongers believe power and resources are more important than results and have already achieved some level of power and status. Their favorite responses to new ideas are "I've already thought of that," "I'm already doing that in my group," and "I hope you can do that with your own people." Power Mongers operate from a viewpoint of scarcity. They believe there aren't enough resources to go around and it's important to hoard and protect assets and information.

Power Mongers are likely to be sensitive to criticism and to reject new ideas, so a good place to start when dealing with them is to give them gracious, authentic praise when they've earned it. The power of suggestion can also be effective with Power Mongers. They need to feel as if the idea came from them. Instead of dictating or directing your ideas, pose them as questions.

The Skeptic

Skeptics are chronic doubters. They remain doubtful that efforts will succeed and often justify their opinions with arguments that there aren't enough resources, time, energy, or expertise available to support new initiatives. Their favorite responses to new ideas include the following: "There are so many problems with that—where do I start?" Don't confuse the Skeptic's behavior with "playing devil's advocate," which may have a constructive role in teasing out the bugs in the proposals. The Skeptic, as an innovation blocker, has no actual interest in or intention of aiding the process. This person socially legitimizes a seemingly innocuous, yet toxic, way of interacting.

One way to deal with the Skeptic is to remain positive. As Marcial Losada[9] demonstrated in studying and evaluating the performance of teams over a ten-year period, the highest-functioning and most innovative teams have a positive-to-negative comment ratio of at least 2.9 to 1. That is, the highest-functioning and most creative and effective teams say positive and constructive things to each other in conversation at least three times more than negative things. And this is the bottom end of what's known as the Losada Zone. The Losada Zone is an area between 2.9:1 and 11.6:1. The highest-functioning teams have at least three times as many positive and constructive comments and questions in their collaboration than negative comments and questions.

If a team remains positive despite adverse environments, this behavior can yield a powerfully high-performing group that, according to Losada and fellow researcher Barbara Fredrickson, possesses broader behavioral repertoires, greater flexibility, more social resources, and optimal functioning—all key ingredients for a high-performance team in a marketquake age.

LET'S RECAP

Remember . . .

- Innovation leaders often gain mastery over something they personally care about and passionately believe can work in the marketplace and in their organization. Being novel about developing this expertise will help put a stake in the ground that identifies a team or organization's unique contributions.

- Innovation is hard work, and while it may start with a spark of inspiration, it must be carried through by true intention and determination, continually probing, prodding, and exploring. It requires sticking with the effort, using dogged perseverance and "grit"—especially when up against adversity.

- The most productive sort of deadline is one in which a clear deliverable is needed and expected but isn't urgent—where the responsible individual has time to thoughtfully consider the project.

- Constant demands, allowing little time for focused effort, give poorer results. Running on a treadmill may require stamina, but running all day, making little progress, and feeling under time pressure are not conducive to an innovative culture.

Your Turn Now . . .

Reach in: Identify a place on your innovation journey that you want to claim as your personal area of expertise. Make it something that fits with your role as a leader, but consider going outside of the bounds of your defined job expectations and aim for something that you truly want to master. Visualize this place. Write a description of what it looks like when you achieve mastery, using words and images that appeal to you personally. Revisit this document throughout your journey.

Reach out: Ask individual members of your team what project or goal they feel deserves a more thoughtful, considered effort. Start by reviewing the desired outcome, and make sure that expectations are clear. Then discuss how to give team members time and space to focus on the project or goal. Avoid being the one to come up with the ideas— let your team members devise what will work for them personally.

Spread out: With your leadership colleagues or team members, agree on one or two specific areas of expertise that your company claims as distinctive. Consider your competitors—what would they say about themselves in terms of distinctive expertise? Examine the differences and look for opportunities for your company to be more novel and innovative in how it expands, communicates, and delivers expertise. Agree to pursue one action that will increase the novelty and distinction of your company.

Remember . . .

- Introducing innovation will inevitably meet with opposition by enemies of change—"innovation blockers." To deal with such opposition, first understand your own reactions and internal dialogue that occurs in the face of innovation blockers. Accepting and managing our own thoughts and emotions makes it possible to understand the thoughts and emotions of others who may block innovation attempts.

- There are four types of innovation blockers: those who are strict in following bureaucratic rules and protocol; those who avoid risk and demonstrate weak sponsorship of new ideas; those who control and protect their power; and those who simply detach from new ideas, holding on to doubt and skepticism. Recognizing that these blockers exist and learning ways to deal with and appeal to their needs is essential for innovation leaders.

Your Turn Now . . .

Reach in: Without judging negatively, identify a person you consider to be an innovation blocker. What type of blocker is this person—Bureaucrat? Wimpy Sponsor? Power Monger? Skeptic? Describe the emotions you experience when interacting with this person. Ask yourself if your internal dialogue is getting in the way of your innovation efforts, and, if so, work on reframing your responses into ones that are more understanding and empathetic. You'll be better able to relate to your "blocker" when you start with yourself.

Reach out: Meet or connect with a person you consider to be an innovation blocker. Have lunch, discuss an article or story of interest, or ask the person for an opinion. Engage in a way that makes the other person comfortable. Remember to consider the type of blocker you are dealing with, and to use specific strategies, such as sticking to rules or protocol (Bureaucrats), asking probing questions to invite support (Wimpy Sponsors), praising honestly (Power Mongers), or instilling positivism (Skeptics). After your meeting, think about what went well and where you must continue to persevere in your efforts to deal with innovation blockers.

Spread out: With your team or work group, hold a mini-seminar on innovation blockers and how to deal with them. Focus on how to be innovation enablers when working across the organization. Discuss how to develop a culture of communication and an openness to innovation with other departments. Organize a lunchtime function specifically geared toward staff mingling and finding out about others' work.

Remember . . .

- In many organizations, a lack of communication can result in duplication of effort and fragmented results. Talent and competence may go unrecognized if leaders do not promote collaboration or mine expertise across the organization. Mining for expertise unearths emerging talent and nurtures the next generation of innovators.

- To reinforce a positive company culture, you need to provide access to and amplify the "voices of distinction"—people who uphold the mores, values, and identity of the organization, are good communicators, and who propel others to act. These leaders are aware of historic precedents while appreciating the value of innovation and forward movement. They model the importance of having passion for the business, sharing success, and balancing culture and performance.

- Great stories, with engaging models and examples, can be more meaningful to people than just descriptions of concepts. Strategic stories convey powerful examples of leadership in action, helping to tap strong internal credibility and sustain company identity.

Your Turn Now . . .

Reach in: Identify three or four people who, in your opinion, epitomize and uphold the values and identity of the organization. Think about your reasons for selecting those people. If you are already communicating and collaborating with them, keep it up. If you are not communicating and collaborating with them, ask yourself "why not?" Turn every reason or excuse into a positive goal. For example, if you don't interface with the person on projects or work assignments, create a reason to do so—even if only to illuminate that person's talents to your team.

Reach out: With your team or work group, identify a few recent successes and ask, "Why did that work?" and "How can we make sure we include that same action next time?" If there are known successes in other groups or departments, assign a team member to reach out to those involved and ask them about their success and how they achieved it. Rotate this assignment and share stories on a regular basis.

Spread out: Identify credible leaders in your industry and search for events, talks, and videos that help bring those people's message to you and your team. Ask these leaders to give a guest talk to your work group in the spirit of sharing stories and examples of innovation that benefit the future of innovation in your work culture. Don't be shy about asking industry leaders and "gurus" to share their inspiration—in most cases, they'll appreciate and understand your request.

CHAPTER 5

ASPIRATION: DREAM WELL— YOU MAY FIND YOURSELF THERE

I used to want to be a Power Ranger, but now I want to be an Olympic champion.

—Aaron Cook, British taekwondo champion

With 12 seconds left on the clock, Andrés Iniesta has the ball. He dribbles past a defender . . . sees Messi . . . passes a long ball across the midfield, which Messi controls easily. Now with the ball, Messi makes a fabulous turn and now he's past one defender, two . . . the goalie steps out—dives! Messi shoots high in the corner—GOAL!!!!!!

This is a description of my sons Charlie and Will (aged 11 and 9 at the time) and me in the backyard reenacting famous soccer players performing astounding feats on the field. My daughter Annie does the same kind of thing as she lip syncs Adele and Taylor Swift. This kind of emulation and aspirational practice is quite valuable, it turns out. When we spend hours envisioning that we possess particular skills and attributes, or emulating the mannerisms or personalities of others we admire, we move in the direction of that aspiration—we become capable of what we envision and aspire to.

Aspirations can come from many sources, but often it's from a person, fictional or real, whom we find heroic. Take Aaron Cook, who was born only a couple years before the television show *Mighty Morphin Power Rangers* debuted in 1993. Although the show was initially criticized for the constant use of violence, Cook, as a boy, found it mesmerizing and inspiring. He wanted to be just like the Power Rangers and would often dress up and wear Power Ranger costumes while practicing his kicks and attacks against his younger brother. His parents talked him out of attacking his brother and instead enrolled him in taekwondo lessons.

The aspiration to become a Power Ranger led Cook on a journey that culminated in his becoming a taekwondo world champion. Such is the power of developing strong role models and aspiring to emulate the skills, attributes, and heightened skills of our heroes.

Emulating the traits of heroes is an important part of realizing the aspirational self and leader. An aspiration is not only an articulated goal but also a feeling of hope and optimism about an intended success as well as a tangible outcome. Aspiration is one of the most powerful ideas leaders can give to others, and a shared aspiration starts with shared truth.

SHARE TRUTH

I was 16 years old at the moment the Space Shuttle Challenger exploded above NASA Kennedy Space Center shortly after takeoff, killing seven astronauts, including New Hampshire schoolteacher Christa McAuliffe. In the months that followed, renowned physicist Richard Feynman was asked to help understand how this happened.

Feynman not only gave famous testimony to Congress describing the O-ring failure that led to the catastrophe, he also led a more quiet inquiry, conducting interviews of the NASA engineers and leaders. He devoted the latter half of his book *What Do You Care What Other People Think: Further Adventures of a Curious Character* to his experience working on the Presidential Commission on the Space Shuttle Challenger Accident, also known as the Rogers Commission (after its chairman).[1] One of Feynman's sober conclusions was that the engineers on the ground build-ing the unique parts of the rocket had a much different perspective than the leaders in the organization regarding assessment of risk.

Clues to the disconnection of perceived risk between the frontline engineers and NASA management started when Louis Ullian, the range safety officer at Kennedy Space Center, began an inquiry into whether or not to place destruct charges on manned rocket flights, including Challenger's. It was common practice at the time to have remote destruct charges placed on unmanned rockets in case something went wrong. The thinking was it would be safer to remotely destruct an out-of-control rocket, rather than have an out-of-control rocket dangerously explode on the ground.

Ullian discovered a 4 percent failure rate among unmanned rocket flights he researched and calculated that manned rocket flights, with their much higher safety standards and preparations, had about a 1 percent failure rate. However, when he asked NASA, he was told the probability of failure for a manned rocket flight was one in one hundred thousand. He told this figure to Feynman, who replied, "That means you could fly the shuttle every day for an average of 300 years between accidents—which is obviously crazy!"

Needing to pick a failure rate on which to base his decision, Ullian settled on one in one thousand as a compromise. However, with NASA management's estimating one in one hundred thousand, Feynman turned to the frontline engineers to find out what they believed the failure rate was.

Feynman requested a meeting with a group of engineers and began asking questions about the rockets, including how they worked and were assembled, to assess their probability of failing. After a couple of hours, he hit on a better idea: instead of trying to extrapolate for himself what the failure probability was, he'd ask the engineers in the room. He said to them, "Here's a piece of paper each. Please write on your paper the answer to this question: What do you think is the probability that a flight would be uncompleted due to a failure in the engine?" He collected and averaged the answers in the room: one in three hundred.

Feynman went on to learn that, unlike airplanes or cars—which are built "bottom up" using integrated systems that have been tried and tested over time—the Space Shuttle, as a unique vehicle, was built "top down." That is, it was conceived as a whole and built from individual and unique parts assembled to suit a specific purpose. In calculating the potential failure probability, the NASA engineers had evaluated the rate of each individual component and extrapolated a probability of one in one hundred thousand. This makes complete sense when you consider that, individually, the failure probability of an engine blade, electrical cable, or bolt is vanishingly small.

What the engineers knew innately from their hands-on perspective was that the failure probability of the dynamically assembled whole structure was far higher. Yet, even with that knowledge available in the minds of the engineers, it didn't come out until Feynman asked the right question. To get closer to the truth and gain higher aspirations of everyone in the organization, first we have to find the hidden truths and share them.

As leaders in the organization, we have the obligation to say out loud when we don't know the intricacies of complex projects, and we expect and demand that those closest to the detail publicly bring to the surface any concerns. If problems are not faced squarely by those in charge, the aspirations of our entire team, and even our organization, can be undermined.

MAKE IT PERSONAL AND HEIGHTEN ASPIRATIONS

Justin Menkes, author of *Executive Intelligence: What All Great Leaders Have*, told me a story about one of Andrea Jung's early business-development efforts at Avon.[2] In the 1990s, Avon was often considered an aging product and a tired brand. Jung came on board as a consultant in 1993 and immediately diagnosed the problem with fresh eyes: the product was considered cheap and associated with low quality and outdated styles.

It was time to take the product upmarket. She launched an ad campaign, "Just Another Avon Lady," to begin to refresh the image of the company as hip, cool, and contemporary. By 1995, she had convinced Olympians Jackie Joyner-Kersee and Becky Dyroen-Lancer to become spokespersons and wear the products. She also positioned Avon as the official cosmetics company of the Olympic Games. Never satisfied, in 1997, Jung led another rebranding campaign with the slogan "Dare to Change Your Mind about Avon." Less than two years later, she was named as the CEO.

From the beginning of Jung's efforts at Avon, she knew choosing a course of action and getting everyone onboard were two different matters, as she learned earlier, in her first effort of rebranding at Avon.

Jung had called a big town-hall-style meeting to introduce the new branding and product enhancements. As her product team was introducing the new flashy colors, packaging, products, and branding, Jung looked at the audience and saw a sea of confused and angry Avon women who didn't understand the reason for all this seismic change. All they could think about was their reliable customers' disappointment and the loss of their own Christmas bonuses. In the minds of these women, Jung was proposing to take away their livelihoods and introduce enormous change that would affect the relationships they had with their customers. Indeed it would, and that was the point.

Jung stopped the presentation and asked the audience to raise their hands in response to a simple question: "How many of you use Avon products?" As the Avon ladies looked around the room, they saw how few among them actually used their own products. This was the deciding moment. Something clicked. They understood how much trouble the company was in, and took on a higher aspiration for the company because it became personal.

In one singular moment, Jung empathetically understood the point of view of these women and was able to pose a question to enable them to realize the urgency of their situation and the need for change. She engaged them on an emotional level, giving them a sense of ownership. The rest was easy. Now Avon had thousands of ambassadors for the new brand and product.

OFFER HOPE

In a 2010 interview, Nick Morgan told me the story of Robert Desnos, who was born in 1900 in Paris and had become a poet and member of the French Resistance in World War II.[3] Near the end of the war, he was arrested by the Gestapo and interred in Auschwitz. In the concentration camp, he and his companions observed that, over the weeks, their fellow inmates were gathered in groups and put on trains to be taken away. The Gestapo said nothing of their fates, but as no one returned, the other prisoners knew that those put on the trains were being sent to die.

One day the guards came to gather Desnos and a few hundred others to put them on the trains. Everyone knew with sullen despondency what was going to happen, and the trains became filled with a heavy, thick sadness as the prisoners were put onboard and the train got underway.

In a flash of impulse, Robert reached to the man next to him and grabbed his hand. "I will read your fortune!" he said. As he held the man's hand and gazed down while touching the crooked lines of his palm, Robert told the man he would live a long life, with marriage and children. He reached out to the next man's hand and declared a fortune of wealth and entrepreneurship and love was destined in his future. Again and again he grabbed each man's hand and conjured a fortune full of life and joy and expectation. And as he passed from each person to the next, announcing a soaring future of adventure and promise, the train car gradually grew louder with the excited talk of swelling jubilation.

The Gestapo became disoriented and unsure of their charge. They had been ordered to send the men away to certain execution, but the guards became tentative and unsure of how to proceed in the face of this excitement. They ultimately reversed the direction of the train, returning to the concentration camp, and opened the locked doors.

"What Robert Desnos was able to do was tell a huge truth about hope in that moment, and he saved the lives of himself and everybody on the train," Morgan concludes.

Not only did Desnos offer hope, but he also saved his own life and the lives of others by using his imagination, writes author Susan Griffin in an essay about the same event: "Robert Desnos was famous for his belief in the imagination. He believed it could transform society."[4]

A beautiful story indeed. Imagine how this vision of joy might translate to your work, to your life, to your capacity to inspire and give hope to others.

I had the honor of working with John Hope Bryant, author of *Love Leadership*, who also sees hope as a powerful force for change. I discovered that, in person, he is incredibly present and focused on the immediate interaction in progress. For example, when I first met him, I made a few introductory comments and then suggested he might prefer some time to focus and prepare for his presentation.[5] Instead, he said, "Hang on, this is the experience we're having now. We have plenty of time. Let's talk."

Bryant made it clear that he was willing to free up mental space in order to spend time focused, in the moment, on his conversation with me. As you might imagine, I was not only honored but even more determined to give my best energy and focus to the interaction. I'm glad I did, because he said something that really stuck with me: "At the point of greatest despair, if you can conjure hope, it will resonate around you and change the world."

Like Robert Desnos and John Hope Bryant, innovative leaders recognize their capacity for inspiring greatness in those around them. One of the greatest gifts you can offer other people is unconditional and open sharing of ideas and wisdom to help them grow their own ideas and talents. Everyone benefits greatly from the experience—not only the person receiving advice and direction from a trusted mentor but also the coach. Make no mistake, when we focus our energies on developing the potential of those around us instead of pandering to those above us, we, our team, our department, and our entire organization become far more successful.

FOCUS ON THE TEAM, NOT THE BOSS

"I'm sorry, what did you say?" I asked.

Ken Hicks, CEO of Foot Locker, had just said, "You are more likely to be fired up than fired down." What he meant was that managers are more likely to lose the trust of their team before their superiors terminate them for incompetence. I was interviewing him at the company's headquarters in New York City about how new managers and leaders could best make a difference in their first weeks and months on the job.[6]

Hicks had just finished a boardroom discussion with about 20 Princeton undergraduates on how to effectively build a brand and the lessons Foot Locker had learned on this subject. A generous man, he had invited these students to share in what he had learned from having led Foot Locker through immense changes. Then he took even more time to let me interview him.

In our conversation, he provided the sound advice that, if we go in with a grand plan to make a difference and expect people to execute on it without involving them in its development, we've lost their buy-in. That is, we've lost the opportunity to benefit from the ideas of those who will be executing the plan while simultaneously securing their engagement.

Hicks believes this strongly and practices what he preaches. In his own first early days with Foot Locker, he traveled to the company's stores, met a lot of people, and listened to what they had to say before making any sweeping changes.

Going back to his statement about being fired, Hicks explained that too often managers get so caught up in pandering to the imagined interests of superiors that they fail to engage those around them, and as a result lose the support of their teams. Building that support comes from listening to the ideas of those around us rather than getting them to say what we want to hear. As Hicks put it, "Many executives and leadership people think that their job is to be better than their people. Their job is to make their people better than them."

When we don't engage our team members, a complete paralysis can set in, or a catastrophe can occur that keeps us from delivering on a project—long before milestones are missed—because we've essentially been fired by our team. Instead of bringing a grand vision to fruition, we lose our ability to be effective as leaders.

In addition to supporting and helping the people around us grow, it's also critical that we acknowledge the importance and positive influence a mentor can have in helping to accelerate our own thinking, experiences, and decision making. While we can be a role model to others, if we want to grow, we should also constantly be seeking opportunities to learn from role models, from those we trust and admire. When we take the time to seek out a talented coach, ask for advice, and aspire to a particular habit, behavior, or way of life typified in another, we can better

- figure out what matters most to us, what will help us grow, and what will enable us to have a greater positive effect on those around us;
- amplify our focus by removing lesser priorities;
- connect with people and ideas more closely aligned with our own ideas; and
- identify and remove blind spots.

In learning to be good mentees, we can become more effective mentors. To teach anything effectively, we must first learn it deeply enough to share it in a meaningful and articulate way and be able to handle penetrating questions. If someone we are advising develops a greater curiosity, we also should know where to direct his or her next inquiry when we don't have all the answers.

PLAY TO AN INDIVIDUAL'S ASPIRATION AND STRENGTHS

The best coaches develop a deep emotional fluency such that they have a strong understanding of their players' strengths. John Wooden, one of the most successful college basketball coaches of all time, coached so personally and directly that he spoke, on average, for only four seconds at a time, and most often only to individual players.

In the movie *The Blind Side*, Sandra Bullock's character takes an interest in Big Mike, a teenager on her son's high school football team, and eventually becomes Big Mike's guardian. Big Mike is on the offensive line and is supposed to protect the quarterback from being tackled, but in play after play, despite his enormous size and power, he does a poor job in blocking defensive players. Bullock's character discovers that when he took a psychological-profile test, Big Mike scored 98 percent on having "protective instincts."

In a defining scene in the movie, Bullock—who has been watching from the sidelines as Big Mike once again fails to protect his quarterback—interrupts the practice to speak directly to him. She asks him to imagine that the quarterback is a member of their own family, even his own brother. When the practice resumes, Big Mike ferociously defends the quarterback.

Bullock's character helped Big Mike move mentally from simply playing a game to envisioning that he was protecting a family member. She had him aspire to a higher, more powerful self, simply by tapping into his strength of having a strong protective instinct.

As we coach and lead to each individual's strengths and aspiration of themselves, we must always expect his or her success as well.

EXPECT THE BEST OF EVERYONE

We have learned that managers, by simply changing very small things about how they interact with their teams and the expectations they have of them, can change their teams' performance immensely. By simply expecting the best of those around us, they can live up to that higher expectation, even if that higher expectation isn't even explicitly stated. People around us respond to our body language, nonverbal cues, and vocal intonation in addition to what we actually say.[7]

A classic study identified individual managers in a large group as having either a "Theory X" or "Theory Y" disposition.[8] Theory X managers believed that employees were essentially lazy, found work to be toiling, only performed it for the money, and had to be constantly watched or they wouldn't perform at all. Theory Y managers, on the other hand, believed that people were intrinsically motivated, creative, and could best decide how to get their work done with little supervision.

It was no surprise, then, to discover that Theory X managers had Theory X employees, and Theory Y managers had Theory Y employees. Interestingly, as they followed these managers over time as they moved into leading different teams, the researchers found that the managers had the ability to change the orientation of the people on their teams. That is, a Theory X manager could inherit a Theory Y team and turn its members into Theory X employees.

This is the Pygmalion or Rosenthal effect, named for psychologist Robert Rosenthal, in which the greater the expectation we place upon people, the better they perform.[9] Some of the more well-known experiments by Rosenthal involved telling teachers that particular students (selected randomly) were exceptional and very intelligent. On the basis of what they'd been told about the students, the teachers then changed their attitudes toward them, expecting them to perform better—and the children did. It turns out that the teacher's biased expectations had real-life effects.

DEVELOP THE GURU IN OTHERS

The meaning of the word "guru" is derived from the Sanskrit word for teacher or master. I had a wonderful interview in May 2012 with

Dr. Sujaya Banerjee, chief learning officer for Essar Group, one of the fastest-growing companies in India.[10] In my experience working with Dr. Banerjee, I found her immensely insightful and thoughtfully present.

As Dr. Banerjee described to me, her ability to allow the conversation to evolve, without external pressures, comes in part from the Hindu culture, which predominantly believes in the eternal cyclicality of life. Therefore, built into human connections and conversations is an allowance for space for reflection and consideration. As a result, our engaging interview went on for more than an hour and, when it was officially over, we continued to carry on our conversation down the hallway for another 20 minutes.

As Dr. Banerjee described, Essar has developed a remarkably successful coaching and mentoring program by appealing to the cultural influences of believing in rebirth and the cyclical nature of life, and of aspiring toward being immortal—in Hindi, becoming "amar." The philosophy of mentoring at Essar is that a way to become immortal is to coach and mentor. Senior executives and managers are encouraged to develop their immortal self through developing the wise guru within another, younger associate. By tapping into this intrinsic motivation to build an eternal legacy of wisdom, executives see clearly that they have a path to create a legacy, and preserve their own immortal wisdom through others. As Banerjee described in our interview:

> You know, you often have a joke about Indians and "Indian Stretchable Time." So Indian Standard Time is often described as "Indian Stretchable Time," because the truth is that Indians have a cyclical concept of time. So they believe in rebirth and the cycle of rebirth, and therefore there isn't a terrible hurry to do or complete anything in this world, and I think coming from there, therefore, is a compelling belief in immortality. So we positioned this program as a great opportunity to remain immortal within the organization, by transferring their knowledge and coaching, grooming, training, mentoring other people, and living, through them, inside the organization for long after they have left and retired from the organization. And I think it worked beautifully well.

Dr. Banerjee and her colleagues effectively used the innate philosophy of their culture to bring out the aspiration of immortality through guiding others.

In developing our aspirational mindsets and methods, we must always reach to influence larger audiences and bigger structures. To be successful, the entire organization must adopt a higher aspiration.

DEVELOP HIGHER ASPIRATIONS AS AN ORGANIZATION

Following on my discussion with Dr. Banerjee, let's consider what would happen if our companies inquired less about making a profit and more about other aspirations, such as the following:

- the personal and professional development and livelihood of employees
- the health and well-being of employees' families
- our local communities' civic integrity
- the broader environmental impact of the company's footprint
- building a positive value chain in which all stakeholders in our product's journey are supported

What if the company's decision making was viewed through a long lens with the expectation that decisions today have immense brand impact downstream?

If all of this were true, the company's incentive and value system would reflect an expectation that we would contribute in these dimensions in proactive and meaningful ways. We might be expected to take time to exercise or attend conferences and workshops to develop our own physical and mental capacities. There might be some peer pressure to talk more about the difference we and our teams made in developing sustained customer value, rather than high-fiving fat commission checks and bonuses. There might be some big initiatives measuring our teams' contribution to civic well-being.

The subject of our inquiry determines the direction in which we grow, develop, and achieve. Our stated aspirations become the shared goals against which we measure our success. But what if we change the aspirations and goals?

Gary Erickson, CEO of Clif Bar, founded the company in 1992 with partner Kit Crawford. They had a vision to make a great-tasting, healthy, organic snack bar, and while they did achieve this, Gary's mind kept drifting to the places outside of work that inspired him and his employees: where they rode their bikes, where they spent their free time, and the communities and beautiful country they lived in. As a result, Clif doesn't have one bottom line, it has five:

- sustaining the brand
- sustaining the business
- sustaining the planet
- sustaining the people
- sustaining the community

These metrics are discussed, debated, and edified in writing such that each associate understands the stated metrics on how Clif will evaluate performance against them, but how they are valued remains up to the employee community to define. To pursue these goals, employees might organize their colleagues to support local charities, or collaboratively measure their progress at the gym, or maybe share details of the time and energy they've devoted to coaching little league.[11]

When we pursue such aspirations in our own lives, the reactions from our colleagues are often, "Good for you, but how do you find the time?" That's because the implicit professional expectation is that performance is measured against contribution to profit alone. If you have any time to make considerate, thoughtful decisions by taking a break and trail-running with your dog, that's just because you've already fulfilled the profit punch-list—you've already fed the hungry maw of fattening investor equity.

Clif has empirically demonstrated that by sustaining (and measuring) not only the business but also other dimensions that drive social and environmental value, companies can prosper successfully in multiple dimensions. In this way, by simply changing the shared aspiration of the organization, we change the behavior and outcomes of those within it.

We explore the value of having this sense of purpose more in chapter 11.

LET'S RECAP

Remember . . .

- Emulating perceived heroes and role models can lead to realizing our own aspirations.

- Aspiring to an intended outcome guides our selective inquiries toward the outcome we seek. It promotes hopeful and optimistic success, leading to a tangible result.

- Aspiring to greatness requires uncovering and exploring truths— including hidden truths—and sharing them with others.

- Leaders have a great capacity for giving aspirational hope to others and inspiring greatness. As John Hope Bryant, author of *Love Leadership*, puts it, "There are only two things in this world—love and fear. At the point of greatest despair, if you can conjure hope, it will resonate around you and change the world."

Your Turn Now . . .

Reach in: Recall a person who helped you to become a leader and helped you aspire toward greatness. What big or small actions did that person take that made a difference to you as a leader? Make time to talk about this with others—colleagues, family members, or friends— and inquire about their leadership models and heroes. Examine themes that arise from your conversations and incorporate them into your own leadership efforts.

Reach out: Challenge your team to talk about projects openly, sharing hopes as well as truths that can bear on the project's overall success. Help balance the discussion by allowing discussion of potential problems and concerns as well as facilitating hopeful expectations and optimism.

Spread out: Find examples in the news, community, and history that exemplify the power of hope, especially in the face of despair. Share these examples with your team members and encourage them to locate and share similar stories and examples that keep aspiration alive.

Remember . . .

- Leaders and mentors have a positive influence on accelerating our thinking, experiences, and decision making. These leaders glean advice from others and learn from people at all levels of the organization.

- Innovative leaders focus energy on their team, department, and organization. They listen to the input of the people who perform the work, and involve them in projects and ideas. In order to gain support, learn, and be role models, leaders must understand and engage with their employees.

- Simply changing very small aspects of our interactions with our teams, and our expectations of them, can create immense performance differences. Negative input fosters negative output. Positive support engenders more productivity and greater job satisfaction.

- The team leader is the deciding factor in promoting a positive or negative outcome. The greater the expectation we place upon people, the better they perform.

- "Guru" is the Sanskrit word for teacher or master—"one who dispels the darkness of ignorance." Coaching and mentoring can bring out the "guru" in others and is believed, in Hindu philosophy, to assist toward immortality. This eternal legacy of wisdom is thus preserved through transfer to young initiates.

Your Turn Now . . .

Reach in: Remember that you are guiding each member of your team toward reaching his or her personal greatness. This is your goal and responsibility. Ask yourself: "How am I doing this now, what's working, and what do I hope to do better?" Identify two or three things you could learn from members of your team that would help you be a better guide, coach, or mentor.

Reach out: Arrange individual meetings with your team members to highlight their strengths and achievements, urging them to ever greater but attainable heights. Make sure that when you invite them to meet with you, you are upbeat and transparent about your intentions. Before the meeting, think about each person carefully—what you observe as strengths, efforts, and achievements. Connect these to the work of the team and the organization. Ask how you can further support the individual and make a verbal commitment to do so.

Spread out: As a team, discuss individual strengths and how each person is a master, teacher, or guru. Allow each person to declare one or two things that he or she does well and would be willing to help others improve, as a coach or mentor. Suggest learning partners, discussion boards, or other ways the team can help one another aspire to greatness.

Remember . . .

- Organizational leaders who develop higher aspirations do not concentrate only on profit but also inquire more about aspirations, such as:
  - promoting personal and professional development and livelihood
  - supporting family health and well-being
  - contributing to the local community's civic integrity
  - attending to the broader environmental impact of the company's footprint
  - building a positive value chain of support for our stakeholders
- Today's decisions are expected to have immense future impact. The company's incentive and value system would reflect every employee's contribution in proactive and meaningful ways.
- What we measure is what we get back in return. The subject of our inquiry determines our future growth, development, and achievement.

Your Turn Now . . .

Reach in: Think about your role in developing higher aspirations for yourself, your team, and your organization. Besides the aspiration to help your organization make a profit and succeed, what is one other dimension—professional development, health, family, community, environment—that you could truly get behind and support? Make one measurable goal for yourself—to achieve in the next 6–12 months—that will show a positive return.

Reach out: Encourage every member of your team to include a higher aspiration goal in his or her annual goal-setting efforts. Make this goal specific, measurable, actionable, relevant, and time-bound. Ask team members to share their goals with one another and provide mutual support for their achievement.

Spread out: Identify and research companies that are models for developing higher aspirations, and learn how they are contributing to the betterment of lives. Even through your everyday activities—driving, shopping, working on a home project—think about the companies that provide the products and services you use. Are they contributing to the betterment of your life?

CHAPTER 6

EDGE: EMBRACE NEW KINDS OF RISK

Borders? I have never seen one. But I have heard they exist in the minds of some people.

—*Thor Heyerdahl, innovator, adventurer, and border-smasher*

I have a friend who installed the same invisible dog fence I did, but he admitted he didn't bother training his dog. He simply installed the underground wire and shackled his dog with the collar that would shock the dog whenever he got near the line. My friend thought that the dog would just learn the boundaries himself and voilà—a dog self-trained to stay in the yard.

When I asked him how that worked out, he said that, as his young, boisterous dog started to run and play as usual, he would get shocked. However, since the dog didn't associate the pain with any clear boundary, he eventually sat in the middle of the yard shaking in fear, too paralyzed to move. From that point on, all the dog wanted to do was stay in the house.

There are many dimensions to this story—not least the owner's behavior—but what I want to address is the dog's perspective. The dog, not understanding why he was getting shocked, arrived at a state that psychologists call "learned helplessness." It's the point at which we are capable of believing that nothing we do matters and, regardless of our action, the outcome will be bad for us.

Having a sense of control, that our behavior matters, is one of the most important predictors of happiness, and, in turn, of workplace productivity, collaboration, and innovation. When we believe that our actions matter, we are more inclined to take action and use our initiative, to fully engage. And once we choose to engage in an activity, particularly a new one, we begin to accelerate our learning.

FIND THE EDGE

In the innovation process, the edge is where we experience a heightened sense of engagement, accelerated learning, and creativity. Mihaly Csíkszentmihalyi, the former head of the department of psychology at the University of Chicago, calls this being "in flow." According to him, "Flow is completely focused motivation."[1] It is the mental state in which a person is fully focused on what he or she is doing, where he or she is totally immersed in an activity. Musicians call it being "in the pocket," and athletes call it being "in the zone."

The point of flow is that delicate place where the task is neither too difficult nor too easy. If the challenge exceeds our ability, we move into greater states of stress and anxiety, and eventually paralysis. If our ability

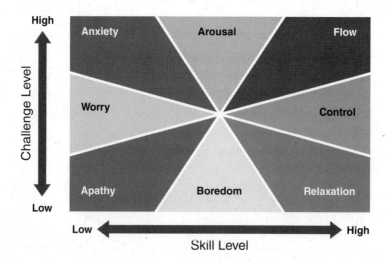

Figure 6.1   Find Flow

Source: Mihaly Csíkszentmihalyi

greatly exceeds the challenge with which we are presented or choose, we enter states of comfort and ease, and eventually boredom and apathy. As Figure 6.1 illustrates, "flow" occurs at the intersection of challenge and skill level.

Being truly engaged frees those in flow to be deeply curious and explorative. They are more about solving a puzzle—finding out what lies beneath the surface of a problem—than about power, position, and money. Being in a state of flow leads to deep hyperfocusing, which in turn leads to finding more creative solutions.

Accelerate Learning through Mindful Practice

We don't often think of learning as having velocity, but it does. The classic notion of practice involves putting in the hours, right? But putting in time is strikingly different than the kind of practice that leads to accelerated learning. It isn't about watching the clock, but more about *purposeful* practice, where we are successful 50 to 75 percent of the time.

The aim shouldn't necessarily be to stop the way we've been doing things, but instead to think about starting new habits, particularly when we're trying to acquire new skills or behaviors. The important thing is to take action.

In December 2011, I worked with Daniel Coyle, author of *The Talent Code*, in a filming collaboration to find out what he had learned from visiting some of the premier talent hotbeds around the world. From tennis and soccer academies to violin conservatories to behavioral clinics, Coyle sought to understand how the best coaches work, and how the most skilled and talented musicians, athletes, and business professionals practice and learn.

Coyle told me a marvelous story (also profiled in his book) about visiting the Shyness Clinic in Palo Alto, California, which focuses on building new habits toward developing "social fitness," as the clinic calls it.[2] The folks that come to the shyness clinic often have arrived at a point where their social anxieties and shyness have become a real hindrance and barrier to connection. The clinicians and psychologists there believe that, much like developing physical fitness, or leadership or creative capacities, people can develop social fitness—but it takes practice and experience. The clinicians believe the best way for their patients to overcome their social anxieties is through deliberate practice of increasingly difficult social behaviors—to move them closer to the edge of their social abilities and fears and eventually expand their tolerance for risk.

A simple exercise at the clinic might involve getting participants to approach two people per day in a public place and simply ask them the time of day. Participants then graduate to asking a store manager where the restroom is, for example. The following week they might be asked to go out to lunch each day and ask for something special with their order—mayonnaise on the side, for example.

For a final exam, a participant might be asked to go to a supermarket and intentionally drop a whole watermelon on the floor, then apologize and work with the market employees to deal with the mess. Such a scene would be an appalling thought to someone suffering from acute shyness. But, over time, the participants could build the social and emotional capacities to effectively deal with such an incident in the future.

Ask Those Closest to Help You Identify Your Strengths

In an interview, Charles Handy—a renowned author, philosopher, and co-founder of the London Business School—described his teaching practices.[3] He would ask students to choose interesting investigations and projects, and then he would sit in the back of the class and let the students teach each other. Instead of lecturing from the front of the classroom, he claims he would periodically ask provocative questions from the back row. The power of such a teaching tactic is that it allows the students to find and develop their own strengths by defining their own inquiry, and then has them take risks by defending their ideas before their peers.

Handy said that sometimes we can become blind to our own greatest capabilities and strengths. Often, as our actions and behaviors become habitual, we come to the belief that we have particular strengths, and we translate that assortment of strengths into a self-identity. We may decide that we are sales professionals or talent scouts or marketing managers or such because by adopting a particular title, set of behaviors, and language, we believe we are defined by this self-imposed persona.

As a result, we can become blind to opportunity and closed to self-reinvention because we overvalue what we have invested in, and undervalue what our friends, family, and colleagues find most appealing and powerful about us. Handy's advice is to trust other people's assessment of our strengths and to take time to ask them what they think our greatest strengths are—and to believe their response.

REDEFINE YOUR LIMITS

> A smart strategist gravitates toward ill-defined and ambiguous opportunities. That is because once everything has been defined and reduced to standard operating procedure, there is no money left to be made.
>
> —*Stuart Hart*

Stuart Hart, one of the world's top authorities on the implications of environment and poverty for business strategy, argues that treading along the same safe path, not looking outside the norm and taking risks, can mean survival but rarely leads to growth in an individual or an organization.

In the early 1990s, Frank Farley, professor of educational psychology at the University of Wisconsin, coined the term "Type T," ("T" is for "thrill-seeking") to describe people who seek out and participate in higher-risk activities and succeed because of this focus.[4] While Type Ts can flame out from self-destructive behaviors (think Janis Joplin), many go on to invent cars, build businesses, construct new surgical techniques, and do much more.

Type T people—such as Erik Weihenmayer, the world's leading blind athlete and the only blind person in history to reach the highest mountain peaks, or British business magnate Richard Branson—redefine our understanding of the limits of possibility while creating businesses, inspiring people, and building jobs and value. Type Ts aren't always about more or faster or higher but about reinventing and redefining the "how" that leads to invention. They are our primary creators and can also inspire all of us to be creative. We may not hit the headlines like Mark Zuckerberg, but we can tap our own hidden potential to get the most out of who we are.

While being able to take risks is important in a creative environment, we as leaders need to make it clear that we and our team members must also be accountable for the decisions we make. Dan Glaser, president and CEO of Marsh & McLennan Companies, described to me in an interview an experiment Marsh & McLennan conducted in Rotterdam.[5] The company renovated a warehouse and set up an open, nontiered environment where associates could collaborate as they felt appropriate, depending on what projects they were working on. There were no schedules, no punch-cards, and no mandatory office hours.

In our interview, Glaser made it clear that, while Marsh employees are encouraged to explore possibilities and opportunities, they are also held accountable to specific business initiatives that create value for the customer, build growth for associates, and create shareholder profits. Glaser emphasized to associates that they honor and value processes that lead to results, not simply showing up in the office for the required hours each day.

While the creative process can be sparked many ways, it usually begins with a challenge we're facing. To meet the challenge and find a solution, the issues at hand have to be identified and understood, then defined and redefined. The lucid defining of the challenge forms the foundation on which to build our ideas for solutions and reveals the materials needed.

Sometimes the best way to spark creativity is by intentionally making the work environment unstable, reconfiguring resources, roles, and business architectures regularly to create a moderate amount of creative tension. Should a team seem to be settling into a comfort zone, we as leaders need to step in and change its makeup, ensuring that the environment is always stimulating. Such intentional disruption can aid strategic agility—the ability to constantly be inventive when it comes to strategy—rather than following the norm of having brief strategy sessions periodically followed by longer-term implementation and execution.

PRAISE EFFORT AND GRIT, NOT TALENT

Talent is cheaper than table salt. What separates the talented individual from the successful one is a lot of hard work.

—*Stephen King, author*

Carol Dweck, the Lewis and Virginia Eaton professor of psychology at Stanford University, led a fascinating study in 1998 in which she and her colleagues gave four hundred fifth graders a series of tests, mostly puzzles.[6] The researchers then praised the students using one of two sets of six words each. With half of the group they said, "You must be smart at this," and with the other half they said, "You must have tried really hard."

The first word set awarded intelligence and innate talent, similar to how many of us parents and coaches (me included) get trapped into talking about, and to, our kids. We say how smart or how naturally gifted they are. The second word set praised effort, determination, preparation, and grit. What the researchers were interested in was how the kids, depending on the type of praise they received, would view their abilities—as fixed and unchanging, or as malleable and able to grow and change with work.

In the next round of puzzles, the kids were offered a choice: they could try harder problems or easier ones. Perhaps surprisingly, the kids praised for talent selected the easier problems while the kids praised for effort chose to attempt the harder ones. Why? While we might think that receiving praise for innate abilities would inspire confidence, instead Dweck found that we create a form of status—a height from which to fall. If people believe they have special talent and are expected to perform well, the thought of failing expectations becomes a liability. To protect themselves as "gifted and talented" individuals, they will choose easier tasks to ensure they have high performance.

In the next part of the study, both sets of kids were given harder problems to solve and both sets of kids performed more poorly. Not surprising; but here's the interesting thing: When the researchers asked the kids how they did on the problems, the kids praised for talent lied or exaggerated their performance almost 40 percent of the time, presumably to maintain their social status as "talented." However, when the kids praised for effort were asked the same question, closer to 10 percent of them exaggerated their performance, presumably because their ego was not wrapped up in their performance.

Here's where it gets *really* interesting. In the next phase of the study, both sets of kids were given problems comparable to the original set of problems. In terms of difficulty, this next set was just as challenging as the first. The group praised for talent had just had an ego setback in the earlier round and did significantly worse than they did the first time around. They were told they were smart, then they performed poorly, and now when they attacked the same level of difficulty with decreased confidence, they performed significantly worse. The second group, on the other hand, did much better—nearly 30 percent better—this time around. For those kids, success was about effort, and failure just meant they needed to work harder instead of worrying about loss of status.

While the difference between these two groups of kids was just six words, keep in mind there are a lot of ways to say, "You must have tried really hard." Dweck and her colleagues use this kind of effort or "process praise" for encouraging engagement, perseverance, and improvement. Here are some examples of how to convey recognition of grit and perseverance in those around you, modeled on Dweck's suggestions:

- "You really prepared for that meeting, and your presentation showed it. You researched the customer's company and interests, outlined the problem perfectly, and presented solutions very well. That really worked!"
- "I like the way you tried all kinds of strategies on that reporting problem until you finally got it."
- "It was a long, hard research assignment, but you stuck to it and got it done. You stayed at the task, kept up your concentration, and kept working. That's great!"

- "I like that you took on that challenging project for the new business group. It will take a lot of work—doing the research, designing the integration, acquiring the resources, and building it. You're going to learn a lot of great things."

Next time we see excellence, we should praise the effort it must have taken to get there. In doing so, we not only will be rewarding excellence but also building growth and confidence, so those praised will be willing to go to the edge of their capabilities.

EMBRACE SOCIAL RISK

Whether we are engaged in creating a new product or improving our business mechanisms, we face risk to ourselves and our companies in every component of the innovation process. We can risk our ability to operate—to produce, deliver, and support our products and services in the market. We can also take social risks—to our reputation, brand identity, and social integrity. Risk can increase exponentially as we push ourselves and our companies to the edge of our creative capacity, but it can also hone our innovative abilities, enabling us to bring back amazing new ideas from that edge. To sustain innovation, we must embrace risk throughout the innovation process.

While we have lots of time-tested tools to help calculate risks on the operational side of business, social risks, which affect our relationships with other people—from fellow workers to customers—are harder to calculate. We take on social risk early in the innovation process, when we first float an idea for innovation. Depending on how open our work environment is, we may risk looking foolish or worse, especially when we shoot out ideas that, in retrospect, even we recognize as being bad. The more we diverge from the norm and take our thinking to the edge, the more likely we are to risk our credibility, but taking such risks, especially in an open environment where creativity is encouraged, can lead to breakthrough innovation that reaps great rewards.

Social risk can affect companies at many levels and can have tentacles that reach into the operational side, but it's most likely to confront us in the process of building relationships inside an organization and with customers. In both arenas, trust is critical—internally, to engage employees and enable them to feel free to express their ideas and, externally, to engage customers and build their loyalty.

Face Social Risk within the Organization

Fairly soon after my father and I sold our company, Targeted Learning Corporation (TLC) to Skillsoft, I was invited to nominate a keynote speaker for our annual global sales meeting. Most organizations have such an occasion where they celebrate victories and plan and design the future. It's an event typically for just the sales and support people in organizations. It's a rah-rah kind of event in which we welcome new contributors, celebrate the company, and give out awards to the big contract winners and sales successes. That year, I had heard that Salesforce.com had booked the Red Hot Chili Peppers for entertainment and Tony Robbins to pump up the sales group and give them some ideas to put to work.

For our event, I picked Keith Ferrazzi, who wrote a couple of business bestsellers about the importance of building relationships and networks of deep trust. I knew his work, but didn't know him very well and doubted he knew who I was much at all, other than the guy who invited him to speak at the conference.

In the weeks leading up to the conference, I was trying to think of interesting and novel ways to introduce him. I wanted to make an impression and deliver something unique to the audience instead of something like, "I am pleased to introduce Keith, author of . . ." I wanted to avoid the mundane, and instead offer something memorable.

One day, while running and listening to music, I suddenly thought to myself, "I'll perform a rap to introduce him!" As soon as I said those words to myself, I knew instantly it was both insane, and yet a dare to myself. Could I write and deliver a rap before my entire company that would be exciting and memorable and not absurd? What a ridiculous idea, and yet I had an inkling it could work, and I had the confidence to at least start composing something to see if it held true in my own mind.

Using Ferrazzi's book and his signature expression, "no one is allowed to fail," for content, I wrote, memorized, rehearsed, and envisioned performing the rap before delivering it.

Keith Ferrazzi Rap

Good morning, good morning to you all
It's my pleasure to introduce someone who will completely enthrall
He's going to blow the roof off; he might even change your life
Put an end to insecurities, doubt, and strife

He's known as a master of connection
And it's true his database is an enormous collection
But what you'll learn is it's not about how many people you know
It's about how many great relationships you grow

It's not just about how many people you can ping
It's about how many people who will sing
Your praises whenever they are asked
How was it to work with you on a project or the Big Task

First build a community, a network built on mutual respect
And these peeps, your posse, you must never neglect
Building that core team becomes the holy grail
For this is the place where NO ONE IS ALLOWED TO FAIL

Then maybe just when you think that big contract fell through
You'll turn that close shave into a WOO-HOO
You'll start to reach higher because it feels like there ain't nothing you can't do
Because your team is tight, bonded like glue

Then build your identity, your very own brand
One that is credible, distinctive, yet easy to expand
A brand that reflects the beliefs and talents that you know most
And soon you'll be inking contracts from coast to coast

But wait before you focus on improving your standard of living
Remember you earn trust and proximity first by giving
With a big head you'll think you turn everything to gold
Be careful in your success, don't let hubris take hold

Your final task, should you choose to accept
Is share this wonderful gift, without pause or regret
For if it's true legacy you want to approach
Teach and share, become a mentor, a coach

People in the house
Open up your hearts and minds, there is nothing to fear
To deliver this message Keith Ferrazzi is here!

When I delivered this rap at our global sales event, it produced the intended effect of surprising and impressing Keith, who brought me back onstage and demanded a standing ovation of the audience. But more important, the stunt also created something of an identity for our team within the company. It was a fun moment and also branded me for a while. At subsequent company events, I was often asked if I had prepared a rap to deliver.

My point is not that I can rap. I can't. If you review the tapes, you'll see I wouldn't get past amateur karaoke hour. The point is that I was willing to risk looking foolish to present an idea in a creative way. In performing such a comical show, there was nothing that would threaten the integrity of a Skillsoft product I was responsible for, nor did I suggest a change in delivery, production, or fulfillment of a product.

My foray into presentation innovation was unlikely to have big repercussions for me or my company. I simply took a personal social risk of looking a bit foolish at the moment. And the reward could be heightening the profile of myself and my product group in the company.

Vineet Nayar, the CEO of HCL Technologies, a leading provider of business solutions, took a bigger social risk when, years ago, he posted his own 360-degree feedback assessment publicly for everyone in the company to see.[7] In this kind of assessment, employees are evaluated by their peers and subordinates on a variety of criteria assessing relative strengths and weaknesses in various job functions, from time management to communication to goal setting.

Typically such assessments are kept private for the person being assessed, or perhaps are made available to just the person's immediate supervisor to see and take action on. Nayar made his own 360-degree assessment publicly available for all 70,000 HCL employees to see. Taking such a heightened and audacious social risk enabled the associates to see Nayar as human, fallible, and constantly striving to improve. In that act, Nayar modeled the way forward for all employees. Such modeling through transparency is critical to building a culture that encourages people to take risks and find the edges of their abilities.

Embracing innovation means embracing risk. It starts when we first share our ideas with others. Even in the most open, welcoming environment, we risk the opinion others have of us, our credibility, even our jobs. While what seems like a wild idea at first can ultimately bring hugely positive results, it can also make others, even ourselves, question our common sense, if not our sanity.

If we carry this willingness to risk our personal reputations to the way we interact with our customers and speak to markets, we can recognize a significant upside without risking operational integrity. Done the right way, with honest intent and creative design, social risk can take on new meaning to those who hear the message and how it's delivered.

Embrace Social Risk in Connecting with Customers

Kerry Smith is a gregarious, talented, and warm sales director for the southeast region of Skillsoft. A couple of years ago, he and his team decided that, instead of offering their customers a typical pro forma half-day customer event that might feature light sales pitches from company representatives and presentations from customers on how our products and services are so great, they'd rent out a beautiful Viking kitchen appliance showroom, stock it with delectable ingredients, and host a wine-tasting and cooking evening led by experienced chefs.

Kerry didn't attempt to change anything about the product or service offered but instead changed the way we as an organization interacted with our customers and how we facilitated their building new relationships with one another. This delightful customer experience involved some social risk, but now our customers have come to expect and eagerly anticipate this kind of event with Kerry's team.

Reward Creative Subversion in Your Company

Whether we're doing business in countries across the globe or closer to home, the ability to connect on a more personal level to a large number of people at one time has grown exponentially with the rapid evolution of the Internet and social media. The stories below illustrate how innovators have taken on social risks to mine the opportunity these technologies present to connect with people inside and outside their companies.

HCL Technologies and Meme. HCL Technologies has some emerging social-risk practices that are led not by the CEO or other senior executives but instead by the frontline associates themselves. According to Nayar, who writes about these practices in his blog, Krishnan Chatterjee, HCL's vice president of marketing, was approached in 2011 by a group of young associates who wanted to create their own social media sharing environment accessible only to the company's employees.[8] Chatterjee objected, advising them it was a waste of time, since social platforms such as Facebook were already readily available for HCL associates, and the company wasn't responsible for managing the hosting and maintenance.

The young leaders in the company thought about Chatterjee's advice, and then did it anyway. They built an online forum, Meme, "to enable HCL employees, to interact with their colleagues in HCL and across all HCL affiliate companies."[9] The forum quickly attracted more than 50,000 members to the community. Reviews of the social media sharing site have been positive, and now Chatterjee himself confesses to being a big fan and active member.

With an average employee age of 26 and consistent double-digit growth, HCL Technologies may well represent the future of innovative companies that encourage innovation in all things, including embracing new social media at all levels of the organization, modeled from the top. And this particular project would not have happened if those junior programmers in the company had heeded the advice of their managers. Instead they chose to persist in their creative subversion.

Taking on social risk to innovate in marketing. Marketing strategist David Meerman Scott tells a story of how Universal Studios risked the marketing of a new theme experience by using an approach that took advantage of the Internet and viral marketing.[10] The company gave a few key people a marketing message, hoping they'd spread the word to their contacts.

Universal had invested considerably in licensing the coveted Harry Potter intellectual property and in building "The Wizarding World of Harry Potter," a unique and signature experience in Orlando, Florida.

After the realistic Quidditch game was designed for the resort, a frightening Voldemort was cast to scare visitors, and butterbeer was brewed for their enjoyment and delight, all that remained was the marketing effort to tell the world about the new experience at the resort.

A more typical marketing operation might include Times Square billboards, expensive advertisements on prime-time networks, and perhaps full-page ads in prominent newspapers. At the time Cindy Gordon, vice president for new media and marketing, chose a new approach of using viral marketing through the Internet to reach customers. She and her colleagues at Universal told just seven people about the new addition to the resort. But they didn't tell just any seven people.

The Harry Potter fan community can be zealous and unsparing in their attention and understanding of detail, and often fanatical in debating the nuances of the Harry Potter universe. Universal Studios knew that, in order to appeal to the key demographic of rabid Potter fans, they needed to be named legitimate by those already credentialed. They needed to be appraised and respected by the most revered curators of the Harry Potter universe—those who managed the most visited Potter online blogs and fan sites, such as Mugglenet.com, and commanded an immense Potter following. For Universal Studios to claim such legitimacy would ring hollow among the Potter fan base.

Universal Studios invited these seven Harry Potter curators for a first peek in a super-secret webcast meeting with Scott Trowbridge, vice president of Universal Creative, and Stuart Craig, Academy Award–winning production designer for the Potter films. The curators attended, felt honored to be the first to have a look, and then reported to their fan base that, indeed, Universal Studios got it right.

Gordon estimates that those seven reached more than 350 million Potter fans around the world. It would have been impossible for Universal Studios to buy such access, much less the rousing endorsement of the Harry Potter royalty.

Inviting seven highly influential members of the target demographic offered no real risk to the operational side of building and running a Harry Potter exhibit, although it did present an audacious challenge to the designers to ensure they got it right before they invited Potter dignitaries to scrutinize. This was more of a social risk, one associated with a carefully targeted community of customers whom the marketers wanted to influence.

LET'S RECAP

Remember . . .

- Finding the "edge" is similar to "finding flow," being "in the zone," or being "in the groove." These are states conducive to heightened engagement, accelerated learning, and creativity. In these states, tasks are neither too easy nor too difficult, allowing deep curiosity, exploration, and highly focused activity to occur. Coupled with a sense of control and a belief that our behaviors have meaning, we are more apt to use our initiative and engage in innovative activities.

- Learning has its own velocity. Learning new skills requires employing deliberate, purposeful practice and taking action—marrying both application and experience.

- Out of habit, we may believe we have certain strengths that form part of our self-image. Deciding to play a particular professional or personal role can impose limits on our thinking beyond that role. We become blind to opportunities beyond the persona we imagine ourselves to have. Trust others' assessments of your strengths and worth.

Your Turn Now . . .

Reach in: Everyone has a comfort zone. You know when you are in your comfort zone, whether it is within your technical area of expertise or in how you communicate with others. List four professional activities or skills that you associate with that sense of comfort and ease. In one word, describe the positive feelings you have when you are performing each of these activities. Then list four activities that lie outside of your comfort zone and the negative feelings associated with them. From that list, select one activity that you truly want to acquire or develop. Set aside 10–15 minutes every day for purposeful practice of this new skill or activity. After 30 days, revisit your initial feelings associated with the activity and reflect on the progress you've made.

Reach out: Ask the members of your team to rate you on four or five activities or skills you consider to be within your comfort zone. You might also include four activities or skills you deem as outside of your comfort zone. Give your team members a simple rating system to use, such as high-medium-low level of performance, or 1–2–3 with 3 representing a high level of skill or performance. Encourage your team members to provide their ratings to you in person, to allow for the productive discussion and feedback you need to develop a plan for learning and practice. This might feel uncomfortable to your team members— and perhaps to you—but it's a worthwhile exercise in learning that some level of discomfort often accompanies change.

Spread out: Ask your team to identify three or four areas of team expertise they possess and with which they believe others in the organization would concur. Where there is disagreement, put those areas aside. Focus on the areas of expertise that have full consensus, even if the team can only agree on one or two areas. Then ask the team to identify one professional activity, skill, or area of performance that is desirable but still outside of their comfort zone as a team. Discuss the benefits of finding their "edge" in this area, and what you as the leader could do to help them move toward that edge. Agree to do something—even if (especially if!) it is a stretch. This activity may also be conducted with individual team members.

Remember . . .

- Treading the same safe path, without ever taking risk, rarely leads to growth—in an individual or an organization. Creation usually begins with challenge and often spurs tension or disrupts the equilibrium of the workplace. Innovators dare to move to the edge of creative chaos while remaining accountable and responsible.

- Risk has a broad scope that ranges in impact. Traditionally, we take risks that affect how products are made, where business is conducted, and how we market to our customers. We can also take risks that have a more social impact on our company's reputation and social integrity.

- Some examples of taking social risks include surprising your audience, targeting a few key customers or stakeholders who then "go viral" with the message, offering novel customer experiences, and setting an example regardless of conventional thought. These types of social risks can pay off significantly, without altering an organization's core expertise or products.

Your Turn Now . . .

Reach in: From your list of current challenges, select one that you feel is well defined and understood but still without a solution. Draw a circle, placing "safe" solutions you've considered in the center. Then place the "risky" solutions more toward the edge of the circle, and even beyond (outside) the circle. For the purposes of this exercise, put a large X through the safe solutions. Then challenge yourself to act on the solutions that are closer to the edge or over the edge, while retaining your responsibility and accountability.

Reach out: Review examples of social risk with your team members. Relate stories of surprising the audience, going viral by targeting a few messengers, offering novel experiences, and setting examples. Then pick a current or future team project or challenge that could benefit from a dose of social risk. Decide on a specific action that represents social risk and opens up possibilities for innovation. Ask for volunteers who are willing to spur the effort and encourage all team members to participate even if only to act as "cheerleaders." Play an encouraging role, stimulating and supporting the team's risk-taking efforts.

Spread out: Select several of your organization's key customers and obtain a concise profile of each, using their websites or other publicly available material. With your team or work group, brainstorm risks that your company could take to make an impact on these customers. Ask participants to "wear the customer's hat." Encourage a range of ideas, from the simplest "local" approach to more complex corporate risks. Facilitate conversation about both straightforward and far-fetched ideas and build on them. Review the ideas and select one that is feasible for your team to actualize.

CHAPTER 7

CONNECTION: COLLABORATE TO INNOVATE

If you have an apple and I have an apple and we exchange these apples, then you and I will each have one apple. But if you have an idea and I have an idea and we exchange these ideas, then each of us will have two ideas.

—*George Bernard Shaw*

In early 2011, in developing a plan for combating her lymphoma, my mother built a rich constellation of help from people throughout her network, community, and personal history to help her. In addition to the chemotherapy and medicinal therapies employed by the doctors and oncologists at the hospital, friends with medical training were called in to advise on various medical issues depending on their expertise.

For physical therapy, yoga instructors were summoned to build physical restorative plans and stretching exercises. For nutritional therapy, chefs and gardeners appeared with dietary plans and meals for nourishing her body. Her pastor and church members gathered at her bedside to guide in spiritual therapy. Artists and musicians would often appear with healing tokens or musical presentations for cultural therapy. One of my personal favorite activities was to help find and deliver jokes or funny movies to support the daily laughter therapy.

Through the rich network my mother called "Team Hunter," each individual applied his or her own talent and expertise to support my mother through her cancer journey.

An innovative effort based on trust, with appreciative inquiry, great aspiration, and deep exploration, can only be realized through the help and collaboration of others—through connection. It is the process component in which we, as individual contributors or leaders, reach out, engage, and collaborate with those around us to discover powerful new ideas, leverage external expertise, and co-opt like-minded collaborators on the Out Think journey.

While we may start with our immediate and intimate circles of colleagues and friends on this part of the journey, we must go beyond that to connect with people who can bring new nuance, insight, and skill to bear on the innovation challenge. Only by reaching beyond—and creating bridges from—our own immediate domain of expertise to cross-pollinate ideas, processes, and components can we move forward in the innovation process.

Results of the Towers Watson Global Workforce Study show that there is a vast reserve of untapped employee potential.[1] Now, more than ever, organizations must engage and inspire the creative talent within them. Organization leaders can help in this process by having respect for employee ideas, connecting to employees emotionally, asking the right questions, and listening carefully. By first engaging each individual, we can build innovative teams that lead us to success. Such engagement can only be developed and sustained in a culture that encourages every employee to participate in the innovation process.

THE CULTURE DEFINES THE OUTCOME

Although the historical business model dictates that a few wield the insight and the others provide the mental brawn of execution, this model squanders the potential collective insights of people who make up the bulk of the executing talent we employ. Thinking, planning, making decisions, and working out action plans are all best done collectively through teamwork.

Flatten the Company

Google CEO Eric Schmidt, when asked about organizational success, says, "The culture defines the outcome."[2] And as Jennifer Chatman of the University of California, Berkeley, and her colleagues assert, "Leaders shape the culture."[3] Therefore the traits, behaviors, and character of the CEO will largely define the culture within the organization, and the culture will drive the results.

Google's leaders believe their company thrives in an organizational environment that is flat (rather than hierarchical), devoid of any pressure, and enables and encourages collaboration. They find that groups make better decisions than individuals on their own and that employees should be passionate about what they do, believe that what they are doing matters, and know that they will be rewarded and recognized. Google attracts highly inventive people and then often assigns managers up to a whopping 60 direct reports. This system is unmanageable by design, giving each team member more autonomy.

Such autonomy also dominates the culture at Disneyland, where employees have the authority and discretion to solve any customer dilemma on the spot. They can comp a penthouse suite if they choose, relying on their peers and colleagues to provide feedback on the quality of these decisions. There are no punitive measures.[4]

This growing trend in giving employees autonomy puts the focus on results rather than on punching a time clock. Netflix has recognized that, as a business that never sleeps, they in fact have no standard working hours for the company. They therefore need to respect the discretionary decision making of their employees and treat them like adults.

As a slide presentation about the benefits of being a Netflix employee describes, the company pays above average in the industry, provides generous benefits, and works to "attract and retain stunning colleagues."[5] How and when you get your work done is up to you, but they expect results.

Clearly the company creates an environment intended to gain the best and brightest people but functions more like a high-performance professional sports team than a family that forgives every fault.

Netflix managers have a test they perform when evaluating performance. They ask themselves this question, "Which of my people, if they told me they were leaving, would I work hard to keep at Netflix?" If someone doesn't satisfy that question, they are offered the compensation package to open up that position for a star performer. Or as Netflix puts it in its slide presentation, "Adequate performance gets a generous severance package." To punctuate its focus on results, not hours, Netflix's "Freedom + Responsibility" presentation goes on to say, "Sustained A-level performance with minimal effort is rewarded with greater responsibility, and great pay."

By focusing on results rather than mere presence or compliance, employees are more likely to feel accountable and less likely to waste the company's time or money.

WorldBlu, an organization that promotes democratic companies and helps create democratic workplaces, has been on the leading edge of such efforts for more than a decade. Their vision is dedicated to unleashing human potential and inspiring freedom by championing the growth of democratic organizations worldwide. Traci Fenton, CEO and founder of WorldBlu, had an epiphany back in the late 1990s, when she realized that many of our most celebrated organizations and companies were busily treating their employees like commodities. WorldBlu, on the other hand, envisions seeing one billion people working in free and democratic workplaces.[6]

Dan Glaser, president and CEO of Marsh & McLennan Companies, was COO when I met him, and he easily defied the stereotypes associated with that role.[7] Rather than being stentorian and commanding, with an iron handshake, Glaser was calm, alert, and polite. Before a videotaped interview I did with him for Skillsoft, he greeted everyone in the room, including our camera and audio technicians.

Glaser talked with me during the interview about the work he had done to simplify and distribute leadership while he was CEO of the company's risk and insurance unit from 2008 to 2011. Marsh had been a highly tiered environment, where associates often reported to up to four different directors. Consequently, because the focus at each tier often differed, objectives sometimes were in competition rather than being shared.

Adamant about simplifying the reporting environment so employees could develop a clear focus, Glaser regularly walked the halls, asking employees what they were working on and how that fit into Marsh's greater mission and values. He used that knowledge to inform his thinking. When he recognized conflict between the goals of people at different levels of the reporting process, he streamlined the process to get people aligned with the projects and ideas that provide value to Marsh's clients. In the interview, he said:

Big companies have to have some level of management. But I also wanted to instill in my managers the sense that they're leaders of the organization. An effective way of accomplishing that is distributed leadership with clear, personal accountability and straight talk between colleagues. I want a company that's open, participatory, striving.

To Glaser, management's focus on *probabilities* was creating a limiting and reactive mindset among employees, so he asked Marsh leaders to look toward *possibilities* instead, leaving the future open to innovation— a landscape defined only by wide-open opportunity:

From my view, the best thing that a company can do is to offer a shell that encourages smart, creative, energetic, passionate people to develop and create opportunities in a business. I'm absolutely certain that if you went back to Marsh & McLennan Companies—let's say 20 years ago—it would have been very difficult for the leaders of that time to fathom all the development that has since taken place and where the firm is focused today—just like I think what we're working on today can branch into many different directions. And so I'd rather not be prescriptive around the directions that the company could go. I'd rather let winners run; see which areas of the business are attracting interest and attention from clients, and keep developing those areas.

By flattening its organizational structure and letting its "winners run," Glaser unlocked Marsh's potential, leading it through 13 quarters of increased financial and operational performance and positioning it for continued success.

By taking a results-oriented approach that streamlines and distributes leadership and removes unnecessary parameters, companies can create a workplace where grand ideas can incubate. Employees who are more focused, energized, productive, efficient, and flexible, feel a greater sense of ownership toward the organization and greater accountability for its achievements.

Focus on Process Rather than Results

Most organizations today create bonus and reward structures that focus on and reward results. If we want an outcome to be repeatable, we instead need to focus on the process that created the result and reward for that. To truly connect with people in our organizations, we should spend more of our time and energy as leaders asking them to examine more closely *how* they perform their tasks and collaborate as teams, and how the organization, as a whole, operates.

While results matter a great deal, if we as leaders want reliable results, we need to place a greater emphasis on identifying, replicating, and constantly improving a reliable process of getting to success—the means, not the ends. We should focus on taking care in the questions we ask, deeply exploring the related issues, building strong collaborative connections, mashing up disparate ideas, and constantly trying new things. None of the innovation elements in the Out Think journey focus on results only—they are processes, not outcomes.

Mark Johnson is chairman of Innosight, a strategic innovation consulting and investing company, which he co-founded with Harvard Business School professor Clayton M. Christensen. Innosight has offices in Massachusetts, Singapore, and India. Last year, Johnson participated in an interview with Skillsoft to capture some of his ideas on how strategic innovation really occurs and the role of process in driving reliable innovation.[8] As he put it:

> The best organizations that implement truly new ideas, especially for creating new growth, have a disciplined process for innovation. Oftentimes it's a misnomer to think, "Well if we have any process to drive innovation, we're going to stymie creativity," but the reality of it is, the real innovations that ultimately commercialize products that go to market and create new growth follow a very structured, disciplined process, because it's not really the lack of good ideas that stymies the ability of an organization to create innovation—to create new growth through innovation—it's really the shaping process of the organization to take that idea and do something with it.

In looking at the big picture of innovation, Johnson says, we need three primary components: deep inquiry and understanding of the clients' need, the business model (not just product) to back it up, and an adaptive support structure with the fundamental understanding that the process will definitely change. As he understands from experience, most organizations need three or four iterations to get it right, and they are exceedingly unlikely to get it absolutely right the first time. As Johnson points out, we can often misinterpret process discipline as stifling creativity, yet, when an organization has an adaptive mindset, refining the innovative process constantly can in fact yield the most creative and productive results.

Process-driven cultures have many benefits, including those below.

Process is replicable and scalable. When the process isn't clearly identified, evaluated, and constantly improved, the results aren't easily repeatable. When we place results alone as the overarching goal, we de-emphasize the process that got us there. When we de-emphasize the process, we can't easily retrace our steps and examine, dissect, and replicate how we got there.

By drawing attention to the steps along the way that garnered a great result, we have the time and awareness to understand, document, and internalize the steps in the process. This moment of internalizing and sharing what works reinforces a culture that slows down to examine not just the success, but also the milestones along the journey that led to the outcome.

Process emphasizes networks, not heroes. A results-only culture can provide too much focus and reward on sole contributors, creating superstars deemed irreplaceable. Results then can take on a heroic quality. Instead of understanding the steps and circumstances that led us to another profitable sales cycle, we associate the success with an individual and bestow on him or her a marquee status. This overvalues the contribution of the individual and de-emphasizes the necessary infrastructure, support processes, and human networks that all contribute to successful results.

This has a doubly negative effect because it not only relies on the elusive and unqualified "talent" of an individual, but also handicaps that individual with a superstar label. As Carol Dweck has demonstrated in numerous studies, when we praise talent instead of hard work and perseverance, we bestow upon the individual a status that is clearly labeled. Suggesting someone paints like Picasso, plays soccer like Lionel Messi, or sells like Larry Ellison gives that person an iconic vaulted status and creates expectation without either a process understanding or redundancy. Should the person fail along the way, there is little backup to rely on.

The labeled superstar can also suffer a confidence drop in the event of a failure. As a result, often those identified as "talented" tend to choose easier and easier tasks and challenges to avoid being exposed as less than remarkable. Inversely, those praised for tenacity, mettle, and grit are more likely to seek harder challenges, apply themselves more arduously to a task, and achieve better results.

If the process isn't appreciated and refined, innovative results become more like Hail Mary shots than layups.

With an emphasis on process comes integrity. If it's the results that count, not how we got there, then we risk inviting unethical behavior to gain the result. The global financial crisis taught us that predatory lending bankers with little oversight and with quick money as their sole motivation were gleefully willing to game the system to their benefit. Their profit was at the expense and misery of those baited into borrowing more than they should have, and more than they should have been allowed to. When we place the greatest value and visibility on the result, not the system that enabled it to be achieved, we incur the danger of inviting unethical behavior and tactics.

The Ethisphere™ Institute, based in New York, is an "international think-tank dedicated to the creation, advancement, and sharing of best practices in business ethics, corporate social responsibility, anti-corruption and sustainability."[9] The institute publishes an annual list of the world's most ethical companies. Ethisphere uses comprehensive evaluation criteria that reward process integrity throughout its inquiry when considering companies for inclusion on the list.

The institute's evaluation scale includes consideration of program structure, oversight, monitoring, and auditing. Market reputation, leadership, and consistent evidence of innovation are also assessed. Finally, corporate citizenship, civic responsibility and leadership, and the company's culture of ethics are all carefully appraised in the competitive screening process needed to become named on the World's Most Ethical Companies list.

Not only does Ethisphere hold in high regard the ethical behavior of an organization, but of equal weight in appraisal value is to what degree the company is innovative. Innovation and integrity of process go hand in hand.

Process cultures remove blame and heighten intelligent risk.
Results are the culmination of a series of decisions that are sometimes intricate and often involve many stakeholders. Individuals at all levels of the value process chain contribute decisions that eventually lead to an outcome. It's possible, even likely, that a strong, high-quality decision can lead to a poor outcome for reasons entirely beyond the control of the person who made the decision. Market forces, external circumstances, or a fickle customer can sabotage the best decisions in ways never imagined or anticipated. And yet, if our reward structures only focus on outcomes, then a sound and valuable person in the organization can be neglected, undervalued, or worse, reluctant to act in the face of uncertainty.

Our willingness to make courageous decisions in this ambiguous and chaotic market environment is critical to our ability to create successful innovations and results. And as the complexity of our work environments increase, we must also increase the attempts, chances, and risks we take in order to find a positive outcome. A rewards-centered culture creates disincentives for people to make mistakes at a time when making mistakes is the most reliable way of figuring out what works. As is often said, "fail faster" toward innovation.

When I first met Melbourne Business School dean Zeger Degraeve, I found him to have a stentorian voice, a firm handshake, and a disciplined demeanor. Then, once I engaged him on one of his favorite topics—excellence in decision making—his eyes lit up and his voice rose in enthusiasm about what clearly captures his passion and interest. In our discussion, he strongly reinforced the power of process-driven cultures in eradicating blame tendencies among managers and peers.[10] When individuals and teams are punished on the basis of poor outcomes, despite strong collaboration and decision making, it sends a signal to the rest of the organization that failure is dangerous, and therefore risk should be avoided.

When new ideas are presented, they usually come with the good news—the things that will go well. We know from research that people react positively to those who consistently deliver positive news. Flattery, even false flattery, is consistently effective in currying favor with superiors in organizations. And as Elaine Chan and Jaideep Sengupta demonstrated in their research, consistent false flattery has the added effect of creating intolerance to bad news.[11] As managers come to expect only good news, bad news becomes increasingly unwelcome. The key is to shift the stigma away from associating realistic truth with bad news. Consistent false flattery can lead to irrational exuberance.

Instead, Zeger says, managers should create the expectation that all proposals and ideas come with the top two or three things people believe could go *wrong*. This activity of pitching new ideas, once embedded into the culture of the organization, becomes less intimidating. If leaders don't explicitly create an expectation that ideas be tempered with honesty around potential pitfalls, then honest fears won't be revealed, and potential invisible cracks won't be discovered until they become disastrous chasms.

When honest expression of concern becomes simply part of the process, it also eradicates any sense of blame.

BUILD THE TEAM THROUGH SHARED VISION AND PERSONAL ENGAGEMENT

Successful teams are the result of hiring the right people, building relationships among them based on trust and concern, creating a shared vision of mission, and keeping communication open.

Hire for Service, Not Servitude

Finding those people who will bring a fresh perspective and yet work well within a team is a challenge. For a team to be successful, each member must bring a combination of skill, imagination, belief in the team's mission, and the ability to collaborate. In turn, those we bring onto teams need to feel the freedom to share their ideas without rebuke. Someone with skills who lacks belief in the mission is a flight risk, and the prima donna who refuses to collaborate can squander the potential synergy of the team effort.

I interviewed Morgans Hotel Group CEO Fred Kleisner in the hip basement nightclub of the company's New York City property, The Hudson, in November 2010.[12] We had to do some creative camera framing and lighting, since the walls were covered with vintage 1970s and 1980s pin-up posters.

Kleisner has the enviable job of running some of the coolest hotel properties in the world. When it comes to hiring, he said Morgans is interested in someone's whole personality and all his or her strengths. Instead of a traditional interview, the company has "casting calls" in theaters. After a standard question and answer session, candidates are invited to get up on stage and share anything they want, with an emphasis on something that expresses who they are at heart. As he described:

> We want fun, friendly, gracious, authentic—we want original. So at the end of the interview, we'll say to you, "There's the stage. Go up and do whatever you'd like. Show us who you are." And some people sing a song, some people tell a joke, some people tell a story. That's what cuts away the people who are just attractive from those who are internally attractive and really care about delivering great service, who understand that service is never servitude.

This exercise tells the candidates they are welcome to express themselves and are expected to bring their unique identities to work, while also enabling the interviewers to glimpse the more personal, authentic side of potential hires instead of finding that out six months into the job.

Seek Diversity

The challenge of working together can draw out the potential in each person that is just below the surface, and having more ideas that contribute to the creative stew is more likely to lead to success. Our workplaces today are increasingly virtual environments, where people of diverse cultures, backgrounds, ages, experiences, and ideas work together.

Diversity is the mark of great creative teams, where differences are strengths, not weaknesses. The five people who composed the comedy group Monty Python were very different people, but they had a process where their differences added up to something that was more than the sum of the parts.

While diversity can bring great energy to teams, it will only work in a nurturing, fostering environment where each individual has free expression, free access to information, and the freedom to think and fail. No idea is forbidden from expression, since ideas that are seemingly unworkable or that seem off track may lead to a different approach that solves the problem at hand or may be a solution for a problem or opportunity that has yet to be considered.

Sometimes sharing the worst, most absurd ideas levels the playing field, enabling individuals who are more reluctant to share their thoughts for fear of failure to do so. In a truly collaborative environment, success is shared along with failure. Employees in such companies are emboldened to challenge assumptions and, through collaboration, the individual members stretch their cognitive abilities and grow.

Share Vision

When we give advice to other people, we're often talking to ourselves, reinforcing our vision of the world while sharing what we have learned in different interactions, situations, and challenges over time. The same is true within organizations. Executive teams will construct their own versions of what they believe is best for the employees, the product, the company, and the company's customers, and genuinely believe this story will resonate and hold true in the minds of the employees and contributors within the organization.

This vision sharing is an important exercise in which we, as leaders, must participate with clarity, conviction, and honesty. It helps those on the executive team to reinforce their own beliefs and sagely talk to themselves. They then need to share this vision effectively with the rest of the organization.

In a September 2010 interview, Nick Kugenthiran, managing director of Fuji Xerox Australia, explained to me how he helps his managers create a sense of shared vision through a short collaborative exercise that puts everybody on the same page.[13] First, the team and its leader together write headlines and a press release that reflect what they want to see in the company in five years. Each team member starts independently and then compares notes with the group. Kugenthiran has found that the team will usually immediately see intersections of vision as each person shares his or her personal perspective of the future.

Connect Personally

As Skillsoft's recent study on leadership characteristics shows, being able to build relationships, being able to collaborate, and being open-minded are among the most desirable characteristics for twenty-first-century leaders. The basis of all relationships is respect—even when things do not go the way we expect. If respect is missing at any level, an entire organization is likely to flounder or even collapse.

In the new dispensation brought about by globalization, relationships are the glue that keeps organizations intact. Success depends on relationships both within the organization and with customers.

Michael Stallard, a leading authority on leadership and teams as they relate to employee and customer engagement, illustrates the importance of strong relationships inside an organization through a story he told me about the highly successful rock band U2.[14]

From the beginning, U2 has maintained a mantra of "music can change the world because it can change people." The strength of the band's identity and commitment to each other has driven its success. When the band's members suffered one personal challenge after another, the band slowed down its touring and took a break to support one another.

In 1987, the leader of the band, Bono, was threatened with death if U2 played their song "Pride," a tribute to Reverend Martin Luther King, Jr., at a concert in Arizona. Bono recalled that, as he entered the third verse—"Early morning, April 4; a shot rings out in the Memphis sky"—he closed his eyes, not knowing what would happen.[15] He described what followed:

> Some people want to kill us. Some people are taken very seriously by the FBI. They tell the singer that he shouldn't play the gig because tonight his life is at risk, and he must not go on stage. And the singer laughs. Of course we're playing the gig. Of course we go onstage, and I'm singing "Pride (In the Name of Love)"—the third verse—and I close my eyes.

And you know, I'm excited about meeting my maker, but maybe not tonight. I don't really want to meet my maker tonight. I close my eyes and when I look up, I see Adam Clayton standing in front of me, holding his bass as only Adam Clayton can hold his bass. There are people in this room who'd tell you they'd take a bullet for you, but Adam Clayton would have taken a bullet for me. I guess that's what it's like to be in a truly great rock and roll band.

The band members show unconditional support for each other's interests, pursuits, and beliefs, in all aspects of life. When Bono started humanitarian work, he says he was ridiculed and derided as another rock star looking to create a positive image without caring deeply about the issues and concerns. He persisted and demonstrated that it's possible to reinvent oneself, and his band supported him and helped make his philanthropic work a success.

In our life and our work, we might not be in a rock band galvanized by hardship and triumph. Yet, consider the powerful connection that holds us together and that goes beyond finding the next quarter profit, or hitting the upcoming deadline. If we want to have success in our business and in our lives, we need to focus on building up each other first, helping everyone in our path to grow, work as a team, and collaborate. Only then might our teammates be willing to take a bullet for us.

In Skillsoft's leadership survey, respondents rated the ability to build relationships in the top three desirable characteristics for twenty-first-century leaders. To truly build powerful relationships with other human beings, "We need a genuine sense of responsibility and a sincere concern for the welfare of others," says the Dalai Lama, Tenzin Gyatso.[16] We have to extend the feeling of respect, concern, love, and well-being from our immediate families to those with whom we work, to our community, our nation, and our environment.

My wife recalls an event from more than 20 years ago when she was visiting me and found herself at a gathering among a group of people, none of whom she knew. A friend of mine, Jason Rich, went out of his way to make her feel welcome and invited. He introduced her to people, and included her in the conversation. Visiting Jason years later, I reminded him of this episode and the lasting positive impact and impression it had on my wife. Although he had no recollection of the event, his brief kindness two decades before left my wife with the recollection that he is a fantastic person. He had left an emotional wake—a psychological ripple—that was positive for her, and, as a result, to this day she believes he is a wonderful person, in part because of that first small gesture of kindness years ago.

No matter how inconsequential we think an interaction with another person is, it can leave a strong emotional wake that can affect that relationship and, ultimately, team productivity. We must stay conscious that how we act and behave toward others is likely to be remembered for a long time.

Making a connection—truly engaging employees in the innovation process and leaving a good emotional wake behind you everywhere you go in the organization—can produce better results than focusing on output and spreading fear and stress.

The Conversation Is the Relationship

In her book *Fierce Conversations*, author Susan Scott writes about a story she heard from British poet David Whyte:[17]

> During a keynote speech at TEC International's annual conference several years ago, David suggested that in the typical marriage, the young man, newly married, is often frustrated that this person with whom he intends to enjoy the rest of his life seemingly needs to talk, yet again, about the same thing they talked about last weekend. And it often has something to do with their relationship. He wonders, Why are we talking about this again? I thought we settled this. Couldn't we just have one huge conversation about our relationship and then coast for a year or two?

> Apparently not, because here she is again. Eventually, if he is paying attention, it occurs to him, Whyte suggests, that "this ongoing, robust conversation he has been having with his wife is not about the relationship. The conversation *is* the relationship."

In an interview I had with Scott,[18] she brought this message into the context of connecting with others on the path to innovation:

> Here is what I want you to take away, besides David's brilliant idea. Our most valuable currency, mine, yours, is not money nor is it IQ, nor is it multiple degrees or industry experience or charisma or attractiveness or self-sufficiency or the ability to analyze a case study, read a P&L statement, build a really cool PowerPoint doc. Our most valuable currency is relationship. It is emotional capital. In fact the currency of the millennium is relationship, human connection, emotional capital.

Dr. Mark Goulston is a business advisor, consultant, trainer, and coach who has trained as a clinical psychiatrist and honed his skills as an FBI trainer of police hostage negotiators. In his book, *Just Listen: Discover the Secret to Getting Through to Absolutely Anyone*, Goulston seeks to help people build stronger and more creative relationships through the power of "deep listening."[19] According to Goulston, if you really want to get through to people, what you tell them is less important than what you enable them to tell you.

In his book, Goulston offers tips for encouraging deep listening in others. One simple mechanism is to ask, "Can you show me what you mean by that? Can you draw it for me?" By asking for an illustration, the other person's visual and creative energy is engaged, and he or she is more likely to be open to new ideas. Further, by asking a provocative question, we sharpen other people's listening skills, because we're showing that we expect them to be active participants in the conversation rather than just waiting to talk.

In a conversation with him, Goulston told me a story of how, while interviewing with a CEO to offer consulting services to his company, he asked about how the CEO was working to effect substantial change.[20] While the CEO was telling his story, Goulston counted ten times in which he was tempted to interrupt and offer some keen insight. At each stage of the narrative, he wanted to show that he understood clearly what the company and the CEO were going through, and that he knew how to help. Instead, when the CEO paused, Goulston deepened the conversation by using words such as "Tell me more" or "Yes, please go on."

At the end, Goulston simply reiterated what he had heard and waited for acknowledgment. "Yes, that's what happened" and "Yes, that's what I meant" were the CEO's responses. The CEO clearly felt that what he said had been wholly heard and understood. Goulston had built a relationship of trust and mutual understanding. Instead of trying to solve each emerging issue as it came up, he encouraged and deepened the conversation, and ultimately got the job to help redirect and support a change initiative.

Goulston claims he learned this technique from Warren Bennis, one of this generation's greatest authorities on leadership. Bennis is often quoted as telling a marvelous story about the difference between nineteenth-century British prime ministers William Gladstone and Benjamin Disraeli. As Bennis relates it in an interview with Anna Muoio:

> When you had dinner with Gladstone, you left feeling he was the wittiest, most brilliant, most charming person on earth. But when you had dinner with Disraeli, you left feeling that you were the wittiest, most brilliant, most charming person on earth.[21]

Bennis's message is that leaders get to know each member of their team through wholehearted listening, through knowing what each is trying to say. Then, by their questions, the leaders provoke that person to see the world, inspiring them to reach for a common goal and effect change.

If we slow down and listen, retain our curiosity about the other person's ideas and remain open to them, and ask the right questions to explore more deeply into that other person's views, that person becomes more trusting. As a result, the relationship will deepen, and the conversation will become richer, opening the doors to innovation.

As with the earlier fallacy of outcome-only cultures creating heroes for positive outcomes, we need to be wary of the inverse problem as well. We need to keep in mind that there is an important distinction between those who identify potential problems and pitfalls and constructively suggest remedies, and those who point out urgencies and suggest they are the only ones capable of fixing the problem. Tim Sanders calls the latter the "Chicken Little Syndrome." A "chicken little" creates a crisis and claims to be the only one capable of correcting it.

ALLOW RISK AND DEMAND ACCOUNTABILITY

As Stuart Hart suggests, taking risks is what leads to growth in an individual and an organization. John Hope Bryant adds that, to fully engage employees, leaders should first allow people to find their own place in the organization, instead of being shown specific tasks and procedures. Once they find that place, they will be more likely to have the confidence to take creative risks, as described in the previous chapter, and to accept accountability.

Employees want to know what their roles are. Demographic studies suggest the demand to have a clear understanding of the roles they play in the larger context of the organization started in earnest with Gen X. Gen Y refuses to be part of a work environment that isn't entirely transparent.

In a recent interview, Tammy Erickson, renowned expert on the implications of demographics in the workforce, described a common pitfall of team leaders that I, too, confess falling victim to.[22] As she described, team leaders often set clear goals and measurable milestones to get there, but leave the task allocation to those on the team to divvy up. In these cases, the leaders are either trying to give team members discretionary decision-making authority to empower them or are simply too lazy or uninvolved to participate in role identification.

A lack of clarity can spell disaster. Envision a busy hospital emergency room, where at any moment someone might be whisked in the door with any variety of maladies or trauma. It's absurd to imagine the clinicians discussing on the spot who should intubate, or who should administer fluids or pharmaceuticals. In the high-paced environment of many companies, the same is equally true.

To work successfully within the organization, team goals must also be considered in the context of the organization's goals. This overarching sense of place in the context of the overall mission and goals of the organization is critical to building the engaged workplace. Consequently, each member feels responsible and accountable for the team's achievements.

Collaboration is a contact sport. Studies have demonstrated over the years that the proximity we have to other people directly affects the amount of influence we have in the relationships. Sara Kiesler and Jonathon N. Cummings cite a controversial series of studies in the 1960s by Yale University psychologist Stanley Milgram in which he tested the power of authority to influence someone to inflict harm on another person.[23] In one sequence of the study, a researcher asked a subject to administer shocks to someone described as a "poor learner." When the experimenter and subject were in the same room, about 65 percent of subjects obeyed the experimenter's command to give 450-volt electric shocks. However, when the experimenter left the room and gave his commands by telephone, only 20 percent were obedient.

As an example of the importance of direct human interaction, I had a conversation with a manager based in Germany whose team worked in California. This manager would fly to California several times a year for no other reason than to spend time directly interacting with members of his team—having dinner, talking, and interacting in social settings. He called these trips "the flying handshake." He understood that our direct, human connection plays an invaluable role in developing the power and inventiveness of the team.

LET'S RECAP

Remember . . .

- To create a culture of innovation, leaders must first create a culture of collaboration. This means engaging and inspiring the creative talents of others, respecting employees' ideas, and bringing new insights into group decisions. Engaging employees requires knowing them, developing them, inspiring them, rewarding them, and involving them. In a collaborative workplace, differences add up to something more than the sum of the parts and result in novel solutions.

- Drawing out the potential in each person on the team does more than just create a rich array of insights and diverse perspectives. It stretches employees to contribute their best and feel accountable for the team's process, outcomes, and achievements. Under these circumstances, team members know that what they are doing matters, and that recognition and reward will flow from their contributions. Leaders can help team members build each other up and grow as a team, forming a solid collective front.

- Relationships in the global context are the glue that holds organizations together. The entire universe is built upon relationships—individuals cannot go it alone. Leaders and managers must focus on building healthy and productive relationships and work cultures that are free from counterproductive stress and fear. This requires a genuine sense of responsibility and sincere concern for others, extending family love outward to our colleagues, community, nation, and environment.

Your Turn Now . . .

Reach in: If you're not already striving to create a collaborative work environment and culture, ask yourself "What is in the way?" Be open to the possibility that some of the difficulty may lie within yourself—a hesitancy to give up power, a mistrust of the talents of those on your team, a need to be directive or appear to be the one with all the creative ideas. Give this up for a week—or at least a day! Even though it may be difficult at first, ask more questions, invite suggestions and ideas, and allow team members to decide how they want to approach a particular task or project. Notice changes or insights—not just outcomes in the team, but how you feel about yourself as a leader.

Reach out: Pose a challenge to your team that has implications at the organizational level. This could be something that the organization is working to improve—a less-than-positive finding from an employee survey, a growing market threat, a concern about resources. Select something that has meaning to your team. Ask them to meet for a few hours and work together to derive two or three possible actions that they could take as a team to help with the larger problem or challenge. You may provide some structure for the team meeting, but allow the team to perform the task autonomously and then present their ideas to you. When they share their ideas, be positive, respectful, and reinforcing. Ask about the process they used, and how they felt about it. Do not be surprised if the team felt uncomfortable or awkward, especially if they are not used to working in this autonomous way. Ask about what worked and focus on what they did together to improve something of importance.

Spread out: Suggest to other leaders in your organization that they pose a similar challenge to their teams and work groups, in a meeting venue or using some collaboration tool. Create a way to bring these ideas together in a way that not only surfaces a wide collection of ideas and suggestions, but also strengthens relationships between people and groups. Continue to reinforce—in your own team and across work groups—the difference they are making by working together rather than focusing on "what is in it for them."

Remember . . .

- Many organizations use bonus and incentive structures to reward results. Unintentionally, even unethical behavior may be rewarded in strictly results-oriented companies. To get positive, repeatable outcomes, organizations must focus instead on the process that creates good results—and reward for that. Results do matter, but replication of a successful process of action will ensure continuance of better results. Concentrate on innovative processes—not just the outcomes.

- Strictly results-oriented cultures may overvalue sole contributors who choose to stay in the "safe" role of superstar. These companies may also ignore valuable people who are willing to take risks toward innovation, even though they may fail. Process-oriented cultures remove blame and heighten intelligent risk. They recognize that relationships and networks are needed to make courageous decisions and create successful innovations and results.

- Process-oriented cultures acknowledge that things may go wrong. They allow creative risks, don't lay blame for mistakes, and recognize that mistakes are the way to learn to get things right. When individuals are included in conversations about possible risks and are allowed to find their own way, they share in both the creative process and the accountability, developing more confidence and courage as they go along.

- The process of innovation requires deep inquiry and understanding of the need, the business model to back it up, and an adaptive support structure. Leaders must clarify roles yet allow for autonomy, encourage risk but also demand accountability, and focus less on what people do and more on managing the quality of relationships. This is a challenge that is well served by the timeless skill of listening.

Your Turn Now . . .

Reach in: Recall times in your career when you were rewarded for improving process, building relationships, or taking risks—even if these efforts failed. What was the form of recognition, and what was the impact on you as a person and a leader? Even if you were not rewarded or recognized in a conventional way (pay, promotion, performance rating), recall the feedback, gratitude, or even your own sense of personal satisfaction that resulted. Assess whether you are still upholding the value of recognition for process, relationship, and creative risk. If not, remind yourself to pay more attention to others who are making these efforts.

Reach out: Ask team members to include an innovation or creative risk-taking goal in their work goals. Work with each person to structure the goal so that it measures process more than results. Be clear about the person's role in achieving the goal and who else is involved, and discuss how to measure "success." Discuss what could go wrong and the process for dealing with both positive and negative incidents. Make time to review progress with each individual. If it is not possible to reach out at the individual level, work with the team to create a team goal and follow a similar process.

Spread out: List significant achievements made by your company, especially those you have experienced or played a role in achieving.

Identify the outcome or result that made the achievement notable. Then identify the process used to attain the result. Consider the value of both the result and the process, and what you personally experienced or observed in terms of recognition or reward. Discuss this with other leaders, asking them to identify similar experiences and listening intently to them. Take advantages of "post-mortem" opportunities to facilitate discussions about processes that work and how to use them in current and future endeavors.

CHAPTER 8

MASH-UP: BORROW BRILLIANCE

If I have seen further it is by standing on the shoulders of giants.
—*Isaac Newton*

In conversations in 2011 and early 2013, Venkatesh Valluri, president of Ingersoll-Rand India, talked to me about successful emerging leaders as possessing three distinct qualities:[1]

- the ability to scan a constantly moving stream of technologies and information and pick out the meaningful trends in their businesses to create new markets
- the ability to conceptualize and converge these identified new technologies and capabilities into innovations and solutions that are right for your market
- the strength and capability to lead a team to execution

As he described it:

Today if you asked me, "What would be an appropriate leadership development model at Ingersoll-Rand in India?" it would be a unique model which must address the needs of an emerging economy. My first question would be if the potential leader has a mindset that demonstrates conceptual flexibility and the strength to scan the environment in a manner that seeks out the problem which the customer has not been able to articulate, and build a solution through multiple interventions and convergence approaches of technologies, innovations, and processes.

Now once having defined that, then I guess the next piece which really comes is, would he be able to execute on that? And once you talk about execution, then, at the same time, is he able to rally the entire team behind that concept by suggesting, "This is the right thing for us to do—let us now go and create a market!" It is a risk-taking capability of a different dimension when you begin to operate in a very volatile, undefined, and an ambiguous market that is constantly being redefined through new technological and innovation interventions at price points not conceived before. Value needs to be demonstrated in relatively short-cycle periods in such markets.

Valluri pointed out that industries around the world are developing deep expertise in many fields, including nanotechnology, energy sustainability, food preservation, data analytics, artificial intelligence, and a plethora of other reporting technologies. Ingersoll-Rand doesn't need to develop expertise in each of these, he said, but the organizational DNA must be such that it constantly is aware of, and seeking out, these technologies. The new leader needs to conceptualize ways to leverage them to not only solve customer problems but also use them to create new markets in the domains in which customers operate.

Valluri calls this "innovation convergence," which I call "mash-up." He gives the following example from his own country of India:

Historically, farmers in India have used the technologies available to them to move farm produce to market—namely, carts and wagons pulled by humans or animals. There are many variables that can lead to product loss and missed market opportunity while picking, loading, and conveying farm produce to a buyer's market or distribution center. The farmer may be unaware of deteriorating weather. There may be a lack of buyers in the market, so the produce will spoil. The seasonal rains may have created mud conditions that slow the farmer's progress. There may be a glut of produce at one market and scarcity at another.

Ingersoll-Rand integrated multiple technologies, including ruggedized buggies with four-wheel drive, GPS tracking to monitor the location of shipments, technology that can determine the status of demand at different markets and shipping locations, and refrigeration technology to preserve the produce in transit.

This solution optimizes the entire value chain, reducing loss and maximizing delivery and value to the market—all without needing to have deep niches of expertise within the organization of each of these disparate technologies. All that was needed was for leadership at Ingersoll-Rand to have an awareness of these technologies; strong, networked collaborators; the ability to conceptualize a new solution for the customer; and, perhaps most importantly, the strength and conviction to lead a team to execute on the vision.

According to Valluri, the leader of the future is going to be an expert on figuring out how to stitch a number of possible solutions or possible technologies together to create a solution for the market. The next issue is how quickly that person can execute on that vision, collaborate internally and externally, and construct a new model that has recognized value in the market.

That, to Valluri, is real innovation.

One of the most exciting components of the innovation process is actively combining disparate ingredients to come up with a whole that is greater than the sum of its parts. Once we have connected to people who are doing innovative work in separate domains, we can begin combining these ideas in our work environment by applying what we have learned elsewhere and inviting others to participate in the process. By constantly mashing up ideas, concepts, applications, and other disparate outcomes gathered from our diverging ventures, we invent powerful new combinations.

The Mash-up Equation

Mash-up = Identifying Meaningful Technology + Conceptual Flexibility + Leadership to Execute

BORROW BRILLIANCE

Great ideas are built on the shoulders of giants—that is, most of what seems to be original thought is in fact built on the strength of the thoughts of those who came before us, who in turn based their thoughts on those before them.

Charles Darwin's *On the Origin of Species* didn't arrive fully formed from the cosmic muse. It germinated from the influence of Darwin's grandfather, Erasmus Darwin, who wrote *Zoonomia; or, The Laws of Organic Life* in 1796. In that book, Erasmus Darwin suggested that sexual behavior and competition might affect species change.

In 1971, Ray Tomlinson was working on ARPAnet and mashed up terminal networks with an existing application that allowed users on the same terminal system to share messages. He did this by writing a script that enabled messages to distinguish between different machines and jump from one to another. Thus, Internet-based e-mail was born.

What sets Steve Jobs apart as an industry icon is a combination of his innovation, leadership, and, perhaps more importantly, his ability to recognize a good idea. In the 1980s, he saw a demonstration of the mouse with a graphical user interface and recognized the combination as perfect for a personal computer. The result: Apple's Macintosh computer. Bill Gates got the idea for Windows from Apple's graphical user interface.

In the 1990s, Jobs saw a demonstration of a new animation software program developed by filmmaker George Lucas and his company. He bought the company, combined the software with storytelling, and created Pixar and the first computer-animated film, *Toy Story*.

Ten years ago, Jobs saw the first MP3 player. He combined it with an integrated website, iTunes, and, with cutting-edge design from Jonathan Ive, created the iPod.

The plain and simple fact is that we all borrow ideas. We copy or even steal from competitors, coworkers, friends, children, friends of our children—whoever has an idea that sparks our own creative process. As Einstein put it, with tongue firmly in cheek, "Whoever undertakes to set himself up as a judge of Truth and Knowledge is shipwrecked by the laughter of the gods."

Once we accept the fact that we build on the creativity of others, our creative process becomes deliberate and intentional. Because we never know where a good idea may be lurking, we need to look everywhere—other industries, science, art, music, society . . . everywhere.

Although ideas give us our starting point, and maybe even the raw material, that is not enough. We must take these a step further, through observation and opening up our minds. Karl Popper, the scientific philosopher, claims that all knowledge begins from an observation. For instance, it was the observation of a rock rolling down a hill that gave the idea for a wheel.

As we examine the ideas we borrow, we need to look at them from all angles with a fresh mind and be skeptical. We have to understand their weaknesses so that we can improve on them. The creative process is an evolutionary one, and the mechanism used to take it forward is judgment.

We must also remember that the value of an idea lies in its practicality, and whether it can be implemented. In questioning the validity of the idea and its usefulness, the idea will evolve. A great idea has its implementation built into it. It may not be obvious immediately, but as we work on the idea, it becomes apparent.

In evaluating ideas, we should also open ourselves up to our own intuition. As Jonas Salk, developer of the first polio vaccine, is often quoted as saying, "Intuition will tell the thinking mind where to look next."

Once we have effectively defined the challenge before us, we can look around for people who have encountered a similar challenge and see how it was solved. In this process, we need to think far, think radical, think *wild*. We can first start close at hand, with our competitors, then look at other industries, and finally look outside the business altogether.

In looking at how the solution to a problem was achieved, the bits and pieces that led to success, we're sure to find kernels of innovation that, when combined, will grow into our own unique solution. Ideas evolve through incubation, critique of strengths and weaknesses, and elimination of the weak points and enhancement of the strong ones—as illustrated in the following examples.

Everything Old Is New Again

Almost everything is imitation. The most original minds borrow from one another.

—*Voltaire*

Along with solar, tidal, and geothermal energies, wind is universally considered and acknowledged as a primary source of sustainable, non-polluting energy. In my own state of Maine, former governor Angus King is leading an alternative-energy company, called Independence Wind, to develop wind farms to help offset fossil fuel consumption and harvest Maine's wind-rich coastline.

The wind turbine today represents the evolution of a basic technology design that is centuries old. The earliest uses of horizontal windmills date back to ninth-century Middle East. These later evolved in twelfth-century Europe into the classic tall, vertical shape we recognize today. Along the way, inventors have tweaked the design with various novel modifications, such as the Darrieus vertical airfoil, the Savonius "S-shaped" turbine, and, in 2005, the Quiet Revolution of vertical helical design, invented by Robert Webb and Richard Cochrane.[2] All indeed were improvements upon the last in terms of efficiency, power output, and reliability in variable conditions.

Yet, despite incremental improvements over the last few hundred years, and accelerated improvements over the last few decades, wind turbines still pose a few frustrating problems. Site location for them remains a complicated and political issue, as some local residents object to turbine visibility. Rotating turbine blades are a hazard to migrating birds and to bats, the noise and vibration of rotating wind turbines can be annoying, and some people who live or work in the vicinity have even claimed to be suffering health issues caused by them. (So far, according to a *New York Times* article, at least two panels of independent health experts who have looked into the matter have found no conclusive scientific evidence to support these claims.[3])

And then there is the efficiency puzzle. Way back in 1919, German physicist Albert Betz published a paper demonstrating that the maximum amount of power that can be extracted from the wind, regardless of design, is only 59.3 percent. And today even efficient wind turbines often achieve only half of that.

Two new inventions for harvesting wind power that are more efficient are currently emerging. They are based not on mechanical blade turbines, but on far more ancient technology used to harness the wind— sails. These new innovations leave the current technology-optimization thread and instead leverage different and more antiquated technology to enable new technology to emerge.

One of the two inventions came from Hassine Labaied and his friend Anis Aouini, who teamed up in 2009 to found Saphon Energy and place their faith and passion in an innovative new design that has no rotating blades. Their inspired design, the Saphonian, isn't based on any wind-turbine predecessor and is not merely an incrementally improved turbine. Rather, the Saphonian is a complete departure from historical wind-harvesting devices designed to extract energy for application purposes—again, much more like a sail than a windmill in that regard. It's effectively a circular wind-capture device that then directs the energy captured to storage cells within the apparatus.[4]

Meanwhile, another sail-inspired innovation, the Quixote Project design from York, Maine, emerged simultaneously and independently of the Saphonian project. Similar in structure, the Quixote design uses a spinning turbine familiar to historical precedent, but the blades of the turbine are also modeled on sails—they "tack" like a sail does to maximize power, regardless of their position relative to the wind. Thus, when in motion, the Quixote design maximizes wind power on both the leading and trailing edges of the rotation, something most common designs do not do.[5]

In both instances the emerging innovation married—mashed up— two types of technologies from two disparate sources to yield a new innovation.

Borrowing Brilliance in Action: Lessons from Joie de Vivre

Possibly my favorite example of "mashing up" ideas to create something new and innovative and that has strong product and service value comes from another story from my 2011 interview with Chip Conley, founder of Joie de Vivre Hotels.

When Conley was building his first hotel in the rough meatpacking district of San Francisco back in 1987, he took an enormous chance on the location. He was heavily leveraged financially, and the clock was ticking.

Conley had gathered his team on-site in the run-down building to help envision what the new hotel might look like. Someone suggested a cool Art Deco theme, someone else wanted a calm spa environment, and yet another person suggested a bohemian theme. Each of these ideas was perfectly valid, but the team lacked the agreement needed to move forward.

After a couple of days of talking past one another and with no agreement on direction, Conley arrived and placed a copy of *Rolling Stone* magazine on the table and suggested they imagine a Rolling Stone hotel. With this anchor idea in everyone's mind, it became much easier to generate ideas about what the Joie de Vivre hotel might look like—its flavor, culture, and ambience—and to build alignment among those ideas. And, indeed, the result is a signature solution (a concept I address more fully in chapter 10). Conley and his team went on to build the first Joie de Vivre hotel.

EMPHASIZE WEAK TIES

In this increasingly global economy, where we can collaborate quickly and easily, it is also increasingly important that we develop our external networks to be broad and deep in expertise. The strength of the ties that we have with one another are based on the time we spend together, the intensity of emotion associated with the other person, the intimacy with which we share ideas, and the reciprocity that each of us brings to the relationship.

Our strong ties are with the people we talk to, e-mail, and interact with on a regular and constant basis. They may all be with members of our workgroup or team, where we know how each of the others thinks. Sometimes we can finish their sentences and predict their actions.

Mark Granovetter, a sociology professor at Stanford University, wrote a paper back in 1973, "The Strength of Weak Ties," in which he argues that our best insights, our most powerful new ideas, and sometimes our most productive collaborations come from reaching beyond those strong ties to emphasize weaker ties in our network—those people we know and have collaborated with in the past but with whom we only interact periodically.[6] Perhaps we see them at annual conferences, or at occasional dinner parties, or infrequent meetings. They are people whose background and expertise we understand but with whom we don't collaborate on a consistent basis. In his paper, Granovetter observed that many people referred to these types of relationship ties as "acquaintances."

And because each person with whom we have weak ties has had his or her own adventures, projects, and investigations independent of our own, each brings something different to the innovation effort.

EMBRACE POSITIVE DEVIANCE

In a 2009 interview I had with him, Professor Yves Doz advised reconfiguring resources, roles, and business architectures regularly to create a moderate amount of creative tension.[7] Such intentional disruption can aid "strategic agility," a phrase he uses to describe the importance of constantly being inventive in terms of how we organize strategy, rather than following the norm of having brief strategy sessions periodically followed by longer-term implementation and execution.

While each of us, as leaders, can foster innovation, the organization as a whole must also support innovation through the makeup of its culture and the way it designs its processes. Sometimes the best way to spark innovation is by allowing—even encouraging—activity within the organization that deviates from the norm but that may lead to positive outcomes.

Here's an example I heard of successful deviation from the norm from Howard Behar, former president of Starbucks.[8] In the early 1990s, when Howard was acting as vice president of sales and operations to help expand Starbucks' store locations, he had a district manager named Dina in southern California who called him up one day and asked him to visit her store location in Santa Monica. When Howard went down to visit Dina, she asked him to try a drink the staff had invented. He agreed it was excellent and went back to the Starbucks headquarters in Seattle to propose the company produce and offer this drink throughout its stores. The management group all declined to adopt the drink, so Howard had to call Dina to apologize and ask her to stop offering the drink.

Dina called Behar a few weeks later and asked him to travel to Santa Monica to visit again. When Howard arrived, she presented him with another new drink her staff had been quietly selling at only their store location, which was rapidly becoming popular with their customers. This time, Howard asked Dina to keep making and selling the drink as a test project and returned to Seattle, without telling anyone of Dina's initiative so as not to slow her efforts. Within weeks, the new drink had become a smash hit locally. Howard went to CEO Howard Schultz and said, "We have to do this. Our customers are speaking."

That was the birth of Starbucks' Frappuccino®, which turned out to be one of their most popular—and profitable—drinks. And according to Behar, it happened because someone was allowed, even encouraged, to experiment with a new product that deviated from the company's core product lines.

As Behar's story shows, such "positive deviance"—a concept championed by Richard Pascale, Jerry Sternin, and Monique Sternin in their book *The Power of Positive Deviance*—can open up a whole new pathway to innovation. The authors see seemingly unsolvable problems as actually being solvable by the few individuals in a group—positive deviants—who find unique ways to look them.

In a *Harvard Business Review* article coauthored by Jerry Sternin, Pascale writes about accepting a position working with the pharmaceutical company Genentech in 2003.[9] The stated purpose and a mantra of the company, he writes, is "in business for life." Genentech has consistently been recognized by *Fortune* magazine to be among the top ten places to work for, and people there say the secret sauce is its culture, which encourages initiative and risk taking.

In 2003, after clinical trials and Food and Drug Administration approval, Genentech introduced the genetically engineered intravenous drug Xolair to the asthma medication market. Unlike standard asthma treatments that stop asthma attacks after they occur, Xolair was developed to block the histamines in the immune system that trigger attacks. It is preventative and effective in the short and long term because, instead of simply stopping attacks once they start, it "helps reduce the number of asthma attacks in people with allergic asthma who still have asthma symptoms even though they are taking inhaled steroids."[10] This allows the patient to lead a life without fear of asthma attacks.

As Pascale related in the *HBR* article, six months into the product rollout, sales were well below anyone's anticipation. Then the financial analysts spotted an anomaly—a big sales spike coming out of Dallas–Fort Worth. Out of 242 national sales reps, two women in the Dallas area created a new sales playbook and were selling 20 times the national average.

Genentech had previously built market expertise in cancer medicines, not asthma drugs. Anyone who has visited an oncology or pulmonary unit knows that the oncology specialists routinely administer intravenous chemotherapy and other medicines, but Xolair's target markets were allergists, pediatricians, and pediatric nurses.

Infusions require a different set of protocols than those followed in a child's standard visit to the pediatrician. Clinicians administering Xolair also must be trained in recognizing rare reactions or side effects. The sales reps could spend all day with PowerPoints and graphs talking about the statistical benefit and effectiveness of Xolair, and they still wouldn't get past the client's apprehension about simply administering it.

The crux of the problem was the mindset and methods of pediatric doctors and nurses. The challenge was to expand their skillsets and change the office culture to align with the company's goal, which for Genentech is "in business for life."

The two sales representatives in Dallas and their team created a new playbook in which they became consultants and mentors in administering Xolair. They educated the doctors to focus on the long-term lifestyle benefits—such as their patients being able to own pets or take up jogging. The team also taught the clinic staff how to navigate the new insurance paperwork maze to get reimbursed for this new treatment. In short, the Genentech team stopped applying force and started becoming change artists working in close partnership with their clients. This kind of emotional intelligence, initiative, and creativity working in serving a shared purpose has a much better chance of succeeding within environments that encourage and reward risk.

Like these Genentech sales associates, some individuals are "positive deviants"—outliers who deviate from the norm in ways that create positive results by seeing solutions where others see only an unsolvable problem. To escape from the stranglehold or equilibrium, Pascale suggests making a practice of hiring people who deviate positively from the norm of the organization. While those invested in old processes are bound to react negatively, an injection of fresh ideas can spark innovation and rejuvenate the organization.

Look Globally for Talent

The number-one characteristic identified as needed in today's leaders by the respondents of Skillsoft's leadership survey is having a global perspective. Talent and markets are now spread across the planet geographically and socially. To compete successfully, companies must take advantage of these resources, getting beyond xenophobia and social biases to tap into global talent pools.

InnoCentive created its Global Solver Network to tap into as many diverse minds as possible for innovative solutions. For example, through a challenge by Scientists Without Borders, it brought the best minds together to find solutions to combat the critical malnutrition problem of folic-acid deficiency in women of child-bearing age in developing countries of the world.[11]

Technology entrepreneur and researcher Vivek Wadhwa points out that 52 percent of the information-technology startups in Silicon Valley and 25 percent of all new businesses in the United States are created by foreign-born nationals, such as Indians, Pakistanis, the Chinese, and the Vietnamese. They have been coming to the United States for decades to earn science, engineering, and math degrees and to start their own businesses. They've created a tremendous number of U.S. jobs, inventions, and wealth.[12]

If these foreign-born nationals don't feel welcome here, or if they see better opportunities somewhere else, they leave. And when they leave, they don't just take their bank accounts, but also their energy, creativity, and capacity to create jobs and prosperity.

According to the North American Alliance for Fair Employment (NAAFE) in a 2004 background briefing, debates about immigration focused mostly on low-wage workers until the mid-1980s when that shifted to highly skilled, temporary workers, such as those in the bur-geoning IT business.[13] Following the economic downturn that began in mid-2001, an "increasingly heated" debate ensued concerning the numbers, scope, and impact of educated, foreign-born workers on the high-tech labor markets.

The United States began issuing only 85,000 visas for highly skilled workers (known as "H-1B" visas) annually, and these expire after six years. In the briefing, NAAFE noted the potentially high stakes: "Views about U.S. 'national competitiveness' and the global division of labor underpin much of the debate."

In a March 2011 report titled "Can America Keep Best, Brightest Immigrants?" NBC news correspondent Tom Brokaw reported that half of nearly a dozen young Silicon Valley entrepreneurs who had gathered recently said they were considering going back to their home countries rather than staying in the United States because of visa issues—and that they would take jobs with them when they leave.

Congress began turning its attention to this potential brain drain and came up with the STEM Jobs Act of 2012, which would increase the number of visas going to those with STEM (science, technology, engi-neering, or mathematics) skills by 55,000. According to a report by the Congressional Research Service, about 47 percent of those with H-1B visas in 2012—91,000 workers—were employed in computer-related occupations.[14] Although the United States remains the leading host country for such students, says the CRS report, global competition for talent in STEM fields is "intensifying."[15]

In our own best interests, U.S. businesses need to remain open to new ideas and people, embrace intellectual diversity, and participate in the global collaboration effort. While the United States has been a global leader in innovation, we have been constrained to some extent by our own way of looking at things, our culture. To keep on the edge of innovation, we would do well to recognize that people from other countries can bring a fresh perspective to creativity.

Researchers Richard Nisbett and Takahiko Masuda conducted a study[16] involving American college students and a group of Japanese students who had just arrived in the United States. The intent of the study was to learn how East Asians and Americans might perceive the world differently. In one portion of the study, they asked both groups of students to photograph another student. As the representative photographs on the following page show, the Americans mostly focused only on the student's face (below left) and included little background or landscape information. The Japanese students consistently framed the subjects from a much wider angle to include much more of their bodies, as well as background information (below right). The Japanese students were more inclined to take photographs of others in context of their environment.

"[The] Japanese literally never made photographs with the person taking up as large a fraction of the total space as the American photo, but it was common for Americans to do so," Nisbett and Masuda write in their paper on the study.

The researchers also tracked eye movement of the two groups of students as they examined photographs that included a focal object and background. He discovered that the Americans spent the majority of their time looking at the primary subject—the focal point—of the picture, while the Japanese students spent a greater amount of time looking at the environment and context of the main subject.

Although Nisbett and Masuda don't draw conclusions about cognitive performance or competitive ability associated with contextual thinking, the differing perspectives of the two groups of students can teach us many things about our point of view. For one thing, problems and their solutions do not exist in a vacuum but rather in relation to other things—they have context and form patterns. To meet a challenge, we need to see the main point clearly but also in relation to the whole picture. We need perspective.

Dan Goleman, in *Working with Emotional Intelligence*, described a study in which researchers assessed the performance skills of top executives at 15 large companies.[17] He drew the following conclusion from the results:

> Just one cognitive ability distinguished star performers from the average: pattern recognition, the "big picture" thinking that allows leaders to pick out the meaningful trends from a welter of information around them and to think strategically far into the future.

**Photograph taken by an
American student**

**Photograph taken by a
Japanese student**

A culture of inclusion and diversity has to be built into businesses, bringing everyone into the creative process. The world is changing, and if we persist in being xenophobic, we will alienate some of the very best and brightest talent from around the world—those eager to bring their energy and intellect to bear here in the United States to create wealth, jobs, opportunity, and innovation.

Labor and innovation can be sourced anywhere. In this age of increasing interdependence, where the economic fates of countries are intertwined now more than ever, collaboration across geographic and social boundaries is absolutely essential if solutions to world problems are to be found. It's tempting for leaders to hire people that look, think, and act like they do, and it can be a good way to build efficiencies, because those of the same ilk can usually communicate and execute faster than a group of people with highly diverse backgrounds. However, if we want to encourage divergent thinking and find new perspectives and new ways of executing on projects, we need new ideas that come from disparate cultures and backgrounds.

ENGAGE THE CUSTOMER

Pay Attention to Customers' Unorthodox Use of Products

One of my son Will's favorite *Calvin and Hobbes* cartoons depicts Calvin preparing for school. He comes down to the kitchen and yells to his Mom, "I need some Crisco for school today!" She gives him a jar of Crisco and he returns with his hair sticking up in a pompadour. She screams, "You put it in your hair!" Calvin replies, "Ah c'mon Mom! It's class picture day!"

At Skillsoft, we often discover customers buying and using our products and services for purposes for which they were never designed or intended but that have excellent application for the customer. Unorthodox product use is often the key to unlocking new value potential, as is the case with short messaging service (SMS). According to Cor Stutterheim, of the technology firm CMG, who created SMS, the technology morphed into something different from the company's original intention:

> It started as a message service, allowing operators to inform all their own customers about things such as problems with the network. When we created SMS it was not really meant to communicate from

consumer to consumer and certainly not meant to become the main channel which the younger generation would use to communicate with each other.[18]

CMG never imagined its own customers might like to use the technology to send messages to each other.

Kleenex was marketed in 1925 as a makeup removal cloth. Originally listed in the U.S. Patent and Trademark Office as "absorbent pads or sheets for removing cold cream," by 1930, the product was actively, and successfully, marketed as a handkerchief replacement under the slogan "Don't Carry a Cold in Your Pocket." It turned out the people who bought Kleenex were actually using it to wipe their noses.

As early as the 1950s, Peter Drucker taught the importance of the customer in the success of any business, and yet companies often don't consider this critical part of the creative process. When product developers dream up new products, they typically think in terms of market segments to whom they can sell it or in terms of the product's attributes. Pharmaceutical companies might think in terms of customer market segments based on income level, age, marital status, or gender. Car companies tend to think in terms of the attributes of compact, mid-size, luxury, SUV, minivan, and light truck.

But creating a product or service this way is rapidly becoming passé—and for good reason. In a *Harvard Business Review* article by Clayton Christensen (Kim B. Clark professor of business administration at Harvard Business School), Scott Cook (co-founder and chairman of Intuit), and Taddy Hall (chief strategy officer of the Advertising Research Foundation) characterized executives' focusing too much on "ever-narrower demographic segments and ever-more-trivial product extensions" as "marketing malpractice."[19]

In looking at market segments or product attributes, companies are missing the real purpose of a product—to do a job. As legendary Harvard Business School marketing professor Theodore Levitt famously put it, "People don't buy a quarter-inch drill bit, they buy a quarter-inch hole!"

Christensen and his coauthors, in elaborating on the idea of business malpractice, wrote that businesses need a paradigm shift in thinking, focusing on the *job* customers want done rather than benchmarking the features and functions of our tools against those of rivals. In focusing on the tools rather than the job, businesses "often solve the wrong problems, improving their products in ways that are irrelevant to their customers' needs." One case they cite was the failure of a financial-planning software product Intuit designed to help customers with planning for retirement:

> While the demographics suggested that lots of families needed a financial plan, constructing one actually wasn't a job that most people were looking to do. . . . Making it easier and cheaper for customers to do things that they are not trying to do rarely leads to success.

Instead of asking "How can I make my product more attractive to my customer?" ask "What was my product hired to do?" Christensen, in a filmed presentation for Skillsoft that I produced in fall 2008, illustrates this point in a story about milkshakes. A fast-food restaurant that wanted to improve its sale of milkshakes detailed a researcher to find out the jobs that the customers were trying to get done when "hiring" a milkshake. He found that most milkshakes were purchased in the morning and that's all that was purchased, that most customers were alone and bought the milkshake to go.

In interviewing the customers, the researcher found that most were in a hurry, had a long commute ahead, and needed something to make the commute interesting while not interfering with driving. They also weren't really hungry but knew they would be by 10:00 a.m. and wanted a snack that would not interfere with lunch. Other questions led to finding out that other foods did not fit these criteria.

The researcher found quite a different set of results with parents bringing their children for a milkshake and a complete meal. In this case, the parents bought the milkshake to placate their children. The downside was that because milkshakes are thick, drawing them out of the straw takes time, defeating the concept of fast food.

Although the milkshake was the same, the job it was "hired" to do differed according to the circumstances. The company responded by making two kinds of shakes. For the commuter, they made a thicker one, with tiny chunks of fruit added (giving it a dimension of anticipation and unpredictability) and, to speed up the purchasing process, sold a prepaid swipe card and moved the dispensing machine in front of the counter. For the parents buying for their kids, they made a slightly thinner milkshake so it could be consumed faster.

Beware of Benchmarking

Often the conversations we do have with customers involve benchmarking processes—"How did other companies do it?" Yet most eminent thinkers, researchers, and writers involved with creative product or process development warn of benchmarking to mediocrity.

Around 2001, while leading Targeted Learning, my colleagues and I got our customer research and stories together and dreamed up an online system to teach the learner and leader how to use, apply, track, and campaign on our video learning assets. We built the system, and when we showed it to a few customers, people surprised us by saying, "You've created an LMS, although it's got some stuff we haven't seen before."

We had indeed built a learning management system before we had ever heard of one. Instead of benchmarking LMS vendors (whom we didn't know existed), we listened to our customers and created something unique. We did it with passion and energy, because we believed in our originality and in our ability to create a killer application.

Through engaging customers in the creative process, we can teach them at the same time we are learning from them. IDEO, a design and innovation consulting firm, engages its clients in its highly co-creative, rapid-prototyping process of design while simultaneously instructing and creating these capacities in its clients.

Focus on the Result, Not the App

Software coders can get hypnotized by the killer hack, sales professionals can be entranced by the nuance of well-run client meetings, and project managers can easily be seduced by the latest task-management app. But we need to remember that, while the devil is in the details, the beauty is in the result, the impact, the difference.

Canadian business consultant Don Tapscott, in his book *Grown Up Digital: How the Net Generation Is Changing Your World*, has a marvelous illustration of the power and importance of connecting people with ideas without being encumbered and distracted by the mechanism itself.[20] A few years ago, he was in his house when down the hall he heard his son calling out, "Dad! Dad! Come here—you've got to check this out!" So Don walks down the hall to his son's room and finds him at the computer looking at images of space and his son is saying, "Look Dad, it's Mars! Isn't that amazing?"

Don is pleased with his son's interest in the cosmos, and says, "That's very cool son, where did you get these images?" And his son says, "Dad, I'm looking through this thing called the Hubble Telescope." Meanwhile Don is thinking about how incredible it is that his son is accessing one of the most sophisticated pieces of technology ever invented by humankind—from his bedroom.

Ultimately our purpose in the Out Think journey toward innovation is not about building killer applications: it's about creating experiences, services, products that enthrall, delight, or solve a particular dilemma for our customer. It's about connecting people with ideas—ideas that are recognized as possessing distinct value by others.

MASH THE HUMAN FACTOR INTO YOUR WORK

The profession of radiology has been progressing over the past 50 years in terms of training methodology, equipment and technology, and immediacy of feedback. Yet, despite these advances, error rates often remain statistically significant and frustratingly high. According to Imaging Economics, the reading error rate can vary from 2 percent to as high as 20 percent, depending on the type of scan, the clinician, the environment, and even the time of day.[21] And up to 80 percent of the errors are perceptual errors. That is, the information was present and shown on the film or scan, but not seen or accurately identified by the radiologist.

As described in an *RSNA News* article, Yehonatan Turner was a radiology resident at Shaare Zedek Medical Center in Jerusalem in 2008 when he decided to experiment with humanizing the process of reading radiology scans to learn what effect it might have on the quality of their evaluation by radiologists.[22] He and his colleagues performed an experiment in which they asked 267 patients for their permission to be photographed before their computed tomography (CT) scans. A CT scan is a more detailed X-ray exam that focuses on a specific part of the body and yields a more detailed image of what's inside the body. The 267 CT examinations with photos were among a total of 1,137 CT examinations performed at a tertiary-care hospital that year.

In a blind study, Turner chose 30 of the original CT examination results that had included photos, and in which radiologists had included incidental findings in their evaluation reports of them. The radiologists were also asked to fill out a questionnaire reporting on their experience with the photos. The results of the study were quite surprising:

- Eighty percent of the evaluations did not include incidental findings this time around when photos were not included, and the radiologists strongly agreed with the study statement "The patient photograph prompted me to relate in more detail to the CT."
- Radiologists reported feeling a greater sense of empathy when evaluating CTs that had photos included with them.
- Radiologists reported feeling more engaged as a physician when a photo was included.
- The length of time it took to evaluate the scans did not increase because of the photos.

To sum up, accuracy, thoroughness, empathy, and a sense of connection with the patient all went up, and no additional time was required to get these benefits. This is an example of innovating by connecting with the end result—with the purpose of the work.

Let's Recap

Remember . . .

- Innovation leaders must be able to identify meaningful business trends, adapt them to their own market, and lead a team to execute solutions. This requires more than an ability to react or respond to immediate needs. It requires a way of thinking that conceptualizes and converges concepts and technologies—often disparate, wild, and radical ones—into feasible possibilities and practical solutions. By constantly mashing up ideas, applications, and outcomes, powerful new combinations emerge that have value to customers.

- Often, great ideas are built from the initiatives of prior thinkers, who based their thoughts on those before them. Some of the most heralded innovative geniuses have borrowed brilliant ideas from observing a variety of realms in life, such as nature, people, inventions, and mistakes. Many great ideas began with intuition and curiosity, exploring previous ideas or kernels of innovation and allowing them to incubate and emerge.

- Unorthodox use of products is often the key to unlocking new value potential. Following conventional marketing paradigms of aiming at specific customer demographics may well be outdated. The real purpose of a product is to do a job, and innovative thinking requires engaging the customer in the creative process to discover the jobs that need doing and the adaptations and innovations customers derive to get the job done.

Your Turn Now . . .

Reach in: Identify a person you consider brilliant—a pacesetter, industry icon, admirable leader, or any figure you admire. You might select someone from the business world or scientific community, performing arts, sports, politics—don't limit yourself to someone who is simply popular. Make your choice personally meaningful, a role model. Buy the book, rent the movie, do the online research—whatever method works for you. Discover things you didn't know about the person. Reflect on the person's approach to life, challenges, and innovation. Let these reflections incubate and, after a few days, do something that your brilliant role model would do.

Reach out: Select two or three functions for which your work group is responsible, such as answering customer questions, filing financial reports, correcting errors in software—any of the hundreds of functions performed by teams every day. From these functions, select something that doesn't go as well as desired. This could be a predictable delay, a resource shortage, or a continued flaw in the process or product. With your team, brainstorm all the possible ideas for improving this aspect of the team's work. Toss in wild and crazy ideas to build on! Ask team members to think of similar problems that exist in any realm of life and how they're solved. Make the goal of this activity to simply be the activity itself—not problem solving or pressure to achieve an outcome. Simply use this as an experiment in deviating from traditional approaches to problems.

Spread out: Great ideas are built on the shoulders of giants, and chances are your company's products and services evolved in a similar way—a founding entrepreneur with a new idea, an industry leader who set the stage for future innovation, or perhaps a mash-up of technologies and concepts. Tell the story of your company's birth, development, and growth to your team, friends, and colleagues in a way that reinforces the idea of borrowing brilliance toward innovation.

Remember . . .

- The new global economy demands that we develop our external networks to be broad and deep in expertise, including people we interact with only periodically who can contribute their own experiences, expertise, and background knowledge. Similarly, hiring people who deviate positively from the organizational norm, intentionally destabilizing the work environment, and fostering moderate creative tension can spark innovation and fresh ideas.

- Problems and their solutions do not exist in a vacuum, but in relation to other things. We must view the whole picture, not only the primary subject matter. "Big picture thinking" allows leaders to discern meaningful trends and think strategically far into the future.

- Leaders need the backup of the organization and a global perspective to support the process of innovation. It behooves us to recognize and embrace intellectual diversity and participate globally. Collaboration across geographical and social boundaries is absolutely essential for world problem solving. If we wish to encourage divergent thinking, thereby discovering new perspectives, we must tap into disparate cultural backgrounds.

Your Turn Now . . .

Reach in: Identify a country or culture that has some relationship to your work. This could be part of your global operations, a supplier, or even a customer. Consider why someone from that country or culture might value your personal talents. List several qualities and characteristics that you could offer to this country or culture. If you had the opportunity to meet with a senior leader in that company or within that culture, what would you talk about, and why?

Reach out: Make a list of five people who you know but with whom you don't regularly interact. Think of these people as "respected acquaintances," people with whom you've shared an interesting conversation or worked with on a short-term project. Commit to connecting with at least one of them and ask about their work, their ideas, and their thoughts on any relevant issue, such as industry, economic, political, or environmental. Be aware of your feelings and responses as you connect with the person, and factor the meaning of these feelings and responses into your work and innovation efforts.

Spread out: Position a current challenge in a bigger picture. Write the specific challenge on a sheet of paper and then make concentric circles around it. Think of this problem or challenge as it exists beyond your team leadership or functional sphere. For example, extend the impact of the challenge to your company's vision, your customers, your country, your industry, your natural environment, and finally your legacy. Do this exercise with a visionary mind, thinking about how you and your team can make an impact all the way to the future.

CHAPTER 9

ACTION: GET MOVING OR ACCEPT THE CONSEQUENCES

Success is not the result of spontaneous combustion. You must first set yourself on fire.

—*Reggie Leach*

In late August of 2012, just as spring was emerging and the brisk air of winter was fading around the city of Melbourne, Australia, I interviewed Campbell Jones, COO of Manheim Australia.[1] Manheim is a rapidly growing business that hosts auctions to facilitate the buying and selling of cars, trucks, motorcycles, heavy machinery, and other equipment. They currently have more than 20,000 employees operating in more than 100 locations throughout the world. The company calls itself the world's largest "remarketer" of vehicles, last year handling more than eight million transactions.

As you might imagine, the work is very logistics intensive. The company needs to have a high level of excellence and proficiency in shipping and timing to ensure its inventory is prepared to support the numerous auctions they host throughout the world. They must develop marketing and brand awareness to generate demand, manage back-office infrastructure activities, and, of course, conduct the primary product of the company, which is to host the auction events.

Like any other company, there is work that is routine and perhaps even monotonous, work that is creatively demanding, and a variety of work in between. In the interview, I asked Jones, who has steadily risen in the company and is considered to be an excellent leader, what things he did on a daily basis that contributed to the high level of engagement clearly found throughout the vibrant company.

He explained a series of consistent behaviors he was committed to. He regularly travels throughout the different operating offices in Australia and New Zealand to meet directly with the people in the company and to spend time listening to their ideas and challenges. He gives local control to people in different divisions of the organization to change or refine how they do their work and supports them with people, funding, and other resources as necessary.

He also explained that he intentionally has worked in many different divisions of the company, from marketing to sales, to logistics and operations. This diversity of experience and the first-hand knowledge and understanding of the work required that he has gained from it enables him to relate to, and collaborate with, people in those divisions more easily. He spends as little time as possible in closed-door executive meetings, and as much time as he can working directly with employees and customers in the field. As he described in our conversation:

> We recognize that everywhere has different characteristics. If I'm not in the field with those people and understanding their challenges, the areas that they're struggling with, or the areas that they're really successful with, then I'm not going to be effective because I'm not going to be able to either take the wonderful ideas that they've come up with or take an idea from somewhere else and help that area where they're struggling. And, so it's imperative that I'm out in the field.

All of these behaviors contribute to building a culture of engagement. People clearly trust Campbell Jones because he has demonstrated consistency of action to back up his promises, he has expertise—or at least an understanding of the different parts of the business and how they interact effectively—and he shows a willingness to those in the organization to trust their judgment and support them with the resources they need to improve their work and develop innovation in the products or processes they support.

A few days later I met with Jill Klein, professor of marketing at Melbourne Business School, to discuss her work, and related the interaction with Jones to her. As I explained the story, Jones's success at Manheim was to be expected. After all, it was common sense that, if a leader behaves with integrity, supports and listens to the people in the organization, and supports and trusts the ingenuity of those performing the work, excellence will emerge. In my telling of the story, I recall thinking, "But of course it works! There's nothing remarkable about this story. Obviously a leader with these traits would drive excellence and innovation for the company."

After listening to the story, Klein remarked, "Yes, but what's remarkable is that he *is doing it*. He is actually practicing these behaviors, while many leaders are simply talking about them."

This brings us to action. The critical part of the Out Think journey is the doing—putting action to the words, values, and ideas. All the curious inquiry, deep exploration, thoughtful conversation, and mindful reflection won't amount to any kind of innovation—much less remarkable innovation—unless we act.

Action distinguishes innovation from creativity, or, as Paul Sloane, author of *The Innovative Leader*, put it: "If you have a brainstorm meeting and dream up dozens of new ideas, then you have displayed creativity, but there is no innovation until something gets implemented."[2]

At this point in the Out Think journey, the volume of activity and experimentation is critical, and the innovative leader celebrates failure and success equally, punishing only inaction. This part of the innovative process requires rapid prototyping and active experimentation. Many innovation journeys stall at this point because of failure to actually take out a hammer, put pen to paper, write the code, build the prototype, or otherwise get our hands dirty.

The symptoms of inaction are often found in the language used. As Tim Sanders likes to say, "Stay away from the 'ings' and spend more time with the 'eds.' The 'eds' say 'We tried that. We tested that. We modeled that.' The 'ings' say things like 'We're thinking about that' or 'We're discussing that.'"

One of the most important drivers of innovative outcomes is action that is novel and unique. Unfortunately, a characteristic of being human is a persistent sense of overconfidence when it comes to habitual activities. And, according to a study at Duke University, almost 45 percent of our daily activity is habitual.[3]

We tend to suffer from hubris when participating in the consistent activities that fill our days—from the time we awaken through engaging in all the daily activities that populate our lives. The first step to acting in novel ways is to recognize the learning opportunities in the activities in which we consistently participate. To do that, we need to get out of our own way.

CURB YOUR AWESOMENESS

In my discussion with Jill Klein, we talked about her particular interest in some of the cognitive biases we humans tend to have when interpreting circumstances and events, and how we then make decisions based on our understandings and intuition.[4] She pointed out that we all often suffer from overconfidence in our abilities and knowledge on a wide range of subjects. In other words, we believe that we will be correct more often than we usually are regarding those behaviors and beliefs in which we regularly participate.

There are plenty of examples from available research of this tendency to overestimate ourselves or overestimate the likelihood of something to happen:

- In a survey of high school seniors, 25 percent rated themselves in the top 1 percent in their ability to get along with others.[5]
- Thirty-seven percent of one firm's professional engineers placed themselves among the top 5 percent of performers.[6]
- Ninety-three percent of American drivers rate themselves as better than the median.[7]
- Those who estimate their own accuracy of answers at 90 percent or greater often have an actual accuracy of less than 50 percent.[8]
- In one study, those who estimated their own accuracy at 99 percent were correct only 87 percent of the time—a fairly big difference when we consider jobs that require accuracy.[9]

There are a variety of psychological explanations for our overconfidence bias, but the most compelling reason may stem from our need to believe in our own sense of self-importance and optimism. If we recognized the statistical truth, we might be a little more pessimistic, and that might inhibit us from leading productive lives and pursuing hopeful ambitions.

This overconfidence bias can be a useful motivator in driving action and initiative, and might even further our own careers and success socially. However, if unchecked by organizational culture, managerial oversight, and self-reflection, overconfidence can lead to failed endeavors and poor decisions for us and for our work.

Klein suggests a few actions and behaviors to help overcome decision overconfidence:

- **Solicit the opinion of more people.** As James Surowiecki, author of *The Wisdom of Crowds: Why the Many Are Smarter Than the Few and How Collective Wisdom Shapes Business, Economies, Societies and Nations*, argued in his book, and as the game show *Who Wants to be a Millionaire* demonstrates on prime-time television, when we ask a larger group of people their opinion on a question, their collective judgment is almost always better than our own.[10]

- **Solicit your own second opinion.** When we consider our own second opinion with our first opinion, we find we are almost always headed in the right direction. Try asking yourself the same scenario and decision outcome in a different way and see if you come to the same conclusion.

- **Consider the extremes.** In figuring our odds of success, or effort, or time required at doing X, we should ask ourselves what we consider the extreme positive and negative boundaries of these outcomes. That consideration will likely lead toward moderation—one way or the other—in how we proceed.

- **Separate our "deciding" self from our "doing" self.** When we acknowledge that an estimate we make, however fact-based and analytical, is not actual but hypothetical, we can temper our own judgment by remaining skeptical of our own decisions. This is our "deciding" self. Yet when we conclude a deliberation, shift to our "doing" self, and act on that decision, it's important to remain optimistic, focused, and steadfast in supporting our "doing" self. The reason is that our colleagues and teams need to gain our confidence to support the endeavor. So once we decide, we need to act with confidence.

After reflection and consultation, we need to remember ultimately that *doing* matters. WD-40 is named for the 40th chemical concoction that worked, and, according to Sir James Dyson, it took him more than *5,000* prototypes to build the world-renowned Dyson vacuum cleaner.[11] New ideas have little purpose if they remain merely a creative thought in our minds. Action comes before innovation, but action in the right direction makes all the difference. In other words, stick with the people who take action and who know how to make new mistakes.

Fail Forward

Indiana Jones or Star Wars? New York or Los Angeles? Mustard or mayonnaise? Most people have stock answers to these preferences and can detail the reasons why one is better than the other. "Dude, *of course* the Red Sox are better than the Yankees because . . ." And they can spend an hour telling you why. Once we decide between different products to invest in, or pick between two courses of action, we justify that choice by constructing numerous reasons why our choice of A is better than B. We do this to make us feel better about the choices we make.

To avoid buyer's remorse and decision regret, and make us feel better about the decisions we are making, we discard or devalue any new information that is presented that might suggest we made a poor decision. It's the path of least resistance to back up our own choices by looking for evidence that affirms our decisions and negates or devalues any evidence or argument that detracts. This kind of decision justification makes us feel better about ourselves and our ability to make good choices. It can also send us down a path of throwing good money after bad and pursuing paths that are not constructive or novel.

The key to innovation and progress is to fail forward—to make new mistakes that will ultimately yield the value we're looking for. The critical part of this learning process is to disassociate our decision from our ego. When we associate a choice with our own sense of self-worth and confidence, it can become very difficult to change course once new information arises that suggests we may have been wrong—which, in turn, can lead to foolish consistencies. When we can look at decisions and choices as learning opportunities and micro-experiments, we can remove the association of decision success or failure from our sense of identity.

While a key to experimentation and making new mistakes is to distance the outcome from our own sense of self-worth, how do we convince others in the organization that their own foolish consistencies are hampering our ability to innovate? How do we thoughtfully approach a colleague or boss and convincingly suggest to them that their repetitious actions and behaviors are ineffective—or, worse, damaging—to our efforts at moving the innovation process forward?

It's pretty difficult to march into someone's office and deliver news you know he or she don't want to hear. When we are describing an idea or project others don't want to hear, we need to remember that their objections are likely their own attempts to protect their sense of value and self-worth. Studies consistently show that, when people receive information that they interpret as a threat or that runs counter to their beliefs, the part of the brain that processes information and activates negative emotional responses will engage and they will even have physiological responses, such as elevated heart rate and respiration. It's a protection response. If we say something that challenges the belief system, habits, and behaviors of people, their immediate reaction is to protect their ideas.

The easiest and most common reaction of those hearing bad news is to decide that the person with the bad news is an idiot and has no idea what he or she is talking about. To protect a sense of self-worth and value, the path of least resistance is to simply discredit the other person as being ignorant, wrong, or misguided. This kind of dismissive response is common among those who can't tolerate cognitive dissonance or have conflicting thoughts.

However, there are a couple honest but clever tricks we can use to help change the minds of such people, and lead the change we believe in. First, we can bolster their self-esteem. Couch the information and news we want to communicate inside something we sincerely believe in that they have initiated in the past.

Then, we can tie what we are proposing to something they have proposed in the past, suggesting that we are introducing an idea and a course of action that is, in fact, consistent with what they have championed previously. This makes it much more difficult to dismiss such proposers as idiots, since they would also be discrediting themselves as well.

At this point they will listen, and hopefully accept the new idea, rationalizing it as consistent with their thinking, because dismissing it would create cognitive dissonance by contradicting their previous behavior and belief.

WHEN TO TRUST, BUT QUALIFY, YOUR GUT INSTINCT

I once had an interview with a business analytics expert and researcher who firmly believed in never making a decision based on "fad, faith, or fashion." In his view, the best decision making comes from rigorous study and thoughtful evaluation of sound evidence. Bookstores are stocked with titles, such as *Competing on Analytics* (Davenport and Harris), *Moneyball* (Lewis), and *Super Crunchers* (Ayres), all testifying to the power of evidence-driven decision making. The story in *Moneyball* of how the Oakland Athletics, which had limited financial resources, still built a competitive baseball team by using an analytical, evidence-based approach served to inform and change the way nearly every baseball club fills their rosters.

While such an approach is undoubtedly valuable as a decision-making tool, the current speed of business does not always allow for the luxury of extended deliberation or data collection for a highly analyzed, evidence-based, or empirically based decision. Klein pointed out that a growing amount of research and data suggest our own intuition, or gut instinct, can also be a valuable advisor.

An intuition is a response triggered by a small shift in dopamine in our brains in reaction to a pattern change beneath our immediate consciousness. Our experiences are constant, voluminous, and stored deep in our emotional memory system such that, when sequences or patterns present themselves, we can intuit outcomes on the basis of previous experience. Conversely, our active analytical memory can consciously identify and recall only a handful of active thoughts at once. When we experience something unusual or inconsistent with our emotional memory, it creates a physiological response.

For example, an interviewer of a job candidate might get a suspicious feeling that leads him to check the candidate's credentials. The interviewer discovers the candidate was lying on his resume and during the interview. It was the interviewer's gut feeling, not evidence, that correctly informed him—his intuition and emotional memory picked up on something in the candidate's behavior that triggered an intuition that nudged the interviewer to think, "I don't trust this person." The important thing to understand is that just because it was a gut perception doesn't mean it was irrational. Our emotional systems are as valid as feedback mechanisms as our intellectual and analytical reasoning processes are.

On the other hand, we can have insightful reactions based on emotional cues that mislead us. In that same interview, the candidate could have been wearing something, or said a particular word or reference that triggered a past bad experience in the interviewer's mind. That small red herring in the interaction would trigger a negative emotional reaction having nothing to do with the interview candidate himself.

So there are problems with following our hunches. As Klein described in our conversation, she has four tests she advises when weighing the value of following intuition and gut feeling. She suggests starting with the notion that an intuition may be merely a hypothesis that requires passing the following tests:

- **The Experience Test.** The first critical test of gut reactions is to ask ourselves if we have enough experience in the area to trust our hunch. For example, when evaluating the quality of an engineering idea, someone might have a feeling that the idea is flawed. Only people with a great deal of experience in this field and with this specific situation should trust their hunches. Anyone lacking the necessary experience should reconsider the quality of the gut reaction and move on to the next test.

- **The Feedback Test.** The faster and more direct the feedback, the better and more qualified it is. In the engineering example above, if we can quickly implement and test prototypes against our intuition, we can quickly verify our hunches. Sports are excellent environments to get immediate and vivid feedback. My 12-year-old son, Charlie, has picked up a sport called longboarding (a type of skateboarding, except the board is, well, longer). He comes home with skinned knees almost every day but is improving rapidly because the feedback when trying a trick or making a weight adjustment when riding down a hill is quick and merciless.

- **The Complexity Test.** This test is a bit counterintuitive, but it turns out that the greater the complexity in the environment, the more accurate our intuition tends to be over our ability to cognitively work out a solution. This is because, when evaluating situations with very few components, we can bring our active cognition into play and individually isolate and evaluate the components of a situation. In situations of greater complexity, we exceed the ability of our minds to work out the best solution by deduction and often our intuition becomes more valuable in making decisions.

- **The Fooled-by-Desire Test.** The final test of the quality of our intuition that Klein described involves evaluating how much we want the outcome. She calls this the "Fooled-by-Desire" test, and believes it may be the most difficult test of intuition for human beings because it's quite difficult to discern between what we want to do, and what our emotion is telling us is the right thing to do. An example of this test would be when we have something in our minds we know we want to do, and then suddenly get a bad feeling about proceeding. If we can first recognize our own desire bias, we can more easily isolate it from the decision-making process when evaluating the intuitions we have. In our conversation, Klein suggested a situation in which we badly want to hire someone who has an excellent resume, yet in the middle of the interview we get a feeling of dread. She suggests this is an important cue to pay attention to because it runs counter to our own desire.

Now that we've evaluated the quality of our hunches, let's move to the importance of creating value before risk, and action before talk.

Create Value before Risk

It can be an exciting time when we decide to initiate a project, build an application, or design a compelling solution. The idea may look brilliant and compelling in our minds, and we may feel the urge to tell the world about our latest endeavor. But hang on a minute—telling people that we intend to do something is different than having something to show them.

Telling others of our intent may be valuable to us because it can create an external motivation. That is, if we tell others of our intent, we may feel compelled to follow through. But that expressed intention has little value to those we told and can create a false expectation. I believe it's best to start with value.

Instead of telling someone what we are considering, or committing to, we need to show them what we've already started, the work in progress. We need to give them something to anchor to for two reasons: what we say we will do will likely change once we start doing it—for market, design, budget, or other reasons; and people tend to understand and respond better to hard evidence than to words.

In other words, speak with action, not words. Our action, prototype, or first cut makes for a much more vivid and interesting discussion and collaboration because it provides a conceptual anchor.

The other powerful and compelling reason to start with action instead of talk is that, once we get in motion and actually produce something of value, other people will recognize and respond to that creation. In the best circumstances, those people we show our work to will contribute, collaborate, and spread the word about what we or our teams are working on, which will drive energy and awareness to our project. It's much more difficult and less inspiring to spread the word about what someone *intends* to do.

Do Whatever It Takes

Anyone seeing him in the hallway of the Rosen Shingle Creek Hotel in Orlando, Florida, picking up bits of trash and straightening plants might mistake him for a custodian or perhaps a fastidious guest. Harris Rosen, founder and owner of Rosen Hotels and Resorts might just be the hardest working man in the business. In person he is quiet, thoughtful, and generous with his time. Well dressed, but never ostentatious, and in excellent health, Rosen swims most every day of the week to remain fit and alert.

In conversations with Rosen in 2012 and early 2013, I found out he is also quite generous as a business owner, community activist, and social philanthropist.[12] He offers excellent health care benefits to his employees and their dependents, has initiated a company-wide no-smoking policy, and offers full college scholarships for his associates and their children.

Rosen says he purchased his first hotel in 1974, after being fired from a number of companies because he was told that he did not fit comfortably in their corporate structure. He decided it was best that he strike out on his own and has never looked back. With diligence, care, and an indefatigable work ethic, he has built remarkable hotel and resort properties in the Orlando area. Starting with a premonition in the 1970s that the Orlando area would become a much sought-after leisure and conference destination, he worked hard to develop and grow his hotel and resort company to cater to both the meeting and the leisure markets.

From his very first property—a Quality Inn—to his most recent luxury hotel, Rosen has sustained a remarkable curiosity, which enables him to remain vigilant about changes in the marketplace and to adjust his strategy accordingly. In an interview, Rosen talked to me about the importance of marrying hard work with risk taking:

> How do you teach someone to take a risk? For those of us who do on occasion take risks, you must first convince yourself that everything will turn out OK because you will do whatever it takes to ensure its success. For instance, if you don't have the money to fly to New York, New Jersey, and Massachusetts to meet with potential clients, you hitchhike.

> I think the message is . . . first have a dream, don't give up, and always be honest and respectful—and work harder than anyone else, to ensure success.

LET'S RECAP

Remember . . .

- Recall that innovation is creativity in action. Action counts—not words—especially when that action is novel and unique. Once you are in motion, actually producing something, people will respond, contribute, collaborate, and spread the word, driving energy and awareness your way.

- Performing habitual activities or being overconfident in our abilities and knowledge can get in the way of taking action. Unchecked by organizational culture, managerial mentorship, and self-reflection, overconfidence can lead to inaction, failed endeavors, or poor decisions. To overcome the problems that habitual activities and overconfidence bring, leaders must solicit opinions from others to gain a more collective perspective.

- Our own odds of success should be compared against best- and worst-case possibilities. This helps moderate our choice of how to proceed and separates our "deciding" self from our "doing" self. Visualizing the "doing" part of an endeavor helps take ideas into action.

Your Turn Now . . .

Reach in: Everyone has habits. List three habitual activities you perform on a regular basis in your professional role—checking e-mail, holding meetings, asking members of your team about projects. Decide to reduce or eliminate activities that contribute minimal value, or approach at least one of these activities in a novel or unique way. For example, instead of preparing agendas in advance of each meeting you hold, try constructing a real-time agenda instead. Ask those attending the meeting to identify one or two items they would like to discuss. In this way, people feel more engaged and valued.

Reach out: From a list of key performance areas associated with your job, identify three or four that you feel very confident demonstrating. Rate yourself as confident, very confident, or super confident. Then ask colleagues, your manager, and members of your team to rate you on these same performance areas. Check to see if your self-perceptions match the perceptions of others.

Spread out: In your peer or work group, make a practice of visualizing potential or pending actions. Draw a continuum, with one point being "we are here" and the other point being "we are there." Visualize what it looks like when you get "there" (action taken). Then lay out incremental steps that will get you from here to there.

Remember . . .

- We justify our choices by constructing numerous reasons why they are the best—and thus we feel better about them. Then we discard or devalue new information pertaining to our choice. Thus we may pursue paths that are not novel or constructive. The key to innovative progress is to fail forward, making mistakes that will yield ultimate value, disassociating our decisions with our egos. When working with others, recognize that they too are hampered by their egos and choice values, and that new information that is perceived to be threatening can activate negative emotional responses, accelerate protective responses, or cause resistance. Bolstering the self-esteem of others and tying new ideas to what they have proposed in the past helps to counteract these types of responses.

- Most leaders believe in evidence-driven decision making. However, research and data suggest our own intuition and gut reactions can be valuable advisors. Response to intuitive feelings does not mean irrationality. Recognize this as valid feedback. Yet, beware of emotional cues or hunches that mislead us. We can test hunches by assessing our experience with the situation or problem, gaining timely and direct feedback, recognizing the degree of complexity influencing cognitive and intuitive evaluations, and discerning the personal level of desire to take one course over another.

- Telling others of our intentions may compel us to act toward our stated aim or promise. But that expressed intention has little value to those we told and can create false expectations. Rather than telling people about your intentions or considerations, show them what you have already started. Hard evidence is more convincing than words, eliciting a better response from others.

Your Turn Now . . .

Reach in: Reflect on a tough decision or choice you made in the recent past. Consider any information or evidence that you either ignored or devalued in the process of making your decision, or information that helped you further justify your decision or choice. Identify the themes that tend to influence your decisions one way or another— for example, concerns about cost or money, potential for enhanced or diminished reputation, or the perceptions of others. The next time you face a decision or choice, reconsider any themes that prevent you from taking valuable action—even if it might result in failure.

Reach out: With your team or work group, brainstorm "gut reactions" or hunches associated with specific projects and plans. Review one project or plan at a time, giving it the "experience, feedback, complexity, and fooled-by-desire" tests for quality. Alongside these brainstormed considerations, list the relevant research, data, and evidence associated with each project or plan. Ask how to use these considerations to promote action, even in the face of risks or potential mistakes.

Spread out: Select an innovative activity you are currently performing and create a prototype that represents your fulfilled innovation. Gather several people whose opinions you respect—other leaders and credible experts, for example. Briefly describe your activities, using active language such as "doing, building, creating, facilitating, enhancing, moving," and integrate those responses and reactions into your prototype. Ensure that, while integrating these ideas, you use the expression "we" to signal that you acknowledge and respect their contributions.

CHAPTER 10

SIGNATURE: MAKE IT YOUR OWN

All the leaders we studied . . . were nonconformists in the best sense. . . . They didn't let external pressures, or even social norms, knock them off course. In an uncertain and unforgiving environment, following the madness of the crowds is a good way to get killed.

—*Jim Collins*

Starting back in the mid-1990s, the little company my father and I had started, Targeted Learning Corporation, had been producing and delivering training and education for government and businesses using the space-age magic of satellite technologies. We were forging a path in the market of providing video-based learning to the desktop. The original idea was pretty simple: bring talented instructors into television studios, broadcast live learning to orbiting satellites, and then charge per view for organizations to "downlink" the events and participate. Audiences could call and fax into the program in real time to ask questions.

When the dot-com era started ramping up in the late 1990s, and early video-streaming providers, such as Broadcast.com, came with it, we had video content ready to be digitized and delivered online. TLC was a dynamic and agile little company that had survived the wake of the dot-com boom and bust and was growing. Our first attempt in 2000 at creating a library of online video content was pretty clunky, but it worked.

Late in 2003, nearly all eight of us at TLC were sitting around a table in a cabin in Yarmouth, Maine, to work on our new technology platform that would host and deliver our video content to customers.

We had been working on this project for weeks in small teams. The energy and discussion was rich and spirited. We were convinced the project was big, important, and audacious; now we were assembled to create magic.

Around the table that day, we each had our own perspective and opinion, and as we worked from grand design through to subtle nuance, we each had something to share. Neil, our programmer, was the voice of realistic optimism about what he could reasonably deliver. Taavo had strong ideas on how the content should be shared and applied in team settings. Kim very much wanted a slick, digital marketing tool that could customize and automate the formatting and delivery of upcoming event announcements to our customers' audiences.

All good ideas, these were coming primarily from two perspectives—our understanding of our product and how we envisioned companies using video learning, and listening closely to the customers themselves and integrating their ideas.

This project went on for a few weeks before we had a prototype, which Neil then built as a clickable model online. In short order, we had a working, if not pretty, demo we could start to show our customers—so we used it to launch a tour for our key customers to give them a glance into the future. We were excited to show off this new design that we believed would revolutionize the way video learning was delivered, enjoyed, shared, and applied.

As I mentioned in chapter 8, we had unknowingly built a learning management system. We found out there was a whole industry of providers that build and sell online software that enables companies and individuals to create, track, attend, and complete learning activities. I had never heard of such a thing, and no one at our meetings ever mentioned the existence of an LMS. As a result, we never examined and looked under the hood of such a system to see how it worked. And what we had built was never intended to be a knock-off of one.

What we *had* created was specific to our product delivery, intentional in design, and spare in functionality—a signature innovative solution to a product challenge. We didn't want to create an environment messy with buttons, and we didn't have the engineering staffing power to back up a highly sophisticated delivery engine, anyway.

A signature innovative comprises the core identity of those who have joined in the innovation journey, executed with the unique personalities of everyone participating, and sustained by the mission of the organization. Signature innovation isn't easily copied or pirated, because it comes out of a truly unique cultural identity within an organization.

TLC's signature solution came from our connecting and building ideas within our internal team, soliciting advice and input from our customers, and acting on the best ideas. The result certainly reflected the simple and elegant design philosophies in the origins of the company, as well as its do-it-yourself quality. The development was indeed idiosyncratic and unique to the personalities working on the team, and the platform was sustained and enhanced over time by our leadership team's fundamental belief in delivering quality learning experiences.

GO BEYOND BEST PRACTICES

Most organizations recognize and embrace the notion of modeling best practices—studying operations and teams that exemplify the kinds of traits and behaviors they wish to learn from and adopt. Such modeling of best practices can be useful in many situations to gain market share and adapt quickly to developing technologies. Being a fast follower—a second or third to market—can be quite powerful. Facebook came long after Friendster and MySpace were in the marketplace. The iPhone was eight years late to the smartphone business.

I couldn't agree more that such modeling is important. Yet creating signature solutions is unlike a wholly borrowed, or "best," practice. In examples I've uncovered from talking with leading executives and thought leaders, consistently leveraging "best" practices and creating a copy-cat business model will only get an organization so far. If a company aspires to being the best in its market, it has to lead. And only by the organization's developing its own voice—its signature—can it attain this leadership position.

When our organizations direct more energy, resources, and time in developing signature solutions, they achieve three things:

- **Get products to market faster.** Trying to figure out what the competition is doing can turn into an obsessive distraction for organizations. When we overly burden ourselves with competitive analysis, we not only slow the innovation process but also begin to eradicate the signature characteristics of our products. When we focus on comparison, we begin to copy and, in the process, start to lose the unique and meaningful attributes that were originally attractive to our market. Allowing competitive analysis and worry to hijack our team's attention also reinforces a grass-is-greener mentality and distracts from substantive progress. When we instead trust the deep expertise, intuition, and skill within our organizations, we build confidence and develop solutions faster.

- **De-commoditize products.** When we begin to develop our own signature solutions, we begin to introduce personality that cannot be copied or commoditized. This can be captured in what we provide, and how we provide it. Zappos, a wildly successful online shoe and apparel shop, has built an iconic identity around remarkable service. An iPhone is so truly unique that any copycat product would be instantly detected as ersatz by a faithful iPhone owner.

- **Build brand loyalty.** After interviewing Yvon Chouinard, founder of Patagonia, I'll probably buy the company's outdoor gear rather than its competitors' simply because of how Patagonia runs its business.[1] It takes responsibility for the integrity of its product, conscientiously overseeing all aspects of the company's value chain from fabric source to construction, to market delivery, and even after the point of sale. Chouinard told me he has yet to find a business problem that cannot be solved by increasing quality. For his conviction, and the signature solutions Patagonia has developed, I have strong loyalty to them.

EMBRACE YOUR ORGANIZATION'S IDENTITY

Ever heard of MyEmma.com? In 2002, I was in search of an e-mail management system. I found quite a few immediately, but they all felt sterile, impersonal, and robotic. Then I bumped into MyEmma. A real person answered the phone, led me on a tour of the company's site, and shared a couple of jokes. I signed up.

The company turned out to be just like its advertising—human, direct, authentic, creative, and responsive. Back then it had a dedicated page on its website with quirky personal profiles of all 12 people in the company. If you visit MyEmmas's website today, it still has a profile of every single one of the company's more than 100 employees, and the profiles are in alphabetic, not hierarchical, order.

I identified with MyEmma right away. Like it, TLC at that time was small and fighting for mindshare in a noisy marketplace of giants. We didn't have direct competitors per se, but we had a number of tangential competitors who created quite a bit of noise with the customers. I had a hunch that one of our distinguishing characteristics should be the unique personalities and people within the company and that we should showcase that. Not everyone agreed. Some of my colleagues at the time argued it would reveal how small we were, that big companies wouldn't take us seriously, and that the market would think we were too fragile and unreliable in the long term.

I felt that there was something inauthentic about concealing the real people and engine behind the product. I wanted to be proud of our size and ability to be nimble and responsive. Ultimately, customers came to know everyone in the company—our individual strengths and passions— and as a result, felt a stronger allegiance and relationship with us.

START WITH GOOD INTENTIONS

In an interview, writer and entrepreneur David Penglase, who is based in Sydney, suggested to me that a key success factor for salespeople is going beyond appealing to customers on the basis of their product's uniqueness, its features that will make the customer buy based on emotion, or how it links customers to a social community, such as Facebook.[2] Instead, salespeople should ask themselves *why* they are selling what they're selling. He believes that there is an economic value—"intentionomics"—within the intention of salespeople when they sell something.

As Penglase described in our interview, "I know that the one true differentiator of all people is . . . when people tap into a higher belief, a higher purpose, a higher intention." If potential customers know that a salesperson genuinely wants to know how his or her product can help them—if that's the salesperson's intention, he says, "there'll be a stronger connection and a stronger engagement."

Our customers want us to solve their problems or offer them a needed product or service. If a salesperson's primary intent is deriving profit from a customer instead of solving the customer's problem, the customer will recognize that. If we have the right intentions, and our actions come from those intentions, then even if mistakes are made, the customer is more likely to be forgiving and to continue to trust us in the future. Our good intentions and integrity are something that customers can feel. In this highly visible and competitive age, as information and power continue to shift from the seller to the buyer, people increasingly care about not only what they buy but who they buy from and how that company conducts its business.

INVITE NEW VOICES TO THE TABLE—THEN LISTEN

TLC never felt hierarchical. Although we did have clear division of expertise, we rarely siloed activities and functions—that is, kept them self-contained and independent from the others. As a result, we benefited enormously from the disparate perspectives we always invited to discussions.

In chapter 3, I related the story Matt May told me about how leaders at Toyota thought that the company had an open culture, with all voices heard. Through a problem-solving exercise the leaders learned that this was not the case, that ideas of junior employees were ignored. I spoke to Juan (not his real name), a senior information-technology leader at a large financial services organization, who had a similar experience, but his voice *was* heard. Recently, he was puzzled to be invited to a meeting with two of his colleagues from different departments who were trying to solve a business dilemma. As Juan sat through the opening comments of the meeting, he kept wondering silently what in the world he was doing there. He was leading the IT group, and clearly what these players needed was a business decision structure that had nothing to do with his team.

Despite his puzzlement at why he was invited, Juan stayed and listened intently and shared his best ideas and suggestions during the course of the meeting. Within just a couple days, Juan was included in some follow-up notes and found his colleagues had agreed and implemented the ideas discussed at the meeting.

Juan later discovered, in water cooler and cafeteria conversations, that it was his presence and divergent opinions and perspectives that bridged the understanding gap among his colleagues, who had been too close to the project to see and execute the solution needed. Building a signature solution means listening to all the voices that make our organizations unique.

FUEL PASSIONS

At TLC, everyone on our team naturally had his or her own unique identity, skillset, and passion. As a team, we worked to constantly allow and reinforce assignments that naturally gravitated to the person with the skills best suited for the task at hand.

An early exercise we conducted to explore aspirations within the company stuck with me. In an off-site working session, we asked all team members to name their greatest hopes and fears. My own fear was that TLC would increasingly consume my life. As it was, it was all I thought about and talked about, at home and at work, taking over nearly every minute of my day.

My greatest hope was that the company would thrive and enable me and everyone else the freedom—economically, professionally, and personally—to grow and not feel encumbered (as I was beginning to feel) by the demands of responsibility. Others said they hoped for a particular key contract, or to build close personal bonds in the process of working together.

In all, the exercise yielded a more open and honest discussion of who we were individually and how we could contribute collaboratively to make a difference. It gave us all a much deeper understanding of the motivating factors within our own lives, and in turn led to collaboration on projects in which all participants felt their strengths were in play and their personal long-term interests were respected.

COLLABORATE WITH CUSTOMERS, BUT BE TRUE TO YOUR VISION

When we at TLC set out to design and build our delivery engine, we didn't conduct elaborate interviews or in-depth surveys with customers to discover their functionality preferences. I had seen exercises in idea solicitation that led to a few suggestions that ended up wagging the dog.

Don't misunderstand—we certainly had a core group of key clients with whom we were working and sharing ideas about development of the new platform, so we weren't working in a vacuum. In partnership with our external designers, we would develop a version, share it with a select client group, and then listen carefully to their comments and suggestions. We would then incorporate the ideas that made sense, so the development was collaborative and in partnership with the customer, who was the stakeholder, yet the finished result was clearly recognizable as developed by our team and distinctive to our customers.

AVOID COGNITIVE BIAS BY DROPPING ANCHORS CAREFULLY

From years of leading product-development teams, I've learned that dropping ideas in the middle of conversations certainly has an anchoring effect—it creates a reference point by which future ideas are measured—and it's not always a positive one. For example, a few years ago the owners of a supermarket in Sioux Falls, South Dakota, experimented with putting a marketing label next to cans of soup. Some days the label read "10% off regular price, limit 10 per customer," and on other days it read "10% off regular price, no limit per customer." Shoppers purchased twice as many on the days with limitations. The sense of scarcity created an anchoring effect, and the number ten set a mental anchor of the amount of cans shoppers should buy. Faced with the limited availability, they felt an urge to buy more.

Similarly, if I ask you, "Is the oldest dog in the world older or younger than 60 years?" and then I ask you, "How old is the oldest dog?" your answer will be higher than if I just ask, "How old is the oldest dog in the world?" You know intuitively that a dog living 60 years is completely nuts, but hearing the idea put forth will still likely have a psychological priming effect and sway your guess upwards—significantly upwards, it turns out. Your dog-age guess will likely be more than a decade above what your guess would have been without the suggestion of a 60-year-old dog.

Mental anchors are everywhere and are used quite effectively in negotiations. The example of the 60-year-old dog is adopted from an example in Daniel Kahneman's book *Thinking, Fast and Slow*.[3] In discussing the anchoring effect, he also points out that we are much more susceptible to psychological anchors during times of stress and anxiety. If we are in a stressful state and someone suggests a point of direction, or an idea to consider, we are much more likely to accept and build on that idea, instead of patiently and thoughtfully questioning it.

In another Kahneman-type example, if I'm nervous and someone asks me a question, even a ridiculous one—such as "Is your arm getting numb?"—I'm far more likely to believe my arm might actually be getting numb than reject such a nutty suggestion.

Recently when our team at Skillsoft was actively debating what to call a new product, we sent an e-mail to our executive group advising them of our current thinking and progress. One executive, whose opinion everyone trusts and listens to, sent his vote in an e-mail reply. On our next call, someone on our team said, "Well that's frustrating! I guess we have to call it what he wants now."

I was very clear in responding, saying, "Not so fast. We own this project, not him, and in this situation his vote has no greater or lesser value than anyone else's." It's important to reinforce with the vested team members the belief that they own the project, and that not even suggestions from higher-ups should be allowed to derail that process.

As the example above shows, suggestions can be interpreted as orders, and we need to be careful about when we drop mental anchors that close creative processes and stifle the emergence of signature solutions. However, there are times when dropping anchors can be quite useful. These are the moments when we are ready to make the transition from brainstorming to execution, when intentionally dropping mental anchors can expedite that shift.

AVOID THE POISONING EFFECT OF POWER

Deborah Gruenfeld, from the University of California, Berkeley, conducted a research study in which students were brought together in groups of three.[4] One student was chosen as the "boss" or arbiter, and the other two were asked to construct solutions to various issues on campus, such as making the campus more green or improving transportation or cafeteria services. The task itself was a red herring. What interested the researchers most was the effect that the power just bestowed on the newly appointed "boss" had on the group's dynamics.

In a session in which the "boss" was asked to evaluate the quality of the proposals from each of the two other students, the researchers brought in a plate of five cookies. After each student took a cookie, two were left. Every culture is aware of the social taboo against taking the last cookie, so the cookie that's in play here is the fourth. Consistently, the appointed "bosses" on each team were much more likely to take the fourth cookie, and to exhibit "disinhibited eating," that is, chewing with their mouths open and leaving more crumbs.

A sure way to kill an emerging signature solution is to fall prey to such power poisoning, in which those placed in a position of power begin to believe that their ideas are more important than those working under them.

LET'S RECAP

Remember . . .

- A signature innovative solution is born of the core identity of those who have joined in the innovation journey, executed with the unique personalities of participants, and sustained by the mission of the organization. Signature innovation is not easily copied or pirated, because it comes out of a truly unique cultural identity within an organization—one that seeks, listens to, and acts on the best ideas of customers and the people who comprise the innovative enterprise.

- Most businesses follow best practices, but signature innovation goes beyond this. Signature innovation values and amplifies the unique engine behind it—the founding legacy and identity of the company, the unique personalities involved in its process, and the core sustaining beliefs of the leadership team.

- A company with signature solutions will get unique products to market faster and establish brand loyalty because it doesn't get bogged down in copying others or creating commodity products. Signature innovations are based on a unique blend of individual and organizational personalities, intentions, and convictions.

Your Turn Now . . .

Reach in: You have a personal, unique contribution within your leadership or peer group. Consider how the members of this group would describe your unique contribution to your company's signature solutions. The next time you meet with this group, view each person through a lens of "unique contribution." Take time to remind each person of what you value about his or her unique contributions to the group's efforts.

Reach out: Describe the concept of "signature" for your team, emphasizing that a signature solution originates from the founding legacy of the company, is refined by the unique personalities of those involved, and sustained by the core values of the leadership team. Select an issue, project, or goal that your team is currently working on. Discuss specific actions and behaviors the team demonstrates that fit the signature definition. Identify how the team—and company leaders—can ramp up efforts to make the team's work product more of a signature innovation.

Spread out: List known vendors, suppliers, or customers who have a unique signature innovation. Ask a member of any of these companies to share his or her stories with you and your team members.

In advance and with your team, prepare questions about the invited company's legacy and history, and how people (inside and outside the company) brought their unique skills and personalities to the table.

Remember . . .

- Signature innovations benefit from the inclusion of new voices and disparate perspectives, even those that come from "left field." These perspectives often bridge gaps in understanding and make something interesting happen.

- Questioning deeply and seeking to understand personal aspirations, intentions, hopes, and fears help uncover passions and skills that people can contribute in areas beyond current assignments and activities.

- When asking customers and stakeholders for input, it's wise to be selective, gathering and implementing suggestions and ideas that are relevant. Similarly, suggestions from superiors can stifle signature solutions. While customer, stakeholder, and leadership inputs are important, the team's intuitions and direction have remarkable value.

- Dropping anchors into conversations can provide mental reference points and help individuals and teams rally around and build on ideas. During times of stress or anxiety, mental anchors are most effective, being more readily accepted and acted upon. Leaders should drop anchors carefully, however, protecting the community voice and allowing space for considered contribution.

Your Turn Now . . .

Reach in: List your responsibilities and accountabilities related to a budding "signature" solution or innovation. Then pepper each of those responsibilities with a statement about your aspirations, intentions, convictions, hopes, and passions. If these are presently untapped, take action to bring them into your work efforts. They may have more impact on innovation than simply performing your assignments.

Reach out: In your meetings with team members, ask about more than just their current goals and accountabilities. Ask about personal aspirations, intentions, convictions, hopes, and passions. Discuss how to tap into, leverage, or build upon the capacity and creativity of each person. If team members have difficulty articulating their personal passions, drop a mental anchor into the conversation, such as "Would you say you're passionate about being part of a team?" or "Are you passionate about meeting tough goals?"

Spread out: Identify a person in the organization who holds a great deal of personal or positional power. Ask that person to comment on a team problem or effort, especially one that has the potential to be a signature innovation. Keep your questions general, such as: "What do you think about the idea of . . .?" or "What are your hopes and fears about . . .?" Probe responses to obtain as much specificity as possible. Take good notes and sort out the responses into those that are "guiding" or "potentially poisoning." Share comments with your team that will encourage, support, and motivate them. Hold back on the other comments until you feel you must share them. Let the team grapple with the issues first.

CHAPTER 11

PURPOSE: CONNECT WITH "WHY"

The idea that the sole purpose of the corporation is to create shareholder value is like saying the sole purpose of a human being is to maximize your breaths. It's not a purpose.... [T]he end goal of a corporation, its purpose, is to provide goods and services, and to do that in a way that's sustainable.
—*Rakesh Khurana, Harvard Business School*

More than five years ago, my cycling partner and friend, Erich, contacted me and suggested we should ride in the three-day, 180-mile Trek Across Maine. It seemed like a reasonable and fun challenge, and all for a good cause—to fight lung cancer. I was in. Then Erich added, "We're taking the boys."

He has two boys, Ian and Owen, just about the same age as my two boys (five and seven years old at the time), and I realized immediately this whole expedition had multiplied in complexity. Understand that Erich is a friend whose intensity and drive is higher than most people I know. When invited to ride with him, I learned early on that a "ride" often meant going about twice as far and twice as intensely as I had envisioned. I learned to calibrate expectations to Erich's world, but this audacious challenge was something new.

We rigged up bicycle contraptions featuring a tandem bicycle, plus a "tag-along" (pictured below) to accommodate the three of us. The machine, plus the bicycle bags (panniers)—loaded with rain gear, snacks, water, and probably a few miscellaneous things the kids claimed to need—all weighed in at more than four hundred pounds with us onboard. This was our "triple-bike."

My mental orientation going into this venture was that it was my job to do the work and make sure the kids were safe, fed, dry, and (I hoped) having fun on this expedition. But it quickly became clear, with our covering more than 60 miles per day through the hills across Maine, that their effort was valuable indeed.

While the boys were small, when they chose to pedal, I could definitely feel a difference. Although I started the journey thinking we would accomplish the trek on the strength of my efforts alone, it quickly became clear that the difference they made when they contributed was not only in increased speed and energy conservation, it was also in camaraderie and real teamwork—how well we worked as a team to push through the effort of going over hill after hill on these three days.

For example, when approaching a hill—as my son Will was back there throwing water on his brother and generally goofing off—I could say sternly, "If you don't pedal *now*, then at the top of this hill I'm going to put you in the sag wagon[1] and you can ride the rest of the way in the *wagon of shame!*" This terse warning might motivate him to pedal harder for perhaps 30–60 seconds.

Inversely, using more positive encouragement, I could urge my son Charlie on by saying, "Buddy, if you pedal really hard, we'll get to the top quicker, and I think they are serving ice cream at the next rest stop!" This also might bring an energetic minute or so of focused pedaling.

It became clear, as the hours went by and the ride went on, that there were a number of more powerful motivators that were much more effective, and fun. It turned out that what I had vastly under-estimated—completely overlooked, actually—was the importance of my boys doing this journey with Erich and his boys, their friends. My kids would constantly be aware of where our friends were on the road, either ahead or behind, and we would create ways to interact by riding alongside and chatting, or goading each other to go faster up the hills. And often we would encounter, and ride with, other participants in the event, which fostered a great sense of communal participation.

After the first year that we participated in the Trek Across Maine, when the boys were five and seven years old, respectively, I decided they needed a deeper and more direct understanding of why we were doing the event. To accomplish this, we rode the triple-bike around the neighborhood before the next year's event. The boys knocked on doors, told the story about what we were doing, and asked for donations to help fight lung cancer. That active participation in gathering donations for the event connected the boys, and our family, with the deeper reason of *why* we were participating.

Connecting with friends and with the purpose of the journey—two small, simple changes in mental orientation—created a powerful sense of engagement in the event and translated into big pedal power (read: team performance gains).

UNDERSTAND A GREATER WHY WITH THE RIGHT MINDSET

Christopher Wren (1632–1723) was a famous English architect and builder. As legend has it, he was walking past three stonecutters working on the rebuilding of St. Paul's Cathedral. He asked them what they were doing.

The first worker said, "I am earning six pence a day."

The second worker said, "I am cutting this stone true and square."

The third worker said, "I am helping Sir Christopher Wren build St. Paul's Cathedral."

Business models, manufacturing and distribution processes, brand loyalties, pricing strategies, and even profits are not why companies exist. Companies have these operational mechanisms, and other trappings as a function of existing, but to survive, companies must provide products and services that the market recognizes as valuable, and do so on a sustainable basis.

To do this, companies need the committed creativity and involved passion and initiative of human beings. The surest way of gaining this is to connect people with a greater sense of purpose. No matter how mundane or utilitarian an employee's task may seem, the greatest leaders can help connect that task, and that person, to a greater sense of meaning.

Many business schools recognize this and are adopting teaching philosophies to emphasize to our next generation of business leaders the importance of connecting with a higher purpose, a sense of meaningful progress in their work. The most successful leaders do this intuitively. Great American military generals don't ask soldiers to think about being better marksmen, but rather about defending the Constitution and protecting a way of life.

Rakesh Khurana, the Marvin Bower professor of leadership development at Harvard Business School, described in an interview I had with him in late 2011 how the global financial collapse of 2008 was visible evidence of the erosion of business integrity and dissolution of trust in the marketplace that began with the notorious Enron scandal of 2000.[2] In 2010, he and some colleagues—fellow Harvard Business School professor Rob Kaplan, dean Nitin Nohria, and Thunderbird School of Global Management president Ángel Cabrera—established an initiative, The Oath Project, in an effort to reverse this trend.

The idea of The Oath Project is to encourage graduates to take an oath upon graduation—similar to the Hippocratic oath that physicians take or the oath that lawyers must take to be admitted to a state bar association—that commits them to demonstrating responsible behavior in their business careers. The project's vision statement reads as follows:

> The Oath Project envisions a day when business leaders will hold themselves to the higher standard of integrity and service to society that is the hallmark of a true professional. At this day, both the schools that prepare them and the organizations in which they work will understand the reach, responsibility, and impact managers have on the wellbeing of people inside and outside their organizations.

Once they launched The Oath Project, the professors received some anticipated critiques. Some professionals from health and law communities suggested that creating an oath for business similar to the Hippocratic or lawyer's oath wouldn't work because all businesses are not focused on the welfare of the public as the health care or legal professions are. Such an oath would create a false equivalency with these professions, the argument went.

In our interview, Khurana said he anticipated this kind of critique, but a more troubling one was emerging from some people within businesses—that an oath for business represented a kind of constraint. The argument against The Oath Project was that it shouldn't challenge a company's inherent right to chase profit as its singular purpose. Justification of such an argument included the notion that pursuit of profit would allow for "giving back" later.

The tacit assumption in this argument is that businesses need not actually create sustainable social value because that would happen later, after the profit, after the dividends. Then, while luxuriating in wealth, businesses would give consideration to creating real value.

Should we in business create sustainable value to the larger community, or should our sole motive be profit for individuals? I, and many others in business, say the answer is we should look beyond profit. Ultimately innovative products that have lasting value in the world must be connected to a larger purpose—one beyond self or financial gain—that serves the community touched. Why? Because with purpose we bring something of greater value to our community—local, national, or global.

LET PURPOSE DRIVE INNOVATION

Of the many stories about businesses that were envisioned and have succeeded because of a larger sense of purpose, that of Iqbal Quadir, director of the Legatum Center for Development and Entrepreneurship at Massachusetts Institute of Technology, encompasses the entire arc of the Out Think journey. It starts when he was quite young, growing up with his siblings in a village in Bangladesh.

In an interview in December 2011, Quadir told me of his mother's asking him, when he was quite young, to walk about six miles to another village to fetch medicine.[3] He spent all morning walking to the village only to discover the doctor was out attending to patients in other villages and retrieving supplies. So Quadir spent the afternoon walking home with his pockets empty.

Years later, after moving to the United States and receiving degrees from Wharton, Quadir became a Wall Street banker. He recalls having another unproductive day in the early 1990s transporting data across Manhattan on floppy disks (remember floppies?). Mobile phones—expensive, heavy, and with scarce connectivity—were still in their infancy. But understanding Moore's Law (in the development of computing hardware, the number of transistors on integrated circuits doubles approximately every two years), Quadir knew that in the coming years mobile phones would become cheap, powerful, and ubiquitous. If this was to be true, he reasoned, why not begin the journey now to provide mobile phones to villagers in his home country of Bangladesh?

In Bangladesh, a source of entrepreneurial capital might be a cow or goat to provide milk to sell or convert to cheese. If having a cow or a goat could be the seed of an entrepreneurial venture in a Bangladesh village, then why couldn't a cellphone be one also? As Quadir put it, "Why can't the cellphone be like a cow?"

Why couldn't people in rural environments in Bangladesh use mobile telecommunications technology as an entrepreneurial technology, just as many use land, livestock, and other local resources to start small businesses? If land could yield crops to sell, or a goat to harvest milk and cheese to sell, Quadir rationalized that someone could take out a micro-loan to purchase a mobile phone that could be shared—rented—by members of the community. In this way, a mobile phone could be an asset to an entire village. As Quadir likes to say, "Connectivity is productivity."

Quadir took this argument to Grameen Bank, a micro-credit lender that could realize the potential, as well as to Telenor telecommunications of Norway, which could help provide the infrastructure. As of this writing, Grameenphone has nearly 40 million subscribers and is still expanding.

This system of microlending has vastly increased the productivity and standard of living of the people of Bangladesh, spawned an untold number of entrepreneurial ventures employing cellphones, and of course brought some wealth to Grameen Bank and Telenor. But the impetus for such an innovative initiative started with Quadir's recognition that connectivity equals productivity, and his strong sense of purpose and meaning in giving back to his native country.

RETURN TO YOUR VISION WHEN THINGS GO WRONG

When we lose sight of our purpose, things can go bad quickly. Consider how Merck lost its way. In 1995, CEO Ray Gilmartin described the principal driver for Merck as growth—not profitability, not cutting-edge scientific breakthroughs, nor medical innovation or R&D, but *growth*. That intent continued into 2000, when the chairman's letter to shareholders stated, "As a company, Merck is totally focused on growth."

At the time, Merck had good reason to believe it could in fact accomplish this goal. They were on the cusp of releasing the FDA-approved drug Vioxx which Merck had patented. By 2002, Vioxx sales worldwide approached $2.5 billion, which represented significant growth indeed. But in the same time period, studies were finding an alarming relationship between Vioxx and an increase in "cardiovascular thrombotic events"—heart attacks and strokes.

In 2008, the *New York Times* published an article revealing that research papers on Vioxx were often ghostwritten by Merck writers and then published under the byline of prestigious doctors and scientists in an effort to substantiate the value and public perception of Merck and Vioxx.[4] By early 2005, the FDA had officially attributed up to 139,000 deaths to Vioxx and unofficial estimates ranged upwards from 250,000 globally, although statistics are difficult to gather in developing nations.[5]

While Gilmartin laudably ordered Merck to voluntarily remove Vioxx from the market in the fall of 2004, sending the company's stock from $45 to $33 a share, one must wonder if Merck's goal behind producing Vioxx served the vision of George Merck II. Pursuit of profit over value, of growth over service, can destroy even the mightiest of companies. The company eventually rebounded by learning the lesson that, if we remember the core vision and values, money will follow. Many organizations have suffered from hubris, conceit, and denial of risk, yet returned from the brink of disaster by returning to their core vision.[6]

CONNECT INDIVIDUALS TO PURPOSE

I've had quite a few conversations over the past couple years with executives, authors, and researchers on this contemporary buzzword "engagement." What I find is different versions of the talent manager or executive or team leader trying to articulate a clearer story around selling the company to employees so they will become more "engaged."

They will talk about emphasizing the *why* of what the company does, emphasizing the core vision, mission, and values in the hopes that it will resonate with employees and get them more engaged, more in the game. The CEO will emphasize the altruistic charity work the company contributes to the community in the hopes that its employees might latch on to that with a comforted sense that the company is making a difference locally. Or the CEO will emphasize how the products or services are making a remarkable difference for the customer. The business gurus suggest that employees should be comforted and heartened by the knowledge that the product they are contributing to matters to the customers they serve.

Here's the thing: no matter how hard we try to sell the company to our employees, they still won't buy it until they are sold on who *they* are.

Until people find their own "why"—their own reason for doing what they do—they aren't going to buy the why of their boss or the why of the company they work for. Until people feel wholly fulfilled, focused, and energized by their own core personal mission and focus, they aren't going to care completely about their employer's version of why.

This isn't necessarily about helping people find their strengths, but rather about helping them find what makes them *feel* strong as a person. I might be strong on Excel pivot tables, but that's not likely to make me feel personally strong, fulfilled, or focused on my personal aspirations.

Develop a Global Culture of Shared Values

Don Vanthournout is the chief learning officer of Accenture, a premier global management-services and advisory organization with more than 259,000 associates in almost 50 different countries around the world. Accenture is perhaps not unlike other multinational companies, except that it has no clear headquarters. Accenture's CEOs over the past few years have been based in Paris, Boston, Palo Alto, and Dallas. Its executives operate globally, and its associates are expected to adopt a nimble and global world view. They're supposed to remain effective and adhere to the Accenture philosophy regardless of where they work. How can such a globally dispersed workforce, with no clear headquarters and a CEO with no nationalistic identity, have a strongly held, shared vision?

As Vanthournout explains, the company starts with a simple and clear set of values as its behavioral principles.[7] Accenture ingrains these values in all associates, so regardless of where they are working in the world, the associates' values and behavior are guided by them. As he put it:

> We build core skills into our people on how we want them to collaborate and communicate with each other, how we want them to manage projects, but we're never going to be able to guess every situation that might confront them. And so the why of why you spend so much time focusing on the value side of things is so that we can develop people who, when they're thrown in that situation that they might not have been prepared explicitly for from a content standpoint, will from a contextual standpoint know how to operate in alignment with what Accenture values.

Next, according to Vanthournout, Accenture operates under a principle of facilitating job mobility and growth. As the chief learning officer, Vanthournout knows that people participate at their highest level of engagement and collaboration when they are doing work they love. When a position becomes tedious, he says, it's time to look for growth opportunities. Accenture recognizes the need of its employees for constant development and creates opportunities for them to fill that need. Vanthournout's recommendation is to start local—ask friends and colleagues for advice in developing oneself.

When it comes to aspiration, those around us will understand and help place us in developing positions only if we voice our opinions and ideas about our own best career trajectory. Accenture has worked to build a culture in which managers are expected to identify and listen closely to the development aspirations of associates, with the recognition that those best placed will ultimately perform at their highest level and realize their greatest potential.

Understand that It's Not about the Money or the Credit

Michael Norton, of Harvard Business School, and his colleagues Elizabeth Dunn and Lara Aknin, of the University of British Columbia, researched the relationship between how we spend money and our own subjective levels of happiness. They published their findings in *Science* in 2008.[8] The researchers explored the paradox that, although people spend so much of their time and effort trying to make more and more money, having all that money does not seem to make them happy.

The researchers found that money can buy us happiness—if we spend it on someone else. For example, in studying the impact of receiving bonuses, they found that spending part of the bonus—even as little as five dollars—on others ("prosocial spending") clearly increased the giver's well-being:

Employees who devoted more of their bonus to prosocial spending experienced greater happiness after receiving the bonus, and the manner in which they spent that bonus was a more important predictor of their happiness than the size of the bonus itself.

The Towers Watson Global Workforce Study showed that the main goals for employees were opportunities for growth, fairness, and a balance between professional life and personal life. Employees had to feel that they were contributing and had to feel good about their company and themselves.

Truly creative people are intrinsically motivated. They are working for the sheer joy of it, because they are passionate about and enjoy their work, and because it gives them a great deal of inner satisfaction. In an April 1971 article in the *Journal of Personality and Social Psychology*, Edward Deci reported that his research showed that offering external rewards actually undermined intrinsic motivation.[9]

Other studies have found that intrinsic motivation increases as participants' options and choices in a particular activity increase. Thus, for best results, people need to be allowed to choose what task or activity to engage in next, which team to collaborate with, and what techniques to use.

When we are intrinsically motivated—aiming to do good things for our organization, community, or environment rather than seeking credit—good things happen. My parents, Hal and Beverly Hunter, live in Rappahannock County, a small, rural Virginia community. They have formed and supported several nonprofit organizations in the county aimed at helping the community and the environment. In 2009, the local newspaper, *Rappahannock News*, selected them for its Citizens of the Year award, because, as the December 31 article about their selection put it, they

> put in countless hours looking after the continued health of Rappahannock's watersheds, its farms and viewsheds, its hungry people, and its educational and arts communities. They have done so quietly, relentlessly—and cheerfully.

Such recognition came out of their actions, but recognition wasn't the reason they did what they did in the community. As Hal likes to say, "There's no limit to what you can accomplish if you don't care who gets the credit." It's an apt saying for those aspiring to accomplish remarkable things. With such aspirations, not only can we bring success to our team and our organization, but we can also effect change in our community and the rest of the world.

Ultimately we must ask ourselves, "Does my work matter? Am I making a difference?" It's important that we abandon pervasive selfish attitudes that dominate contemporary thinking—the "what's in it for me?" attitude. Instead we should focus on what we can contribute—how we can ease suffering and enlighten others through offering our time, energy, and friendship. In his work, Hal sees time and again that those who give without concern or interest for themselves always wind up healthier and happier spiritually, and consequently richer economically.

Help Others Find Their Own Personal "Why"

One of the most important and profound gifts we can give to people who work for us is the opportunity to explore and discover their own personal "why." As leaders, instead of investing in learning opportunities that only make people better at doing the tasks, chores, and duties associated with the company's stated outcomes, we must also invest in development opportunities that help people figure out who they are and what they want to accomplish.

We might lose a few people along the way. They might have an epiphany about their values and their greater personal mission in the world and leave the company. That's okay. We should let them go, with our blessing. We've helped them shape their sense of purpose, and they will likely be more productive in an environment that better suits their personal goals.

Make Big Connections to Purpose through Small Interventions

Just a small shift in thinking, in mindset, to help people connect with their own why can translate into immense performance gains. The research of Adam Grant, a talented young professor at the Wharton School, demonstrates this.

A few years ago, Grant led a study in which he worked with a group of students at the University of Michigan.[10] These students were earning a little extra cash by making cold calls to alumni to raise money that would go to scholarship funds for students who were accepted at the university but couldn't afford the tuition.

After observing their behavior and performance for two weeks, Grant and his colleagues divided the students into three separate groups and had them perform activities for just ten minutes before their shifts. The first group could spend that time however they pleased and had no interaction with scholarship beneficiaries. The second group had indirect interactions with beneficiaries of the scholarship fund. They were asked to read letters for a few minutes from people who had benefited from the scholarship fund on which they were working and then talk about the contents of the letter with their peers for a couple minutes.

The third group was also given a handful of letters to read together, but after a few minutes in the break room, they got a surprise. The call organizer would announce that a special guest had arrived to speak with them. This special guest was a real recipient of the scholarship fund on which the students were working. For just a few minutes, the students talked directly with the beneficiary. They could ask questions such as where they were from, what classes they were taking, and what they intended to do after they graduated. At the conclusion of the meeting, the organizer would say, "Remember this when you're on the phone—this is someone you're supporting."

That's it—a five-minute intervention to connect the callers with the impact, the difference, the real goal of their work. The result? A 142 percent increase in persistence (time spent on the phone), and a 171 percent increase in revenue performance (money raised), sustained over a month after that single intervention—171 percent better than their peers who had no direct contact with the beneficiaries.

Just as in this example, we often find that larger purpose when we take the time to talk to the people who actually consume, touch, experience, contact what we offer or what we create. It reminds us of why we do what we do, and prompts us to continually ask ourselves, "Will what we do lead to higher quality, excellence in craftsmanship, and a better relationship with our customers?"

As Grant's study shows, touching base with customers to remind us of the larger purpose of what we do can also lead to higher performance. How does 171 percent higher sound?

When we act despite uncertainty, and encourage others to take action amidst uncertainty, we not only strengthen and grow our own skills but also reinforce the confidence in others to take action. When we inspire those around us to take initiative and to sustain that action and momentum, we must always remember the most powerful motivating factor is a sense of progress in meaningful work. By celebrating and reinforcing a clear sense of measurable progress, we ensure not only progress itself, but heightened sense of meaningful productivity of those around us.[11]

And finally, measurable growth of talent is built through intentional challenge and adversity. Unless we are reaching and stretching ourselves in both our behaviors and beliefs, we will fall short of our own potential. To encourage ourselves and those around us to step further, we should focus our inquiry and action on the real impact we intend to make. As shown in Adam Grant's work, when we connect emotionally and empathetically with the envisioned future impact of what we offer to our customers and community through our work, we connect with the why of what we do.

LET'S RECAP

Remember . . .

- In any endeavor, there should be a purpose behind it if we are to receive maximum enjoyment, fulfillment, and a deeper sense of our own role in its achievement. Working as a team optimizes collective effort-sharing, camaraderie, and combined contribution toward the goal or purpose.

- Business models, manufacturing and distribution processes, brand loyalties, pricing strategies, and even profits are not why companies exist. These are merely operational mechanisms of their existence.

To survive, companies must provide products and services that the market sees value in, on a sustainable basis. This demands a commitment to creativity and the involved passion and initiative of human beings. And the surest way to achieve this is to instill in people a greater sense of purpose and meaning—which the great leader can do.

- The global financial collapse of 2008 was evidence of erosion of business integrity and dissolution of trust in the marketplace. Many companies now reinforce and demonstrate a commitment to responsible behavior and purposeful practices that go beyond profit and individual gain and provide greater value to the local, national, or global community.

Your Turn Now . . .

Reach in: Recall the story of the workers rebuilding the cathedral, and how each worker described what he was doing. Imagine someone approaching you when you are performing your leadership role. What would you say *you* were doing? Reflect on your answer and take it to the highest level of purpose that feels authentic and meaningful to you.

Reach out: Tell the story of The Oath Project to your team and ask them how they would customize the oath of having "reach, responsibility, and impact" on the people inside and outside their organization. Discuss the value of having an oath that helps connect them to a greater purpose and how they might use an oath to inspire their work efforts. Have a healthy discussion about values, purpose, and the importance of understanding the team's impact on others. Be prepared to address questions about results, profits, and other hard measures—they are important, but not without purpose.

Spread out: Working from your team's greater purpose and their collective reach, responsibility, and impact, put words into action. Ask your team to agree to undertake a volunteer activity, work project, or any manifestation of their team's purpose. Provide some reasonable parameters. For example: it can be accomplished in a few hours, must involve all team members, or must include others in the organization. Try to keep the parameters as flexible as possible so it is the team's effort—not yours. Make sure to have a debriefing on the activity and discuss not only what happened but how people felt about it.

Remember . . .

- Losing sight of our purpose, pursuing profit over value, or promoting growth over service can lead to things going wrong very quickly. If we remember the core vision and values of our companies, money will follow. Many companies have learned this the hard way.

- Effective leaders know that just selling the company to employees will not result in true engagement. Employees must experience who *they* are and discover their personal vision and purpose in their work. Leaders can help individuals find their strengths and be more fulfilled, focused, and energized by their core personal mission and function within the organization. Remember that the most powerful motivating factor is a sense of progress in meaningful work.

- A culture of shared values gives every employee a context for his or her work, and conveys the behaviors and skills expected by all members of the organization. This might include how to communicate, collaborate, manage projects, and deal with unexpected or uncertain situations. When employees face uncertainty and adversity, shared values and a sense of purpose help them stretch and reach their potential. Shared values support individuals in making decisions, taking more initiative, and being more innovative.

- Although people spend an inordinate amount of time trying to make money, having it does not necessarily make them happy. Truly creative people are intrinsically motivated, working for the sheer joy of it. As people's options and choices increase, so does intrinsic motivation. Choice of tasks and activities should be encouraged, as well as which team to work with, and what techniques to employ.

- We often discover a larger purpose when we talk to people who actually consume, touch, experience, and contact what we offer to create. It reminds us of why we do what we do. It leads to higher quality, integrity, and excellence of craftsmanship, and to a better relationship with our customers—and higher performance.

Your Turn Now . . .

Reach in: Admit that there are times when you fall prey to striving for profit, growth, and making money. These are not evil pursuits, but can be dangerous when sought without a sense of purpose, vision, and value. Review your performance requirements and associated measures. For each one, attach a statement of purpose, meaning, or value. For example, if you are measured on achieving a certain number of sales or reducing a percentage of costs, identify what the bigger purpose or value is of each of those goal attainments.

Reach out: Start with your immediate work group to develop a small set (four to six) of meaningful shared values. You can do this with your direct reports or a peer group. If your organization has a set of values for all employees, customize them to apply to your team or work group's purpose. Turn each value into representative behaviors, describing what it "looks like" when a person demonstrates the value. For example, if a team values accountability, describe the behavior of an accountable person. Complete the sentence "An accountable person . . ." or "A person is accountable when he or she. . . ."

Spread out: Allow members of your team to play a role or perform a task that they don't ordinarily do but which has interest and meaning for them. Provide some choices or ideas, such as visiting a customer, attending a leadership meeting, working on a problem with another group, teaching something, or attending a short workshop on a subject of interest.

CHAPTER 12

SUSTAINING THE INNOVATIVE MINDSET

Don't stumble over something behind you.

—*Seneca the Younger*

I have a confession. I used to be a tyrant in the morning. Tyrant might be an exaggeration (or not), but my recollection is that, in getting the kids ready for school, I spent all of my energy cajoling, prodding, pleading, scolding, and sometimes ranting at them—to put on their shoes, eat their breakfast, brush their teeth, get dressed, put their lunch in their backpacks, etc.—because *the bus is coming!* My wife has a different, and more effective, style, but on my mornings to handle bus time I would conduct diatribes on the inevitability of the bus and rant that, unlike procrastinating in getting in the car, the bus is coming at an appointed time and they needed to *hurry up!*

One evening after berating myself again for being an ogre of a parent, I decided that the next morning I just wasn't going to behave that way again. I resolved that regardless of whether they missed the bus or not, I simply was not going to be a jerk to my kids. While a nice idea, this did require that I adopt another behavior—to simply advise them of the time and ask them what the next steps were. Instead of "Get your lunch in your bag!" I might say, "Looks like we have about 14 minutes. Is your bag ready?" Or if my daughter, Annie, asked me to play Taylor Swift songs on the kitchen iPod stereo, I might say, "Well, we have about 20 minutes.

Do you think we have time?" Sometimes she decided we did have time to listen to Taylor Swift, sometimes not.

It really worked. On the first few days we had a few close calls catching the bus, but the strategy worked. I would simply point out the time, and almost immediately they learned to watch the clock and developed an awareness of when the bus—which is quite punctual— would arrive. My whole demeanor changed from dictatorial bus baron to simply asking what was left on their checklist in the next X minutes. I would ask if they brushed their teeth or packed their homework, but not command them to do so.

I'm also convinced this shift in my morning behavior worked because I truly didn't care if they missed the bus. I was completely prepared to drive them, but I never admitted it out loud. I kept up the shared expectation that we always ride the bus. I just shifted the accountability from me to them. Making the bus became their responsibility; I was just there to help the process.

Believe me, my wife and I don't claim to be model parents, and I find it almost impossible to manage the logistics of our lives these days (last night I missed a soccer meeting by an hour), but now in the morning we have four kids (three of our own, plus the wonderful exchange student we're hosting, Nico) successfully meeting buses that come at two different times, and the kids rarely get there late. They watch the clock, punch the list, and make the bus.

It wasn't easy to stop barking orders at my kids. It had become an ingrained habit. As in this case, if we are to sustain innovation in our business lives we have to selectively abandon past behavior and pick up new habits and actions in equal parts. What is happening today may not be happening tomorrow, trends come and go, but constantly looking for ways to improve a product or process, or invent a new one, will keep us competitive in an ever-changing marketplace.

FORGET TRENDS AND KEEP INNOVATING

A December 2012 article in *The Atlantic* by Charles Fishman charted what may be the most significant reversal in manufacturing trends in decades.[1] It starts with the story of a General Electric manufacturing facility in Kentucky.

In 1951, GE began construction on what would become the largest domestic appliance manufacturing plant in the United States, aptly named Appliance Park. It is so big that it has its own zip code. Housing the appliance division of GE, and featuring the first-ever use of a computer (a gigantic UNIVAC) in a manufacturing setting, Appliance Park became the centerpiece of the company's appliance production division, and within just a couple years employed 16,000 people.

By 1973, 22 years after opening its doors, the immense plant—with its mile-long parking lot and its own fire department—employed more than 23,000 people and turned out washing machines, dryers, refrigerators, and other appliances to Americans eager to embrace the conveniences of technology.

Within just another 11 years, by 1984, the plant had been nicknamed "Strike City" for the constant divisive and productivity-killing strikes that were pervasive. The working population had dropped back to 16,000 workers, and then fell steadily through the 1990s as GE continued to outsource manufacturing to Mexico and China. Finally, by 2011, a mere 1,863 manufacturing employees remained at Appliance Park.

Then an interesting thing happened. In February 2012, GE fired up a manufacturing line in Building 2 of Appliance Park to build high-tech, low-energy water heaters that had been made by the company in China for more a decade. And then, a month later, in Building 5, another assembly line opened up to begin assembling fancy refrigerators, previously assembled in Mexico.

Why would GE do this? After all, they have been enjoying the cheap labor benefits of outsourcing product assembly for years, and GE CEO Jeff Immelt isn't in-sourcing manufacturing to the United States to help improve the government's employment numbers—he's running a business. Now, just four years after GE tried, unsuccessfully, to sell off the entire appliance division, Immelt explained at an event in September 2012 why GE is moving manufacturing back to the United States: "I don't do that because I run a charity; I do that because I think we can do it here and make more money."

There are a number of marketquake influences contributing to GE's decision to bring manufacturing of the GeoSpring water heater back to the United States. Wages in China are rising, and workers there demand higher pay and a higher standard of living: oil prices, and hence cargo shipping costs, are also rising. Meanwhile, labor costs at Appliance Park have fallen because GE has negotiated with the labor union.

While these factors, on their own merit, make for a compelling spreadsheet argument to bring appliance manufacturing back to the United States, there are other unexpected benefits. With manufacturing basically walled off in China, GE discovered that engineers had lost touch with the actual process of manufacturing, and therefore had lost touch with opportunities to continually innovate in this critical function. Once GE engineers examined the water heater, in the process of bringing the company's manufacturing back home, they decided to completely overhaul the design. This in turn led to even higher increases in its efficiency and performance, and to the speed of the company's it and getting it to market.

The GeoSpring was reengineered to have 20 percent fewer parts and is now produced in Kentucky in 80 percent less time than it was made in China. This increased efficiency is partly because of the device's design, but also because GE has redesigned the workplace and assembly lines themselves. For example, its revamped dishwasher assembly line requires only 20 percent of the physical space previously required and reduces production time by 68 percent.

As Fishman describes the situation:

> So a funny thing happened to the GeoSpring on the way from the cheap Chinese factory to the expensive Kentucky factory: The material cost went down. The labor required to make it went down. The quality went up. Even the energy efficiency went up.

Another key aspect of having the manufacturing process in-house was the loss of what might be considered innovation over the water cooler. With staff from all departments now close by, there were more opportunities to casually share ideas that led to sustained innovation.

By the end of 2012, GE expects to have more than 3,600 professionals employed at Appliance Park, including salaried designers, engineers, and IT professionals.[2] These professionals will work hand in hand with the assembly-line employees to ensure the design conveys efficiently to the actual construction process. As Jeff Immelt writes in the March 2012 edition of *Harvard Business Review*:

> At Appliance Park we have torn down functional silos and replaced them with a "one team" mentality. Designers, engineers, and assembly-line workers together determine the best way to meet their goals; they own the metrics.[3]

Meanwhile, over at Apple, CEO Tim Cook announced to NBC on December 6, 2012, that Apple intends to invest $100 million to begin producing a line of Apple products within the United States in 2013 for reasons similar to GE's.[4]

Seismic changes in the world have brought about increased connectivity, interrelatedness, and interdependency. In such a rapidly changing world, no matter how cataclysmic the change, being optimistic about the future and embracing continual innovation are key to growth and stability. Change and upheaval clears the ground of orthodoxy and primes the pump for an explosion of ideas.

EMBRACE CHANGE AND RISK TAKING

To keep moving ahead, organizations will have to keep rethinking and redefining their systems. Few of the traditional, orthodox methods and systems will be enough to carry us through the century and beyond. Old systems have to be either discarded or reworked, no matter how well they may have worked in the past, and new systems have to be created. New goals have to be formulated along the lines the changes require. Leaders need to accomplish all this while keeping the core values of the organization in mind.

More and more, CEOs want leaders to take risks. With increasing marketquakes and ambiguities that come through globalization, waiting until things settle down before committing to a particular direction may seem a better approach, but responding swiftly to changes and challenges while others hesitate can pay off. In a volatile environment, speed of response is what is required. The key to a successful jump is to follow our true convictions and beliefs, even if they lead us on an unknown path.

How we perceive change is a matter of attitude. Dan Glaser, in addressing a group of insurance industry leaders, suggested how to approach what he sees as "an age of relentless acceleration," where there is greater interconnectedness and a shifting of power centers, and where a single event can greatly affect the world and the environment:

> View today's challenging environment as an opportunity for differentiation, innovation, and the creation of long-term value. . . . Reward and risk are bound together. For those leaders and entrepreneurs who are unafraid of taking risks and are excited by challenges of a global economy, rewards can be in the form of growth of revenue, increased market share, territorial expansion, diversification, flow of commerce, and regeneration of the world's productive prowess.[5]

Current global upheavals spark instability, fear, and the desire to protect ourselves against change and cling to the familiar, leading to "ideacide"—killing creativity. To borrow from Harvard Business School professor Youngme Moon's video *My Anti-Creativity Checklist*, ideacide can happen for many reasons: playing it safe and not taking risks; limiting or pigeonholing ourselves; thinking our job is not about being creative; being skeptical, thinking that past results dictate the future; crushing ideas that crop up naturally, thinking everything is old hat; closing our eyes and minds; blaming failure on external forces; underestimating and undervaluing our customers; being suspicious of those who are creative and don't fit into the box in our minds; and stifling the imaginative child within, thinking "playing is for children."[6]

Although we may stay safe by allowing our audacious ideas to perish, we miss the thrill of seeing where they might lead. This is where dynamic leaders really play an important role. Their optimism is what will keep their organization afloat, keep creativity at the forefront, and enable the organization to move forward.

3M famously created the environment in which Art Fry could invent Post-it® Notes, building a culture in which people in the organization could express their own creativity. After Spencer F. Silver, Fry's colleague, had created a "low-tack" adhesive that would enable paper to be temporarily stuck to objects, Fry had the notion of using that temporary adhesive on small pieces of paper as "temporary bookmarks," as he put it. It took five years to work out the kinks, file the patents, and bring the product to market, but in 1980, Post-it® Notes were introduced in the United States.[7]

BE PREPARED FOR CREATIVITY

I find the more I practice, the luckier I get.

—*Gary Player*

As I said earlier in the book, chance and creativity favor the prepared mind. Broadly speaking, the prepared leader knows what he or she is looking for, makes informed decisions, and simplifies the most complex conditions in order to take clear action. We can't control all variables, but preparedness of mind is within our control, so this is what we should concentrate on. We can then handle the rest.

The prepared mind is not a matter of chance. It is a matter of resolution and intention.

Work environments are becoming dynamic, offering plenty of opportunity for growth. There is no one right way, but many options. The mind has to have the necessary skills to be able to take advantage of these opportunities, be creative, and make the right choices. For instance, with technology, if basic skills can be learned, they soon become a platform for creativity, and growth can be exponential.

Preparedness added to raw talent is a powerful combination. People who are confident in their knowledge are not afraid of going beyond their boundaries and job descriptions to experiment and take risks.

Broadly speaking, preparing the mind requires study and keeping an open mind, reasoning, imagination, challenging assumptions, making decisions, acquiring knowledge and learning, creating an enabling environment, and reflection. A state of preparedness is the basic requisite for inspiration. Those with a prepared mind will know how to use all the ideas that flow around them. They will be ready for that "click"!

As leaders, we need to ask ourselves, "Is our workforce prepared for the future?" In an online debate with Intel chairman Craig Barrett about technical education, Vivek Wadhwa said, "The U.S. is graduating fewer and fewer scientists and engineers."[8] The real problem is that "the majority of these graduates are foreign nationals (who are now increasingly returning home)." If the United States is to compete seriously in the twenty-first century, Barrett added, it has to increase its science, technology, engineering, and math talent pool. A workforce of smart people has to be created, research and development invested in, and the environment made attractive for investment and innovation.

Jeff Joerres, CEO of ManpowerGroup, in an interview I had with him in 2012, described himself as a strong proponent of job training and workforce development initiatives.[9] He likens developing employees at the point of execution of a project to training pilots after taking delivery of the airplanes. He advises a more strategic workforce-development plan, in which we grow our people now and always, to meet tomorrow's challenges.

Training and preparing people for the job they have to do makes sense from a business-development standpoint. It also makes sense from an engagement standpoint. People innately want to learn and grow, and the greater opportunity we provide, the more likely people will stay on the bus.

Joerres also believes that the modern labor market is truly global. Often bright people may not have the skills for a particular job. They may, however, have all the other qualities needed, including the right attitude, adaptability, a keen interest in learning, and a desire to take on problems. He feels that with training they will prove to be assets to the company and contribute to the economy of the country.

In line with the preparedness of prospective employees, ManpowerGroup is working with technical-education institutions to make sure that individuals learn the skills needed to be a part of the global workforce—a talent pool of individuals who can be moved to where the demand is.

Wadhwa and Barrett say that it is the responsibility of both the public and private sectors to create an ecosystem with incentives for deserving talent—regardless of whether the talent is American or foreign—and with lots of opportunities.

PUT IT ALL TOGETHER

We have to continually nurture curiosity to allow creative value to emerge. Brainstorming and divergent thinking are effective techniques that can move us toward innovation, but they're only a part of this complex process. We must remain open to all ideas, all paths to new ways of seeing the world.

To uncover the pleasantly unexpected in something we have known for a long time, or to have a novel interpretation of something we have never seen before, we must remain ever curious. This curiosity enables us to build a growing repertoire of ideas that, when gestated for long enough, can interconnect to create new mash-ups that, hopefully, are recognized by the world as possessing shared value.

When we are in flow—deeply engaged in activity—we can accelerate the time it takes for those idea mash-ups to reach full potential. We do this by reaching out to our network of people, especially those with whom we don't interact regularly. The most powerful new creative mash-ups often come when we share, connect, and collaborate with those with whom we have weak ties or when we make new relationships. In this way, we can borrow brilliance, bringing in new ideas or seeing familiar ideas in a different light. By such cross-pollination of disparate ideas, we can create new value.

And, then, once we have nurtured a sense of focused curiosity—built a tapestry of connected relationships to grow new ideas—we must act. We must put our thoughts in motion. Recall the discussion earlier of how WD-40 was invented. The success of Water Displacement #40 came after 39 failed attempts at innovation.

Finally, we find the best expression of ourselves when we don't wait to be picked by our leadership or our company. In our work, we all see opportunities to be filled, dilemmas to be solved, and possibilities for action—and yet we often hesitate. We're waiting to be asked, ignoring the difficult, or pausing out of fear. That fear is often born out of trying to anticipate what we think the company wants and expects of us and trying to intuit how the company or leadership thinks we should act.

The truth is that we will bring much greater energy and creativity to our work when we take the lead, when we take the first step. Step boldly.

LET'S RECAP

Remember . . .

- Optimism about the future is the key to growth and stability. To sustain forward movement, enterprises must rethink and redefine their systems, discarding or reworking old ways and creating new goals. Leaders must take risks and act with conviction and without hesitation, all the while retaining core values. This attitude is one that views risk and reward as interconnected.

- "Ideacide" is the killing of creativity, sparked by fear of change and adaptation to new circumstances. Although we may stay safe by allowing our audacious ideas to perish, we miss the thrill of seeing where they might lead. The optimism of dynamic leaders with deep creativity at the forefront will enable the organization to move forward.

- The prepared mind is not a matter of chance. It is within our control and requires resolution and intention. Dynamic work environments will challenge leaders to bring their raw talent and deep knowledge into play with their curiosity, discovery, open-mindedness, and reflection. A state of preparedness is the basic requisite for inspiration.

- Remaining curious, growing a repertoire of ideas, creating new mash-ups, and cross-pollinating ideas with others is the new path that leaders must take. The path leads to taking bold actions that create new value. Step boldly.

NOTES

INTRODUCTION

1. Jeremy Gutsche, *Exploiting Chaos: 150 Ways to Spark Chaos During Times of Change* (New York: Gotham Books, 2009).

CHAPTER 1

1. Liisa Välikangas, author of *The Resilient Organization: How Adaptive Cultures Thrive Even When Strategy Fails,* told the story of Bodie to the author in an interview, November 2010, Vienna, Austria. To learn more about Bodie, read Robert C. Likes "Mono Mills to Bodie," *Explore Historic California,* June 2006, accessed December 17, 2012, http://www.explorehistoricalif.com/mono_mills.html.

2. A motive is a short melodic component, also called a motif, a cell, or a figure.

3. Nod to Gina Keating, author of *Netflixed: The Epic Battle for America's Eyeballs* (New York, NY: Portfolio, 2012).

4. Daniel Goleman, *Working with Emotional Intelligence* (1998; repr., New York: Bantam, 2000).

5. Paul Sloane, "What's the Difference between Innovation and Creativity?" *Innovation Excellence* (blog), last modified June 7, 2010, http://www.innovationexcellence.com/blog/2010/06/07/what-is-the-difference-between-innovation-and-creativity.

6. Norm Merritt, telephone interview by author, January 2013.

7. Dhanya Ann Thoppil, "Indian Outsourcing Firms Hire in U.S.," *Wall Street Journal* website, last modified August 7, 2012, http://online.wsj.com/article/SB10000872396390044351710457757293020845318 6.html.

8. Jeff Joerres, interview by author, July 2010, Milwaukee, WI.

9. Bruce Churchill, interview by author, November 2011, New York, NY.

10. Michael Byrne, interview by author, September 2010, Sydney, Australia.

11. Henry William Chesbrough, *Open Innovation: The New Imperative for Creating and Profiting from Technology* (Boston: Harvard Business School Press, 2003), xxiv.

12. Andrew Deonarine, "I'm a Solver," *Perspectives on Innovation Blog*, accessed December 7, 2012, http://www.innocentive.com/blog/2010/09/28/i%E2%80%99m-a-solver-%E2%80%93-andrew-deonarine.

13. "Generation Y Makes Its Own Career Rules," National Public Radio (NPR) website, May 27, 2008, http://www.npr.org/templates/transcript/transcript.php?storyId=90853994.

14. Michael S. Malone, "The Next American Frontier," *Wall Street Journal* website, last modified May 19, 2008, http://online.wsj.com/article/SB121115437321202233.html.

15. Dwayne Spradlin, interview with Taavo Godtfredsen, May 2011, Boston, MA.

16. G. Shawn Hunter, "Actionable Leadership in the Creative Age" (White Paper), Skillsoft Corporation website, June 2012, http://www.skillsoft.com/infocenter/whitepapers/documents/whitepaper_actionableleadership.pdf.

17. IBM, *Capitalizing on Complexity: Insights from the 2010 IBM Global CEO Study*, 2010, accessed December 29, 2012, http://www-304.ibm.com/businesscenter/cpe/download0/200422/ceostudy_2010.pdf.

18. See examples at the Jones Soda website, http://www.jonessoda.com/gallery.

19. Peter Andrew Georgescu, "About Peter," Peter Georgescu website, accessed December 6, 2012, http://theconstantchoice.com/about-peter.

20. Peter Georgescu, interview by author, November 2011, New York, NY.

CHAPTER 2

1. Paul Hiltz, interview by author, May 2011, Cincinnati, OH.

2. Bob Sutton, interview by author, April 2011, Santa Clara, CA.

3. Howard Behar, interview by author, July 2008, Seattle, WA.

4. Garry Ridge, interview by author, May 2011, San Francisco, CA.

5. Paul Stebbins, interview with Taavo Godtfredsen, November 2009, New York, NY.

6. Ken Robinson and Lou Aronica (contributor), *The Element: How Finding Your Passion Changes Everything*, (New York: Viking Adult, 2009).

7. Col. John R. Bourgeois, e-mail messages and telephone conversations with the author in fall 2012. For more about the colonel and the band, go to www.jrbourgeois.com.

8. Robert Cross and Andrew Parker, "The Core," chap. 3 in *The Hidden Power of Social Networks: Understanding How Work Really Gets Done in Organizations* (Boston: Harvard Business School Press, 2004).

CHAPTER 3

1. Yves Doz, interview by author, November 2009, Vienna, Austria.

2. Paul Sloane, *How to be a Brilliant Thinker: Exercise Your Mind and Find Creative Solutions* (London: Kogan Page Limited, 2010).

3. Nelleke Don and Jader Tolja, "The Story of the Five Fingers," BodyConsciousDesign.com, 2006, last accessed March 21, 2013, http://bodyconsciousdesign.com/uploads/interview_fliri_for_publication.pdf.

4. Bert Hölldobler and E. O. Wilson, *Journey to the Ants* (Cambridge, MA: Belknap Press, 1994), 1.

5. Chris R. Reid, David J. T. Sumpter, and Madeleine Beekman, "Optimisation in a natural system: Argentine ants solve the Towers of Hanoi," *Journal of Experimental Biology* 214 (2011): 50–58, also available at http://jeb.biologists.org/content/214/1/50 (doi:10.1242/jeb.048173).

6. Lee Sweetlove, "Number of species on Earth tagged at 8.7 million," *Nature* website, last modified August 24, 2011, http://www.nature.com/news/2011/110823/full/news.2011.498.html.

7. Sarah Jane Gilbert, "The Accidental Innovator: Q&A with Robert D. Austin," Harvard Business School website, last modified July 5, 2006, http://hbswk.hbs.edu/item/5441.html.

8. David L. Cooperrider and Diana Whitney, "What is Appreciative Inquiry" (excerpted from *Appreciative Inquiry: A Positive Revolution in Change*), Appreciative Inquiry Commons, last accessed December 13, 2012, http://appreciativeinquiry.case.edu/intro/whatisai.cfm.

9. Appreciative Inquiry Commons, ASTD online, "Interview with David Cooperrider," February 1, 2009, http://appreciativeinquiry.case.edu/learning/whatsnewDetail.cfm?coid=12557.

10. Todd Kashdan, *Curious?* (New York: Harper-Collins, 2009).

11. "Seligman Speech at Lincoln Summit," University of Pennsylvania Positive Psychology Center website, accessed December 21, 2012, http://www.ppc.sas.upenn.edu/lincspeech.htm.

12. Shawn Achor, webinar interview by author, June 2012.

13. Norman Doidge, *The Brain That Changes Itself: Stories of Personal Triumph from the Frontiers of Brain Science* (New York: Viking Adult, 2006).

14. Alan B. Krueger et al., "National Time Accounting: The Currency of Life," National Bureau of Economic Research, available at http://www.nber.org/chapters/c5053.pdf.

15. Todd Kashdan, *Curious?* (New York: Harper-Collins, 2009).

16. Daniel Kahneman, *Thinking, Fast and Slow* (New York: Farrar, Straus and Giroux, 2011), 122.

17. Richard Wiseman, *The Luck Factor: The Four Essential Principles* (New York: Miramax Books, 2003).

18. Jaak Panksepp and Lucy Biven, *The Archaeology of Mind: Neuroevolutionary Origins of Human Emotions* (New York: W. W. Norton & Company, 2012), 328.

19. Matthew May, interview by author, December 2009, Los Angeles, CA.

20. Lincoln Crawley, interview by author, September 2010, Sydney, Australia.

21. Sheena Iyengar, *The Art of Choosing* (New York: Twelve, 2010).

22. Sheena Iyengar, interview by Taavo Godtfredsen, April 2012, San Diego, CA.

CHAPTER 4

1. Carl Woideck, *Charlie Parker: His Music and Life* The Michigan American Music Series, (Ann Arbor, MI: University of Michigan Press, 1997).

2. Angela L. Duckworth et al., "Grit: Perseverance and Passion for Long-Term Goals," *Journal of Personality and Social Psychology*, 92 (2007): 1087–1101, also available at http://www.sas.upenn.edu/~duckwort/images/Grit%20JPSP.pdf (doi:10.1037/0022-3514.92.6.1087).

3. John Grant, interview by author, September 2010, Sydney, Australia.

4. Teresa Amabile and Leslie A. Perlow, "Time Pressure and Creativity: Why Time Is Not on Your Side," Harvard Business School website, last modified July 29, 2002, http://hbswk.hbs.edu/item/3030.html.

5. Teresa Amabile and Steven Kramer, *The Progress Principle: Using Small Wins to Ignite Joy, Engagement, and Creativity at Work* (Boston: Harvard Business Review Press, 2011).

6. Teresa Amabile, interview by author, December 2011, Boston, MA.

7. "This Is Your Life: Looking at the Big Picture," featuring Sir Howard Stringer and Brad Anderson, *CEO Exchange Program* (episode 507), PBS.org, March 14, 2007, video clips available at http://www.pbs.org/wttw/ceoexchange/episodes/507_episode.html; transcript available at http://www.pbs.org/wttw/ceoexchange/episodes/transcripts/CEO_EXCHANGE_TRANSCRIPT_episode507.pdf.

8. Chip Conley, interview by author, April 2011, San Francisco, CA.

9. Barbara L. Fredrickson and Marcial F. Losada, "Positive Affect and the Complex Dynamics of Human Flourishing," *American Psychologist* 60 (2005): 678–686, also available at http://www.unc.edu/peplab/publications/Fredrickson%20&%20Losada%202005.pdf (doi:10.1037/0003-066X.60.7.678).

CHAPTER 5

1. Richard Feynman, *What Do You Care What Other People Think: Further Adventures of a Curious Character* (New York: W. W. Norton & Company Ltd., 1988).

2. Justin Menkes, webinar interview by author, March 2012.

3. Nick Morgan, interview by author, December 2010, Boston, MA.

4. Susan Griffin, "To Love the Marigold: Hope and Imagination," in *The Impossible Will Take a Little While: A Citizen's Guide to Hope in a Time of Fear*, ed. Paul Rogat (New York: Basic Books, 2004). The essay is also available online at http://www.commondreams.org/views05/0127-21.htm.

5. John Hope Bryant, interview by author, April 2011, Charlotte, NC.

6. Ken Hicks, interview by author, November 2011, New York, NY.

7. Albert Mehrabian, *Nonverbal Communication* (Boston: Walter De Gruyter Inc., 1972).

8. Douglas McGregor, *The Human Side of Enterprise* (New York: McGraw-Hill, 1960).

9. Robert Rosenthal and Lenore Jacobson, *Pygmalion in the Classroom: Teacher Expectation and Pupils' Intellectual Development* (New York: Irvington Pub, 1992).

10. Sujaya Banerjee, interview by author, May 2012, Orlando, FL.

11. Heffernan Insurance Brokers, "Beyond the Bottom Line: Clif Bar & Co. Measures Success Five Ways," accessed December 21, 2012, http://www.heffins.com/contact-us/california-offices/heff.voL3.8.1.clif.pdf.

CHAPTER 6

1. Mihaly Csíkszentmihalyi, *Creativity: Flow and the Psychology of Discovery and Invention* (New York: Harper Collins, 1996).

2. Daniel Coyle, interview by author, December 2011, Chicago, IL.

3. Charles Handy, interview by author, November 2010, Vienna, Austria.

4. *Psychology Today* staff, "How to Be Great!" *Psychology Today* website, November 1, 1995, http://www.psychologytoday.com/articles/199511/how-be-great.

5. Dan Glaser, interview by author, November 2009, New York, NY.

6. Carol Dweck, *Mindset* (New York: Ballantine Books, 2008).

7. Vineet Nayar, "EFCS 2.0—Employees Driven Management Embraced," Vineet Nayar: In Search of New Leaders website, accessed November 16, 2012, http://www.vineetnayar.com/leadership-and-business-lessons/next-management-revolution-at-hcl-%E2%80%93-hq-asia-october-2011.

8. Ibid.

9. HCL Technologies Ltd., "Terms of Use," accessed December 13, 2012, https://meme.hcl.com.

10. David Meerman Scott, "The New Rules of Viral Marketing," David Meerman Scott: Marketing and Leadership Strategist website, 2008, accessed December 17, 2012, http://www.davidmeermanscott.com/documents/Viral_Marketing.pdf.

CHAPTER 7

1. Towers Watson, "The New Employment Deal: How Far, How Fast and How Enduring; Insights from Towers Watson's 2010 Global Workforce Study," accessed December 13, 2012, http://www.towerswatson.com/global-workforce-study.

2. Management Lab® (MLab), "Management the Google Way," Lab notes 9, September 2008, http://www.cecmi.org/files/article-google-management.pdf.

3. Charles A. O'Reilly III et al., "The Promise and Problems of Organizational Culture: CEO Personality, Culture, and Firm Performance," Haas School of Business, University of California–Berkeley website, accessed December 11, 2012, http://faculty.haas.berkeley.edu/chatman/papers/CEO%20Personality%20Final%20Ms.pdf.

4. Margery Weinstein, "Keys to the Kingdom: Part II," *Training* magazine website, September 8, 2008, http://www.trainingmag.com/article/keys-kingdom-part-ii.

5. "Netflix Culture: Freedom & Responsibility," Netflix website, accessed December 11, 2012, http://jobs.netflix.com/jobs.html.

6. Traci Fenton, keynote address, WorldBlu LIVE: Spreading Freedom at Work, May 19–20, 2011, San Francisco, CA.

7. Dan Glaser, interview by author, November 2009, New York, NY.

8. Mark Johnson, interview by Taavo Godtfredsen, December 2010, Boston, MA.

9. Ethisphere, "About Ethisphere," accessed December 14, 2012, http://ethisphere.com/about.

10. Zeger Degraeve, interview by author, September 2012, Melbourne, Australia.

11. Elaine Chan and Jaideep Sengupta, "Insincere Flattery Actually Works: A Dual Attitudes Perspective," *Journal of Marketing Research* 47 (2010): 122–133.

12. Fred Kleisner, interview by author, November 2010, New York, NY.

13. Nick Kugenthiran, interview by author, September 2010, Sydney, Australia.

14. Michael Stallard, interview by author, August 2010, Boston, MA.

15. Bono (Paul David Hewson), "U2 Hall of Fame Induction Acceptance Speech," *Bono Speaks* (blog), posted by Dave Waltman, last modified March 14, 2005, http://bonospeaks.blogspot.com/2005/03/u2-hall-of-fame-induction-acceptence.html.

16. Tenzin Gyatso, "Compassion and the Individual," His Holiness the 14th Dalai Lama of Tibet website, last accessed December 11, 2012, http://www.dalailama.com/messages/compassion.

17. Susan Scott, *Fierce Conversations* (New York: Berkeley Publishing Group, 2002).

18. Susan Scott, interview by author, July 2008, Seattle, WA.

19. Mark Goulston, *Just Listen: Discover the Secret to Getting Through to Absolutely Anyone* (New York: AMACOM, 2009).

20. Mark Goulston, interview by author, February 2009, Los Angeles.

21. Muoio, Anna, ed., "Your Boss: Interview with Warren Bennis," Zinezone.com, accessed December 18, 2012, http://communitybridge.com/zz/zones/wealth/fastcompany/1999/Aug/30/interview2.html.

22. Tammy Erickson, webinar interview by author, September 2012.

23. The study is cited in S. Kiesler and J. Cummings, "What do we know about proximity in work groups? A legacy of research on physical distance," chap. 3 in *Distributed Work*, P. Hinds and S. Kiesler (Cambridge, MA: MIT Press, 2002), 57–80.

CHAPTER 8

1. Venkatesh Valluri, interview by author, November 2011, Vienna, Austria, and e-mail exchanges with author, January 2013.

2. "Vertical Axis Wind Turbines: A Relevant Solution for Urban Areas," *JEC Composite Magazine*, July–August 2007: 22, also available at http://www.quietrevolution.com/downloads/pdf/media/JEC_Composites_Jul-Aug_2007.pdf.

3. Leslie Kaufman, "Wind Turbines and Health Hazards," *Green: A Blog about Energy and the Environment, New York Times* website, last modified January 18, 2012, http://green.blogs.nytimes.com/2012/01/18/wind-turbines-and-health-hazards.

4. Carl Franzen, "From Tunisia, The Future Of Wind Power?" *TPM*, TPMIdeaLab page, last modified June 20, 2012, http://idealab.talkingpointsmemo.com/2012/06/tunisia-wind-power-saphon.php.

5. The Quixote Project, "An Introduction," last accessed December 29, 2012, http://jpssis.com/the-quixote-project.html.

6. Mark S. Granovetter, "The Strength of Weak Ties," *American Journal of Sociology* 78 (1973): 1360–1380.

7. Yves Doz, interview by author, November 2009, Vienna, Austria, and e-mail exchanges with author, January 2013.

8. Howard Behar, interview by author, July 2008, Seattle, WA.

9. Richard Tanner Pascale and Jerry Sternin, "Your Company's Secret Change Agents," *Harvard Business Review*, May 1, 2005, also available at http://hbr.org /product/your-company-s-change-agents/an/R0505D-PDF-ENG.

10. "How Xolair May Help," Xolair.com, accessed December 28, 2012, http:// www.xolair.com/xolair/about.html.

11. "Scientists without Borders Challenge Offers 10,000USD for Solutions to Combat a Critical Consequence of Malnutrition," Innocentive website, last modified November 15, 2010, http://www.innocentive.com/scientists-without -borders-challenge-offers-10000usd-solutions-combat-critical-consequence -malnutrit.

12. Vivek Wadhwa, "A Better Formula for Economic Growth: Connecting Smart Risk Takers," *The Chronicle for Higher Education* website, last modified November 18, 2010, http://chronicle.com/article/A-Better-Formula-for-Economic/125441.

13. Reem Assil, "The US H1-B Visa Program" (Background Briefing), North American Alliance for Fair Employment, November 2004, available at http:// www.fairjobs.org/archive/sites/default/files/RA-H1Bbriefing.pdf.

14. Ruth Ellen Wasem, "Immigration of Foreign Nationals with Science, Technology, Engineering, and Mathematics (STEM) Degrees," Congressional Research Service, November 26, 2012, available at http://www.fas.org/sgp/crs /misc/R42530.pdf.

15. As of December 2012, Congress was still battling over passage of the STEM Jobs Act, since the new visas would come from demolishing the Diversity Immigrant Visa program, under which visas go to randomly selected, qualified immigrants from countries with low rates of immigration to the United States.

16. Richard E. Nisbett and Takahiko Masuda, "Culture and Point of View," *PNAS* 100 (2003): 11163–11170, published online before print, September 5, 2003, http://www.pnas.org/content/100/19/11163.full.pdfuhtml (doi:10.1073/pnas .1934527100).

17. Daniel Goleman, *Working with Emotional Intelligence* (1998; repr., New York: Bantam, 2000).

18. Emily Turrettini, "Happy bday! SMS txt msgs turn 20," Textually.org (blog), last modified December 1, 2012, http://www.textually.org/textually/archives/cat _sms_a_little_history.htm.

19. Clayton M. Christensen, Scott Cook, and Taddy Hall, "Marketing Malpractice: The Cause and Cure," *Harvard Business Review,* December 2005, 76, also available at http://hbr.org/2005/12/marketing-malpractice-the-cause-and-the -cure/ar/1 or http://www.digitaltonto.com/wp-content/uploads/Christensen MarketingMalpractive.pdf.

20. Don Tapscott, *Grown Up Digital: How the Net Generation Is Changing Your World* (New York: McGraw-Hill, 2009).

21. "Quality in Management Radiology," *Imaging Economics* website, accessed December 13, 2012, http://www.imagingeconomics.com/all-news/16144-quality -in-management-radiology.

22. "Photos Increase Radiologist–Patient Connection," *RSNA News,* March 2009, 12–13. Also available at http://www.rsna.org/publications/rsnanews/march -2009/photos_feature.cfm.

CHAPTER 9

1. Campbell Jones, interview by author, September 2012, Melbourne, Australia.

2. Paul Sloane, "What is the Difference between Innovation and Creativity?" *Innovation Excellence* (blog), June 7, 2010, accessed December 17, 2012, http://www.innovationexcellence.com/blog/2010/06/07/what-is-the -difference-between-innovation-and-creativity.

3. David T. Neal, Wendy Wood, and Jeffrey M. Quinn, "Habits—A Repeat Performance," *Current Directions in Psychological Science* 15 (2006): 198–202, also available at http://dornsife.usc.edu/wendywood/research/documents /Neal.Wood.Quinn.2006.pdf.

4. Jill Klein, interview by author, September 2012, Melbourne, Australia, and follow-up conversations by e-mail in January 2013.

5. Mark D. Alicke and Olesya Govorun, "The Better-Than-Average Effect," in *The Self in Social Judgment,* edited by Mark D. Alicke, David A. Dunning, and Joachim I. Krueger, 5–106, *Studies in Self and Identity Series* (New York, NY: Psychology Press, 2005).

6. T. R. Zenger, "Why do employers only reward extreme performance? Examining the relationships among performance, pay, and turnover," *Administrative Science Quarterly* 37 (1992), 198–219.

7. O. Svenson, "Are we less risky and more skillful than our fellow drivers?" *Acta Psychologica* 47 (1981), 143–151.

8. J. B. Soll and J. Klayman, "Overconfidence in interval estimates," *Journal of Experimental Psychology: Learning, Memory, and Cognition* 30(2)(2004), 299–314.

9. B. Fischoff, P. Slovic, and S. Lichtenstein, "Knowing with certainty: The appropriateness of extreme confidence," *Journal of Experimental Psychology: Human Perception and Performance,* 3 (1977): 552–564.

10. James Surowiecki, *The Wisdom of Crowds: Why the Many Are Smarter Than the Few and How Collective Wisdom Shapes Business, Economies, Societies and Nations* (New York: Doubleday, 2004).

11. Chuck Salter, "Failure Doesn't Suck," *Fast Company* website, last modified May 1, 2007, http://www.fastcompany.com/59549/failure-doesnt-suck.

12. Harris Rosen, interview by author, May 2012, Orlando, FL, and follow-up conversations by phone and e-mail in January 2013.

CHAPTER 10

1. Yvon Chouinard, interview by author, October 2010, New York, NY.

2. David Penglase, interview by author, August 2012, Sydney, Australia.

3. Daniel Kahneman, *Thinking, Fast and Slow* (New York: Farrar, Straus and Giroux, 2011), 122.

4. Dacher Keltner, Deborah H. Gruenfeld, and Cameron Anderson, "Power, Approach, and Inhibition," *Psychological Review* 110 (2003): 265–284, also available at http://socrates.berkeley.edu/~keltner/publications/keltner.power.psychreview.2003.pdf.

CHAPTER 11

1. The term "sag" comes from "sagging behind." In events with lots of nonprofessionals (including running events), the sag wagon picks up people who have fallen behind or are dropping out.

2. Rakesh Khurana, interview by author, December 2011, Harvard Business School, Allston, MA.

3. Iqbal Quadir, interview by author, December 2011, MIT, Cambridge, MA.

4. Stephanie Saul, "Ghostwriters Used in Vioxx Studies, Article Says," *New York Times* website, last modified April 15, 2008, http://www.nytimes.com/2008/04/15/business/15cnd-vioxx.html?_r=1&.

5. *FDA, Merck and Vioxx: Putting Patient Safety First? Hearing before the Comm. on Finance, Thursday, November 18, 2004, before the Senate Comm. on Finance,* 108th Cong., 13–17 (2004) (statement of David Graham, M.D., M.P.H, Associate Director for Science, Office of Drug Safety, Center for Drug Evaluation and Research, Department of Health and Human Services,

Food and Drug Administration), U.S. Senate Finance Committee website, available at http://www.finance.senate.gov/hearings/hearing/download/?id=0c63bcec-bde2-4763-9dd6-2f6d5422cd85.

6. Jim Collins, *How The Mighty Fall: And Why Some Companies Never Give In* (New York: HarperCollins Publishers, Inc., 2009).

7. Don Vanthournout, interview by author, October 2011, Elk Grove Village, IL.

8. Elizabeth W. Dunn et al, "Spending Money on Others Promotes Happiness," *Science* 319 (2008): 1687–1688, also available at http://www.sciencemag.org/content/319/5870/1687.full (doi:10.1126/science.1150952).

9. Edward L. Deci, "Effects of externally mediated rewards on intrinsic motivation," *Journal of Personality and Social Psychology* 18 (1971): 105–115.

10. Adam M. Grant et al., "Impact and the art of motivation maintenance: The effects of contact with beneficiaries on persistence behavior," *Organizational Behavior and Human Decision Processes* 103 (2007): 53–67, also available at http://rcgd.isr.umich.edu/seminars/Winter2007/Grant%20Paper.pdf (doi: 10.1016/j.obhdp.2006.05.004).

11. Adam M. Grant, "Leading with Meaning: Beneficiary Contact, Prosocial Impact, and the Performance Effects of Transformational Leadership," *Academy of Management Journal* 55 (2012): 458–476, also available at http://amj.aom.org/content/55/2/458 (http://dx.doi.org/10.5465/amj.2010.0588).

CHAPTER 12

1. Charles Fishman, "The Insourcing Boom," *The Atlantic*, December 2012, also available at http://www.theatlantic.com/magazine/archive/2012/12/the-insourcing-boom/309166.

2. Terry Boyd, "The Atlantic: 'Insourcing' at GE Appliance Park sparking a new wave of American manufacturing greatness," InsiderLouisville.com, last modified December 3, 2012, http://insiderlouisville.com/news/2012/12/03/the-atlantic-insourcing-at-ge-appliance-park-sparking-a-new-wave-of-american-manufacturing-innovation.

3. Jeffrey R. Immelt, "The CEO of General Electric on Sparking an American Manufacturing Renewal," *Harvard Business Review*, March 2012, also available at http://hbr.org/2012/03/the-ceo-of-general-electric-on-sparking-an-american-manufacturing-renewal/ar.

4. Associated Press, "Apple CEO Tells NBC that Line of Macs Will Be Produced in the US Next Year," *The Washington Post* website, last modified December 6, 2012, http://www.washingtonpost.com/business/technology/apple-ceo-tells-nbc-that-line-of-macs-will-be-produced-in-the-us-next-year/2012/12/06/e968b94e-4009-11e2-8a5c-473797be602c_story.html.

5. Marsh Inc., "Marsh CEO Dan Glaser Addresses Need and Opportunity for Innovation and Differentiation in the Insurance Industry," press release, last modified May 12, 2012, http://usa.marsh.com/NewsInsights/MarshPressReleases/ID/513/Marsh-CEO-Dan-Glaser-Addresses-Need-and-Opportunity-for-Innovation-and-Differentiation-in-the-Insurance-Industry.aspx.

6. Youngme Moon, *"The Anti-Creativity Checklist,"* *HBR Blog Network*, video, *Harvard Business Review* website, last modified March 18, 2010, http://blogs.hbr.org/cs/2010/03/the_anticreativity_checklist.html.

7. "Inventor of the Week: Art Fry & Spencer Silver, Post-it® Notes," Lemels N-MIT website, accessed December 14, 2012, http://web.mit.edu/invent/iow/frysilver.html.

8. "Craig Barrett Takes On Vivek Wadhwa in the Tech Education Debate," TechCrunch.com, last modified March 14, 2010, http://techcrunch.com/2010/03/14/craig-barrett-takes-on-vivek-wadhwa-in-the-tech-education-debate.

9. Jeff Joerres, interview by author, September 24, 2010, Milwaukee, WI.

BIBLIOGRAPHY

Achor, Shawn. *The Happiness Advantage*. New York: Crown Business, 2010.

Alicke, Mark D., and Olesya Govorun. "The Better-Than-Average Effect." In *The Self in Social Judgment,* edited by Mark D. Alicke, David A. Dunning, and Joachim I. Krueger, 5–106. *Studies in Self and Identity Series*. New York: Psychology Press, 2005.

Amabile, Teresa, and Steven Kramer. *The Progress Principle: Using Small Wins to Ignite Joy, Engagement, and Creativity at Work*. Boston: Harvard Business Review Press, 2011.

Amabile, Teresa, and Leslie A. Perlow. "Time Pressure and Creativity: Why Time Is Not on Your Side." Harvard Business School website. Last modified July 29, 2002. http://hbswk.hbs.edu/item/3030.html.

Arneson, Steve. *Bootstrap Leadership*. San Francisco: Berrett-Koehler Publishers, 2010.

Appreciative Inquiry Commons, ASTD online. "Interview with David Cooperrider." February 1, 2009. http://appreciativeinquiry.case.edu/learning/whatsnewDetail.cfm?coid=12557.

Assil, Reem. "The US H1-B Visa Program" (Background Briefing). North American Alliance for Fair Employment, November, 2004. Available at http://www.fairjobs.org/archive/sites/default/files/RA-H1Bbriefing.pdf.

Behar, Howard, and Janet Goldstein. *It's Not About the Coffee*. New York: Penguin, 2007.

Blumenthal, Noah. *Be the Hero*. San Francisco: Berrett-Koehler Publishers, 2009.

Bono (Paul David Hewson). "U2 Hall of Fame Induction Acceptance Speech." *Bono Speaks* (blog), posted by Dave Waltman. Last modified March 14, 2005. http://www.be-the-hero.com/hero.html.

Boyd, Terry. "The Atlantic: 'Insourcing' at GE Appliance Park sparking a new wave of American manufacturing greatness." InsiderLouisville.com. Last modified December 3, 2012. http://insiderlouisville.com/news/2012/12/03/the-atlantic-insourcing-at-ge-appliance-park-sparking-a-new-wave-of-american-manufacturing-innovation.

Branham, Leigh. *The 7 Hidden Reasons Employees Leave*. New York: AMACOM, 2005.

Bryant, John Hope. *Love Leadership: The New Way to Lead in a Fear Based World*. San Francisco: Jossey-Bass, 2009.

Buckingham, Marcus. *Now, Discover Your Strengths*. New York: The Free Press, 2001.

Buckingham, Marcus, and Curt Coffman. *First, Break All the Rules*. New York: Simon & Schuster, 1999.

"Burn Your Resume, And Create a Job." *Tell Me More*. National Public Radio. January 18, 2011.

Capitalizing on Complexity: Insights from the 2010 IBM Global CEO Study. IBM. 2010. Accessed December 29, 2012, http://www-304.ibm.com/businesscenter/cpe /download0/200422/ceostudy_2010.pdf.

Carl Franzen, "From Tunisia, The Future Of Wind Power?" *TPM*, TPMIdeaLab page. Last modified June 20, 2012. http://idealab.talkingpointsmemo.com/2012/06 /tunisia-wind-power-saphon.php.

Chan, Elaine, and Jaideep Sengupta. "Insincere Flattery Actually Works: A Dual Attitudes Perspective." *Journal of Marketing Research* 47 (2010): 122–133.

Charan, Ram. *Leadership in the Era of Economic Uncertainty*. New York: McGraw-Hill, 2009.

Chesbrough, Henry William. *Open Innovation: The New Imperative for Creating and Profiting from Technology*. Boston: Harvard Business School Press, 2003.

Christensen, Clayton M., Scott Cook, and Taddy Hall. "Marketing Malpractice: The Cause and Cure." *Harvard Business Review*, December 2005. Also available at http://hbr .org/2005/12/marketing-malpractice-the-cause-and-the-cure/ar/1 or http://www .digitaltonto.com/wp-content/uploads/ChristensenMarketingMalpractive.pdf.

Chua, Hannah Faye, Julie E. Boland, and Richard E. Nisbett. "Cultural variation in eye movements during scene perception." Gordon Research Conferences website. Last modified August 22, 2005. http://www.pnas.org/content/102/35/12629.full (doi:10.1073/pnas.0506162102).

Conley, Chip. *Emotional Equations*. New York: The Free Press, 2012.

Cooperrider, David L., and Diana Whitney. "What is Appreciative Inquiry" (excerpted from *Appreciative Inquiry: A Positive Revolution in Change*), Appreciative Inquiry Commons. Accessed December 13, 2012, http://appreciativeinquiry.case.edu/intro /whatisai.cfm.

Coyle, Daniel. *The Talent Code: Greatness Isn't Born. It's Grown. Here's How*. New York: Bantam. 2009.

"Craig Barrett Takes On Vivek Wadhwa in the Tech Education Debate," TechCrunch .com. Last modified March 14, 2010. http://techcrunch .com/2010/03/14/craig-barrett -takes-on-vivek-wadhwa-in-the-tech-education-debate.

Collins, Jim. *How The Mighty Fall: And Why Some Companies Never Give In*. New York: HarperCollins Publishers, Inc., 2009.

Csíkszentmihalyi, Mihaly. *Creativity: Flow and the Psychology of Discovery and Invention*. New York: Harper Collins, 1996.

Cross, Robert, and Andrew Parker. *The Hidden Power of Social Networks: Understanding How Work Really Gets Done in Organizations*. Boston: Harvard Business School Press, 2004.

Darwin, Erasmus. *Zoonomia; Or, the Laws of Organic Life*. London: J. Johnson, 1796.

Deci, Edward. *Why We Do What We Do*. New York: Penguin Group, 1995.

Deci, Edward L. "Effects of externally mediated rewards on intrinsic motivation." *Journal of Personality and Social Psychology* 18 (1971): 105–115.

Deonarine, Andrew. "I'm a Solver." *Perspectives on Innovation Blog*. Accessed December 7, 2012, http://www.innocentive.com/blog/2010/09/28/i%E2%80%99m-a-solver-%E2%80%93-andrew-deonarine.

Deutchman, Jeremy. "Bennis and Panel of Experts Discuss the Future of Leadership in Light of the Economic Crisis." USC Marshall School of Business website. Last modified November 30, 2009. http://www.marshall.usc.edu/news/releases/2009/bennis-and-panel-experts-discuss-future-leadership-light-economic-crisis.

Doidge, Norman. *The Brain That Changes Itself: Stories of Personal Triumph from the Frontiers of Brain Science*. New York: Viking Adult, 2006.

Don, Nelleke, and Jader Tolja. "The Story of the Five Fingers." BodyConsciousDesign.com, 2006. Last accessed March 21, 2013. http://bodyconsciousdesign.com/uploads/interview_fliri_for_publication.pdf.

Duckworth, Angela L., Christopher Peterson, Michael D. Matthews, and Dennis R. Kelly. "Grit: Perseverance and Passion for Long-Term Goals." *Personality Processes and Individual Differences* 92 (2007): 1087–1101. University of Pennsylvania website. Also available at http://www.sas.upenn.edu/~duckwort/images/Grit%20JPSP.pdf (doi:10.1037/0022-3514.92.6.1087).

Dunn, Elizabeth W., Lara B. Aknin, and Michael I. Norton. "Spending Money on Others Promotes Happiness." *Science* 319 (2008): 1687–1688. Also available at http://www.sciencemag.org/content/319/5870/1687.full (doi:10.1126/science.1150952).

Dweck, Carol. *Mindset*. New York: Ballantine Books, 2008.

Economist, The. "The New Masters of Management." April 15, 2010.

Ethisphere. "About Ethisphere." Accessed December 14, 2012. http://ethisphere.com/about.

Feynman, Richard. *What Do You Care What Other People Think: Further Adventures of a Curious Character*. New York: W. W. Norton & Company Ltd., 1988.

Fishman, Charles. "The Insourcing Boom." *The Atlantic*, December 2012. Also available at http://www.theatlantic.com/magazine/archive/2012/12/the-insourcing-boom /309166.

Florida, Richard. *The Rise of the Creative Class*. Cambridge, MA: Basic Books, 2002.

Fredrickson, Barbara L., and Marcial F. Losada. "Positive Affect and the Complex Dynamics of Human Flourishing." *American Psychologist*, 60 (2005): 678–686. Also available at http://www.unc.edu/peplab/publications/Fredrickson%20&%20Losada% 202005.pdf (doi:10.1037/0003-066X.60.7.678).

"Gallup Study: Engaged Employees Inspire Company Innovation: National Survey Finds That Passionate Workers Are Most Likely to Drive Organizations Forward." *Gallup Management Journal*, October 12, 2006. Also available at http://gmj.gallup .com/content/24880/gallup-study-engaged-employees-inspire-company.aspx.

Gebauer, Julie, and Don Lowman. *Closing the Engagement Gap*. New York: Penguin Group, 2008.

"Generation Y Makes Its Own Career Rules." National Public Radio (NPR) website. Last modified May 27, 2008. http://www.npr.org/templates/transcript/transcript .php?storyId=90853994.

Georgescu, Peter Andrew. "About Peter." Peter Georgescu website. Accessed December 6, 2012. http://theconstantchoice.com/about-peter.

Gerber, Scott. *Never Get a Real Job*. Hoboken, NJ: Wiley, 2011.

Gilbert, Sarah Jane. "The Accidental Innovator: Q&A with Robert D. Austin." Harvard Business School website. Last modified July 5, 2006. http://hbswk.hbs.edu /item/5441.html.

Goleman, Daniel. *Working with Emotional Intelligence*. 1998; repr., New York: Bantam, 2000.

Goulston, Mark. *Just Listen: Discover the Secret to Getting Through to Absolutely Anyone*. New York: AMACOM, 2009.

Granovetter, Mark S. "The Strength of Weak Ties." *American Journal of Sociology* 78 (1973): 1360–1380.

Grant, Adam M. "Leading with Meaning: Beneficiary Contact, Prosocial Impact, and the Performance Effects of Transformational Leadership." *Academy of Management Journal* 55 (2012): 458–476. Also available at http://amj.aom.org/content/55/2/458.

Grant, Adam M., Elizabeth M. Campbell, Grace Chen, Keenan Cottone, David Lapedis, and Karen Lee. "Impact and the art of motivation maintenance: The effects of contact with beneficiaries on persistence behavior." *Organizational Behavior and Human Decision Processes* 103 (2007): 53–67. Also available at http://rcgd.isr.umich.edu /seminars/Winter2007/Grant%20Paper.pdf (doi:10.1016/j.obhdp.2006.05.004).

Gratton, Lynda. *Hot Spots*. San Francisco: Berrett-Koehler Publishers, 2007.

Gratton, Lynda, and Sumantra Ghoshal. "Beyond Best Practice." *MIT Sloan Management Review* 46 (2005): 49–57. Also available at http://www.bus.iastate.edu/nilakant/MIS538/Readings/Gratton2005.pdf.

Gretes, Mike. "Making Medicines for People, Not Profit," TED Terry talks, February 2, 2009. http://www.terry.ubc.ca/2009/02/02/terry-talks-video-mike-gretes-making-medicines-for-people-not-for-profit.

Griffin, Susan. "To Love the Marigold: Hope and Imagination," in *The Impossible Will Take a Little While: A Citizen's Guide to Hope in a Time of Fear*, edited by Paul Rogat. New York: Basic Books, 2004.

Grossman, Lev. "Person of the year 2010: Mark Zuckerberg." *Time*, December 15, 2010. Also available at http://www.time.com/time/specials/packages/article/0,28804,2036683_2037183_2037185,00.html.

Gutsche, Jeremy. *Exploiting Chaos: 150 Ways to Spark Chaos During Times of Change*. New York: Gotham Books, 2009.

Gyatso, Tenzin. "Compassion and the Individual." His Holiness the 14th Dalai Lama of Tibet website. Accessed December 11, 2012, http://www.dalailama.com/messages/compassion.

Hamel, Gary. *The Future Of Management*. Boston, MA: Harvard Business School Publishing, 2007.

Hart, Stuart. *Capitalism at the Crossroads*. Upper Saddle River, NJ: Prentice Hall, 2010.

Hearing before the Comm. on Finance, Thursday, November 18, 2004, before the Senate Comm. on Finance, 108th Cong., 13–17 (2004) (statement of David Graham, M.D., M.P.H, Associate Director for Science, Office of Drug Safety, Center for Drug Evaluation and Research, Department of Health and Human Services, Food and Drug Administration). U.S. Senate Finance Committee website. Available at http://www.finance.senate.gov/hearings/hearing/download/?id=0c63bcec-bde2-4763-9dd6-2f6d5422cd85.

Heath, Chip, and Dan Heath. *Switch*. New York: Broadway Books, 2010.

Heffernan Insurance Brokers. "Beyond the Bottom Line: Clif Bar & Co. Measures Success Five Ways." Accessed December 21, 2012. http://www.heffins.com/contact-us/california-offices/heff.voL3.8.1.clif.pdf.

Hoff Macan, Therese. "Time Management: Test of a Process Model." *Journal of Applied Psychology* 79 (1994): 381-391. Also available at http://mef.med.ufl.edu/files/2009/02/time-management-article.pdf.

Hölldobler, Bert, and E. O. Wilson. *Journey to the Ants*. Cambridge, MA: Belknap Press, 1994.

Hunter, G. Shawn. "Actionable Leadership in the Creative Age" (White Paper). Skillsoft Corporation website, June 2012. http://www.skillsoft.com/infocenter/whitepapers/documents/whitepaper_actionableleadership.pdf.

Hunter, G. Shawn. LottaGuru.com. Last accessed December 29, 2012.

Hunter, John E., Frank L. Schmidt, and Michael K. Judiesch. "Individual differences in output variability as a function of job complexity." *Journal of Applied Psychology* 75 (1990): 28–42.

Immelt, Jeffrey R. "The CEO of General Electric on Sparking an American Manufacturing Renewal." *Harvard Business Review*, March 2012. Also available at http://hbr.org/2012/03/the-ceo-of-general-electric-on-sparking-an-american-manufacturing-renewal/ar.

"Inventor of the Week: Art Fry & Spencer Silver, Post-it® Notes." Lemels N-MIT website. Accessed December 14, 2012. http://web.mit.edu/invent/iow/frysilver.html.

Iyengar, Sheen. *The Art of Choosing.* New York: Twelve, 2010.

Johnson, Mark. *Seizing the White Space.* Cambridge, MA: Harvard Business Press, 2010.

Johnson, Steven. *Where Good Ideas Come From.* New York: Riverhead Books, 2010.

Kahneman, Daniel. *Thinking, Fast and Slow.* New York: Farrar, Straus and Giroux, 2011.

Kashdan, Todd. *Curious?* New York: Harper-Collins, 2009.

Kaufman, Leslie. "Wind Turbines and Health Hazards." *Green: A Blog about Energy and the Environment, New York Times* website. Last modified January 18, 2012. http://green.blogs.nytimes.com/2012/01/18/wind-turbines-and-health-hazards.

Keltner, Dacher, Deborah H. Gruenfeld, and Cameron Anderson. "Power, Approach, and Inhibition." *Psychological Review* 110 (2003): 265–284. Also available at http://socrates.berkeley.edu/~keltner/publications/keltner.power.psychreview.2003.pdf.

Kiesler, S., and J. Cummings. "What Do We Know about Proximity in Work Groups? A Legacy of Research on Physical Distance." In *Distributed Work*, eds. P. Hinds and S. Kiesler. Cambridge, MA: MIT Press, 2002.

Krueger, Alan B., Daniel Kahneman, David Schkade, Norbert Schwarz, and Arthur A. Stone. "National Time Accounting: The Currency of Life." National Bureau of Economic Research. Available at http://www.nber.org/chapters/c5053.pdf.

Land, George, and Beth Jarman. *Breakpoint and Beyond.* Scottsdale, AZ: Leadership 2000 Inc., 1992.

Levitt, Ted. *The Marketing Imagination.* New York: The Free Press, 1983.

Likes, Robert C. "Mono Mills to Bodie." *Explore Historic California.* Last modified June 2006. http://www.explorehistoricalif.com/mono_mills.html.

Malone, Michael S. "The Next American Frontier." *Wall Street Journal* website. Last modified May 19, 2008. http://online.wsj.com/article/SB121115437321202233.html.

Management Lab® (MLab). "Management the Google Way," Lab notes 9. September 2008. http://www.cecmi.org/files/article-google-management.pdf.

Marsh Inc. "Marsh CEO Dan Glaser Addresses Need and Opportunity for Innovation and Differentiation in the Insurance Industry." Press release. May 12, 2012. http://usa .marsh.com/NewsInsights/MarshPressReleases/ID/513/Marsh-CEO-Dan-Glaser -Addresses-Need-and-Opportunity-for-Innovation-and-Differentiation-in-the -Insurance-Industry.aspx.

May, Matthew, and Kevin Roberts. *The Elegant Solution: Toyota's Formula for Mastering Innovation.* New York: Free Press, 2006.

McGregor, Douglas. *The Human Side of Enterprise.* New York: McGraw-Hill, 1960.

Mehrabian, Albert. *Nonverbal Communication.* Boston: Walter De Gruyter Inc., 1972.

Menkes, Justin. *Executive Intelligence.* New York: HarperCollins, 2005.

Meyer, Pamela. *From Workplace to Playspace.* San Francisco: Jossey-Bass, 2010.

Moon, Youngme. *The Anti-Creativity Checklist. HBR Blog Network,* video, *Harvard Business Review* website. Last modified March 18, 2010. http://blogs.hbr.org /cs/2010/03/the_anticreativity_checklist.html.

Muoio, Anna, ed. "Your Boss: Interview with Warren Bennis." Zinezone.com. Accessed December 18, 2012, http://communitybridge.com/zz/zones/wealth/fastcompany /1999/Aug/30/interview2.html.

Murray, David. *Borrowing Brilliance.* New York: Gotham Books, 2009.

Nayar, Vineet. "EFCS 2.0—Employees Driven Management Embraced." Vineet Nayar: In Search of New Leaders website. Accessed November 16, 2012. http://www .vineetnayar.com/leadership-and-business-lessons/next-management-revolution -at-hcl-%E2%80%93-hq-asia-october-2011.

Neal, David T., Wendy Wood, and Jeffrey M. Quinn. "Habits—A Repeat Performance." *Current Directions in Psychological Science* 15 (2006): 198–202. Also available at http:// dornsife.usc.edu/wendywood/research/documents/Neal.Wood.Quinn.2006.pdf.

"Netflix Culture: Freedom & Responsibility Culture." Netflix website. Accessed December 11, 2012. http://jobs.netflix.com/jobs.html.

Nisbett, Richard. *The Geography of Thought: How Asians and Westerners Think Differently . . . And Why.* New York: The Free Press, 2003.

Nisbett, Richard E., and Takahiko Masuda. "Culture and Point of View," *PNAS* 100 (2003): 11163–11170. Published online before print, September 5, 2003. (doi:10.1073/pnas.1934527100).

O'Reilly, Charles A. III, David F. Caldwell, Jennifer A. Chatman, and Bernadette Doerr. "The Promise and Problems of Organizational Culture: CEO Personality, Culture, and Firm Performance." Haas School of Business, University of California–Berkeley website. Accessed December 11, 2012. http://faculty.haas.berkeley.edu /chatman/papers/CEO%20Personality%20Final%20Ms.pdf.

Panksepp, Jaak, and Lucy Biven. *The Archaeology of Mind: Neuroevolutionary Origins of Human Emotions*. New York: W. W. Norton & Company, 2012.

Pascale, Richard Tanner, and Jerry Sternin. "Your Company's Secret Change Agents." *Harvard Business Review*, May 1, 2005. Also available at http://hbr.org/product /your-company-s-change-agents/an/R0505D-PDF-ENG.

"Photos Increase Radiologist–Patient Connection." *RSNA News* March 2009, 12–13. Also available at http://www.rsna.org/publications/rsnanews/march-2009/photos _feature.cfm.

Pink, Daniel. *A Whole New Mind: Why Right-Brainers Will Rule the Future*. New York: Penguin Group, 2006.

Pink, Daniel. *Drive: The Surprising Truth about What Motivates Us*. New York: Riverhead Hardcover, 2009.

Psychology Today staff. "How to Be Great!" *Psychology Today* website. November 1, 1995. Last modified on June 19, 2012. http://www.psychologytoday.com /articles/199511/how-be-great.

"Quality in Management Radiology." *Imaging Economics* website. Accessed December 13, 2012. http://www.imagingeconomics.com/all-news/16144-quality -in-management-radiology.

Quixote Project, The. "An Introduction." Accessed December 14, 2012. http://jpssis .com/the-quixote-project.html.

Ramo, Joshua Cooper. *The Age of the Unthinkable*. New York: Back Bay Books, 2009.

Reid, Chris R., David J. T. Sumpter, and Madeleine Beekman. "Optimisation in a nat-ural system: Argentine ants solve the Towers of Hanoi." *Journal of Experimental Biology* 214 (2011): 50–58. Also available at http://jeb.biologists.org/content/214/1/50 (doi:10.1242/jeb.048173).

"Richard Pascale." *The Economist* website. December 12, 2008. Accessed December 13, 2012. http://www.economist.com/node/12676998.

Ridderstrale, Jonas, and Kjell Nordström. *Karaoke Capitalism*. Stockholm: BookHouse Publishing Sweden, 2005.

Robinson, Ken, and Lou Aronica (contributor). *The Element: How Finding Your Passion Changes Everything*. New York: Viking Adult, 2009.

Rosenthal, Robert, and Lenore Jacobson. *Pygmalion in the Classroom: Teacher Expectation and Pupils' Intellectual Development*. New York: Irvington Pub, 1992.

Salter, Chuck. "Failure Doesn't Suck." *Fast Company* website, May 1, 2007. Accessed December 18, 2012. http://www.fastcompany.com/59549/failure-doesnt-suck.

Sanders, Tim. *Today We Are Rich*. Carol Stream, IL: Tyndale, 2011.

Saul, Stephanie. "Ghostwriters Used in Vioxx Studies, Article Says." *New York Times* website, April 15, 2008. Accessed December 18, 2012. http://www.nytimes .com/2008/04/15/business/15cnd-vioxx.html?_r=1&.

"Scientists without Borders Challenge Offers 10,000USD for Solutions to Combat a Critical Consequence of Malnutrition." Innocentive website. November 15, 2010. Accessed December 13, 2012. http://www.innocentive.com/scientists -without-borders-challenge-offers-10000usd-solutions-combat-critical -consequence-malnutrit.

Scott, David Meerman. "The New Rules of Viral Marketing." David Meerman Scott: Marketing and Leadership Strategist website, 2008. Accessed December 17, 2012. http://www.davidmeermanscott.com/documents/Viral_Marketing.pdf.

Scott, Susan. *Fierce Conversations*. New York: Berkeley Publishing Group, 2002.

"Seligman Speech at Lincoln Summit." University of Pennsylvania Positive Psychology Center website. Accessed December 21, 2012. http://www.ppc.sas.upenn.edu /lincspeech.htm.

Simon, Phil. *The New Small: How a New Breed of Small Businesses is Harnessing the Power of Emerging Technologies*. Caldwell, NJ: Motion Publishing, 2011.

Sloane, Paul. *How to be a Brilliant Thinker: Exercise Your Mind and Find Creative Solutions*. London: Kogan Page Limited, 2010.

Sloane, Paul. "What is the Difference between Innovation and Creativity?" *Innovation Excellence* (blog), June 7, 2010. Accessed December 17, 2012. http:// www.innovationexcellence.com/blog/2010/06/07/what-is-the-difference -between-innovation-and-creativity.

Stallard, Michael. *Fired Up or Burned Out*. Nashville, TN: Thomas Nelson, 2007.

Surowiecki, James. *The Wisdom of Crowds: Why the Many Are Smarter Than the Few and How Collective Wisdom Shapes Business, Economies, Societies and Nations*. New York: Doubleday, 2004.

Sweetlove, Lee. "Number of species on Earth tagged at 8.7 million." *Nature* website. Last modified August 24, 2011. Last accessed December 17, 2012. http://www.nature .com/news/2011/110823/full/news.2011.498.html.

Tapscott, Don. *Grown Up Digital: How the Net Generation Is Changing Your World*. New York: McGraw-Hill, 2009.

Tapscott, Don, and Anthony D. Williams. *Macrowikinomics: Rebooting Business and the World*. New York: Portfolio Penguin, 2010.

"This Is Your Life: Looking at the Big Picture," featuring Sir Howard Stringer and Brad Anderson. *CEO Exchange Program* (episode 507). PBS.org, March 14, 2007. Video clips available at http://www.pbs.org/wttw/ceoexchange/episodes/507 _episode.html. Transcript available at http://www.pbs.org/wttw/ceoexchange /episodes/transcripts/CEO_EXCHANGE_TRANSCRIPT_episode507.pd.

Thoppil, Dhanya Ann. "Indian Outsourcing Firms Hire in U.S." *Wall Street Journal* website. Last modified August 7, 2012. Accessed December 17, 2012. http://online .wsj.com/article/SB10000872396390443517104577572930208453186.html.

Towers Perrin. *Closing the Engagement Gap: A Road Map for Driving Superior Business Performance. Towers Perrin Global Workforce Study, 2007–2008.* TP531-08. Available at http://www.towersperrin.com/tp/getwebcachedoc?webc=HRS/USA/2008/200803/GWS_Global_Report20072008_31208.pdf.

Towers Watson. "The New Employment Deal: How Far, How Fast and How Enduring; Insights from Towers Watson's 2010 Global Workforce Study." Accessed December 13, 2012. http://www.towerswatson.com/global-workforce-study.

Turrettini, Emily. "Happy bday! SMS txt msgs turn 20." Textually.org (blog). Last modified December 1, 2012. http://www.textually.org/textually/archives/cat_sms_a_little_history.htm.

Tyrangiel, Tim. "Tim Cook's Freshman Year: The Apple CEO Speaks." BloombergBusinessWeek.com. Last accessed March 18, 2013. http://www.businessweek.com/printer/articles/88214-tim-cooks-freshman-year-the-apple-ceo-speaks.

"Vertical Axis Wind Turbines: A Relevant Solution for Urban Areas." *JEC Composite Magazine*, July–August 2007. Also available at http://www.quietrevolution.com/downloads/pdf/media/JEC_Composites_Jul-Aug_2007.pdf.

Wadhwa, Vivek. "A Better Formula for Economic Growth: Connecting Smart Risk Takers." *The Chronicle for Higher Education* website, November 18, 2010. Accessed December 18, 2012. http://chronicle.com/article/A-Better-Formula-for-Economic/125441.

Warren, Rick. *The Purpose Driven Life.* Philadelphia, PA: Running Press, 2003.

Wasem, Ruth Ellen. "Immigration of Foreign Nationals with Science, Technology, Engineering, and Mathematics (STEM) Degrees." Congressional Research Service, November 26, 2012. Available at http://www.fas.org/sgp/crs/misc/R42530.pdf.

Weihenmayer, Erik, and Paul Stoltz. *The Adversity Advantage.* New York: Fireside, 2010.

Weinstein, Margery. "Keys to the Kingdom: Part II." *Training* magazine website, September 8, 2008. Accessed December 13, 2012. http://www.trainingmag.com/article/keys-kingdom-part-ii.

Wheatley, Margaret. *Turning to one another: Simple conversations to restore hope to the future.* San Francisco: Berrett-Koehler Publishers, Inc., 2005.

Wiseman, Richard. *The Luck Factor: The Four Essential Principles.* New York: Miramax Books, 2003.

Woideck, Carl. *Charlie Parker: His Music and Life,* The Michigan American Music Series. Ann Arbor, MI: University of Michigan Press, 1997.

World Health Organization. "Essential Medicines." Accessed December 29, 2012. http://www.who.int/topics/essential_medicines/en.

"Your Job May Be Killing You." *Gallup Management Journal*, April 13, 2006. Also available at http://businessjournal.gallup.com/content/22375/your-job-may-killing.aspx.

ACKNOWLEDGMENTS

Numerous people, each in his or her own unique way, contributed to the creation of this work.

I have been extremely fortunate to work with some of the brightest minds in business over the past decade or more. This book is truly the culmination of interactions with executives, authors, researchers, clients, and colleagues. The strength of this book is a testimony to the wisdom of these people, whose names appear throughout the book. I am deeply grateful for their time and insight.

A number of people worked behind the scenes to help make this book happen. Without each of these valuable contributions, I'm quite certain this work would exist in a diminished form.

With patience and clear thinking, my editor, Pam Owen, helped me to unravel and clarify my thoughts, and contributed to fitting them together neatly on the page. She has been with me throughout this journey, and I am grateful for her sure guidance.

My great thanks to Eleanor Guare, who helped translate my ideas into the specific action items found at the end of each chapter. Those guideposts can help readers apply the Out Think process in their organizations.

Tim Sanders has been a dear friend and supporter throughout this journey. I owe a deep debt of gratitude to him for encouraging me to set forth on this endeavor, and for reminding me to write with courage.

Literary agent Lisa DiMona, at Lark Productions, stepped in at just the right time to shepherd this work to the world. She entered the process just as I was getting lost.

Don Loney, executive editor at Wiley, found me and had faith in my ideas and voice. I'm thankful to him for his keen editorial eye and constant support.

John Ambrose, senior vice president for strategy and corporate development at Skillsoft, championed this work and helped clear the way for this book to happen. It was his leadership that enabled me to work on this effort and still keep my job. I thank John for that, and for constantly supporting those around him.

Taavo Godtfredsen conducted a few of the interviews highlighted in this book. Those interviews were immeasurably valuable in filling in some of the gaps. I'm thankful to him for his participation in this journey and his friendship over the years.

Our children—Charlie, Will, and Annie—have been a source of constant inspiration and joy. A few of their stories are sprinkled throughout the book. I hope I didn't embarrass them too much and that they'll cherish these mementos later. I love them dearly.

Most importantly, I thank my wife, Amy. My commitment to this book was made possible by her love, support, and understanding. I admire her more than she may know and am forever grateful for her kindness.

ABOUT THE AUTHOR

G. Shawn Hunter is vice president and executive producer for Skillsoft's leadership video-learning products. In developing these products, Hunter has collaborated with, and interviewed, hundred s of executives, thought-leaders, academics, and authors in the United States, Canada, the United Kingdom, Europe, and Australia. Shawn cofounded Targeted Learning Corp. with his father, Hal Hunter, Ph.D., which was acquired by Skillsoft in 2007. Before founding TLC, Shawn taught skiing in Colorado, worked on a ranch in Montana, taught English abroad, and bicycled throughout America. He lives in Portland, Maine, with his wife, Amy, and their three children, Charlie, Will, and Annie. Shawn can be reached online at www.shawnhunter.com.

Skillsoft is a pioneer in the field of learning, with a long history of innovation. It provides cloud-based learning solutions for customers worldwide, including global enterprises, government, education, and small to mid-sized businesses. Five thousand companies and more than 13 million end-users rely on Skillsoft to provide high-quality, tailored training programs on a wide range of essential business and IT skills. To learn more visit www.skillsoft.com.

INDEX